Markus S. Agerer

COMPOSITION IN DRAWING
THE DESIGN AND COMPOSITION OF DRAWINGS

Impressum

Composition in Drawing
The Design and Composition of Drawings

ISBN-13: 9798560447779

2022

Original Texts: Markus S. Agerer
Translation: Paul Ronning
Editing: Elizabeth Dawson

Illustrations:
S. 28 stock.adobe.com © Irina;
Any other pictures: Markus S. Agerer

Cover Design: Markus S. Agerer

Bürgermeister-Haidacher-Straße 1
82140 Olching
Germany

email: markus-agerer@web.de
web: www.markus-agerer.de

This book, the sections thereof as well as the pictorial material – if not otherwise noted – are protected by copyright. It may not be used or exploited in any manner divergent from the law without authorization from the creator.

The author/illustrator has produced all the contents with the utmost care; nevertheless, liability of any kind cannot be assumed for errors or for the direct or indirect consequences thereof.

This book contains links (also via QR code) to external third-party websites, over whose content the author of this book has no influence. Therefore, no liability can be assumed for this external content. The linked pages were checked for possible legal violations at the time the link was created. Continuous monitoring of the content of the linked pages is not reasonable without concrete evidence of an infringement.

QR codes: The QR codes in this book contain links to various websites. This expands the content of the book. No guarantee can be given for the continued existence of this online content. It should also be noted that the websites linked in this way may contain advertising, affiliate links, etc. The terms of use and the data protection declaration of the respective websites must be observed.

TABLE OF CONTENTS

A Quick Overview	5
Introduction	9
Finding the Right Composition	10
What Does Composition Mean?	14
The Motif – Basic Principles	15
The Organizing Principles	17
Perception and Psychology	21
Basic Psychological Principles	22
Figure-Ground Relationship	23
Design Principles	25
Methods for Subdividing an Image	29
Symmetry	30
The Golden Ratio	32
The Golden Spiral	35
The Rule of Thirds	37
Graphic Design Elements	45
Points	46
Lines as Design Elements	52
Diagonal Lines	55
Surface and Form	67
Structure	76
Further Design Elements	83
The Format	84
Using Contrasts	88
Perspective and Space	94
Plasticity	104
Light and Shadow	107
Direct and Diffuse Light	110
Tricks for the Use of Shadows	112
Movement	114
Balance in Pictorial Composition	117
Closing Remarks	121
Source	123

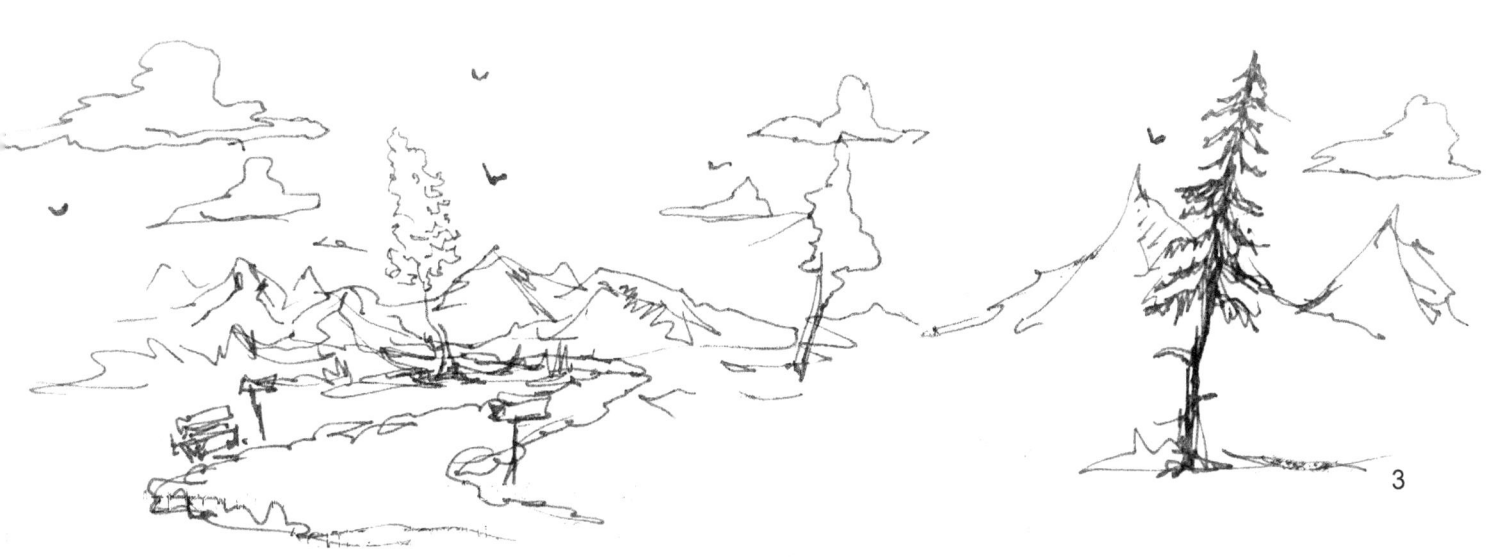

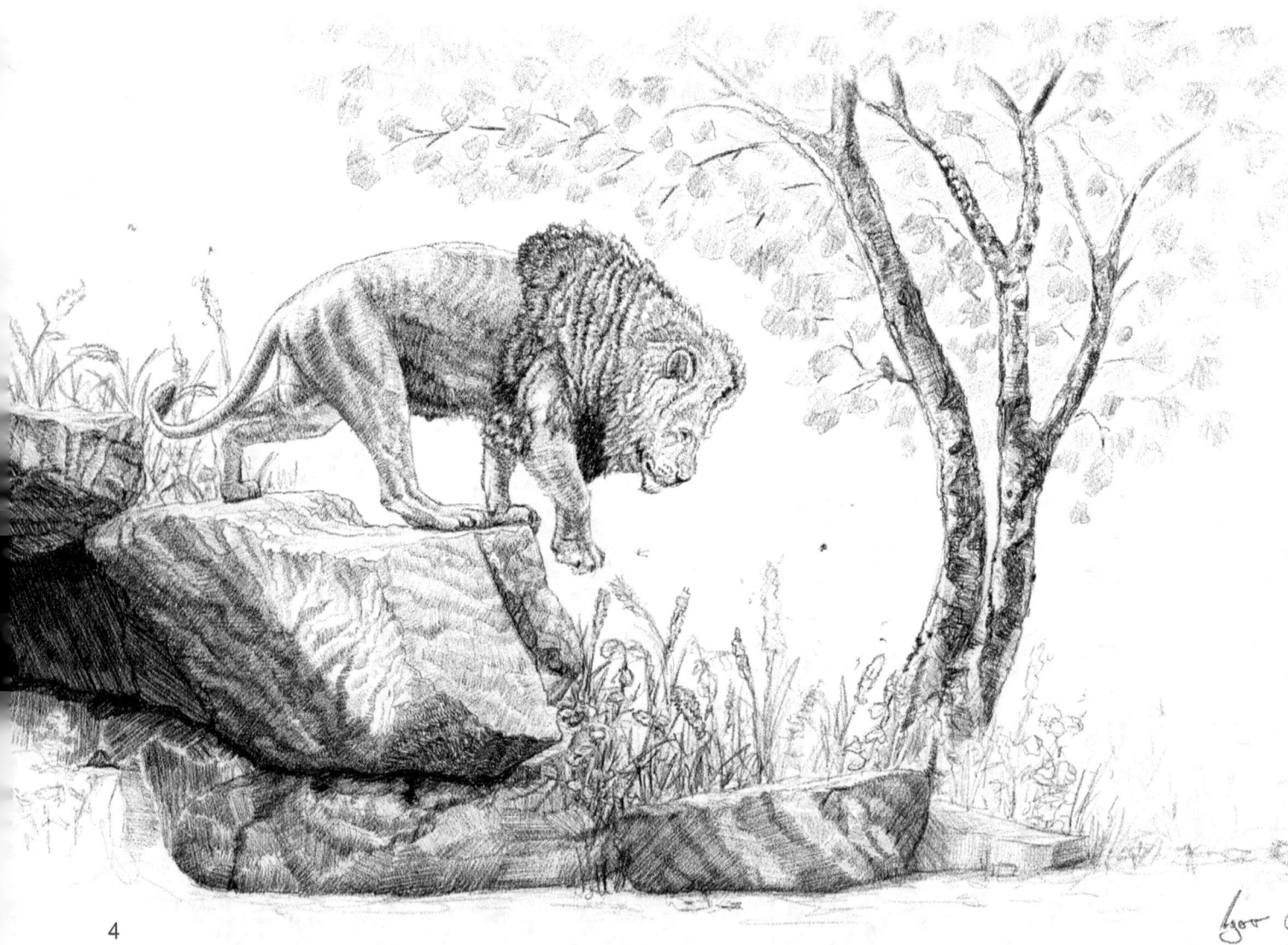

A Quick Overview

» There are actually two people in the soul of a painter – the poet and the craftsman. «

- Émile Zola -

Chapter 1: Introduction

What does pictorial composition mean?

Drawing Technique

Creativity

The Motif

Organizing Principles

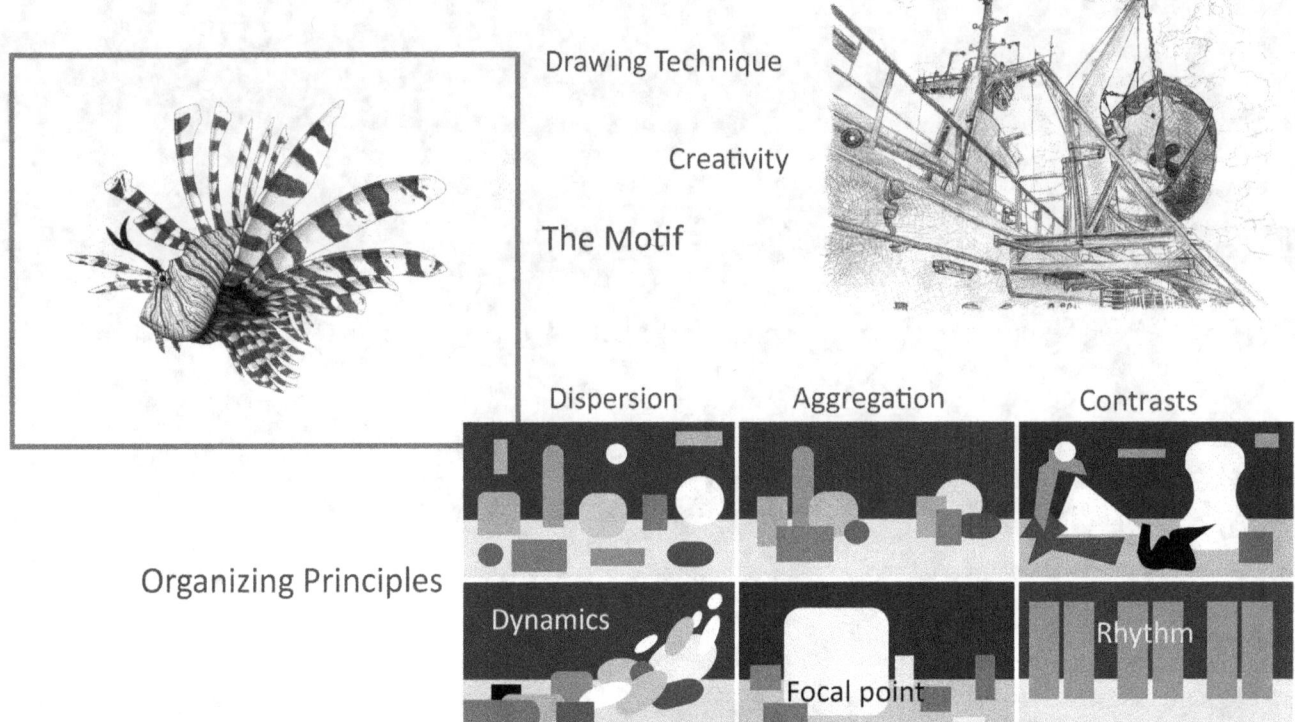

Chapter 2: Perception and Psychology

Figure-Ground Relationship

Design Principles

Law of Common Fate

Law of Closure

Law of Proximity

Law of Continuity

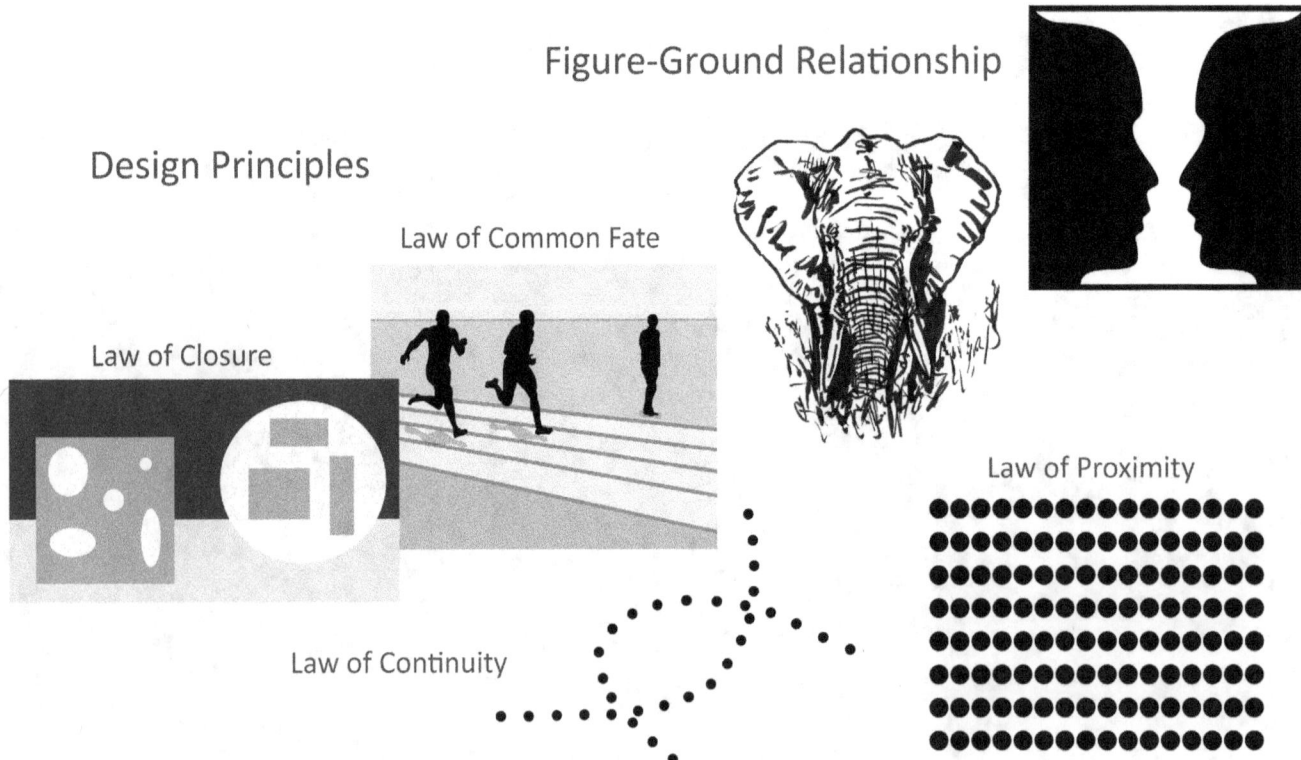

Chapter 3: Methods for Subdividing an Image

Symmetry
Rule of Thirds
Golden Spiral
Golden Ratio

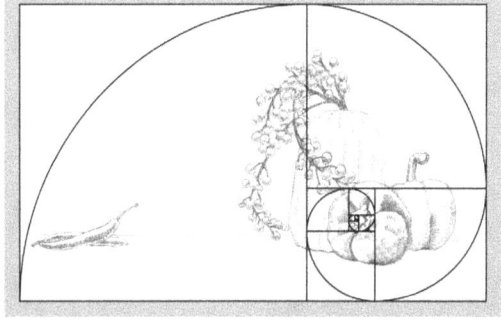

Chapter 4: Graphic Design Elements

Point
Line
Horizontal
Vertical
Diagonal

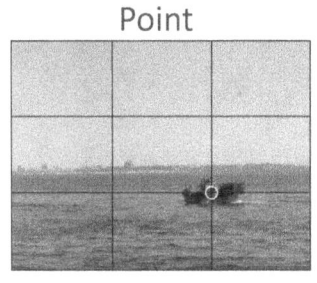
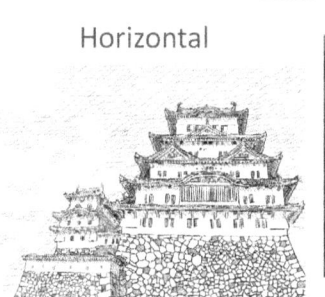
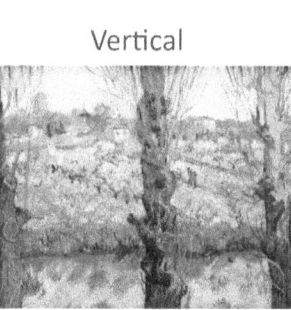
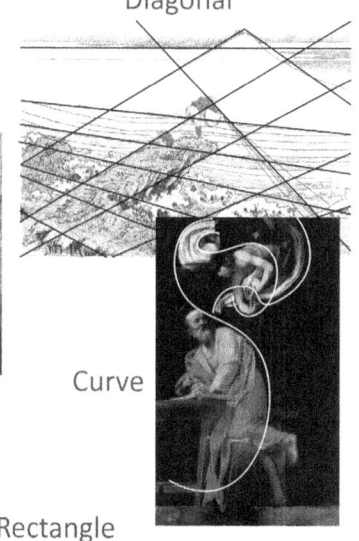

Curve

Surfaces
Form
Triangle
Circle & Oval
Rectangle

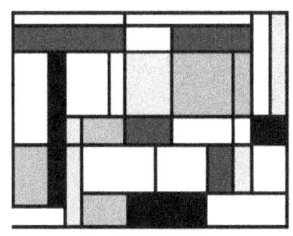
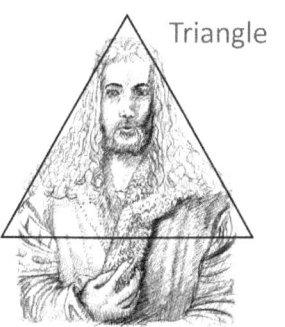
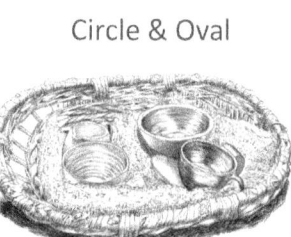
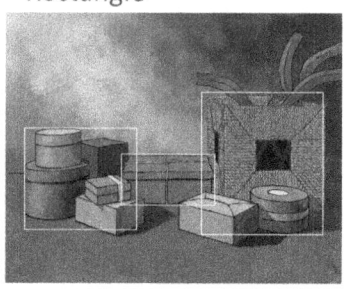

Chapter 5: Further Design Elements

Format

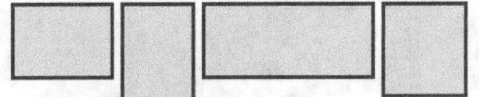

Contrasts
- Light-Dark
- Content
- Form

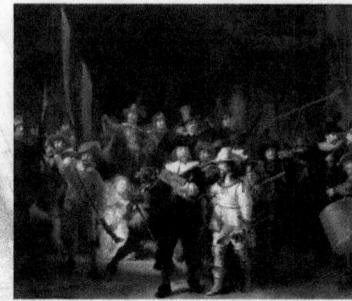

Perspective & Space

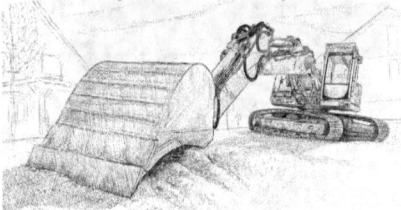

Light & Shadow

Movement

Balance
symmetrical vs. asymmetrical

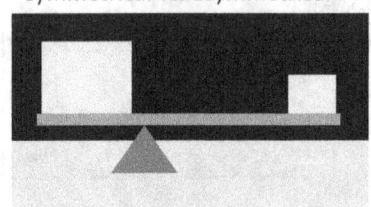

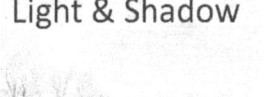

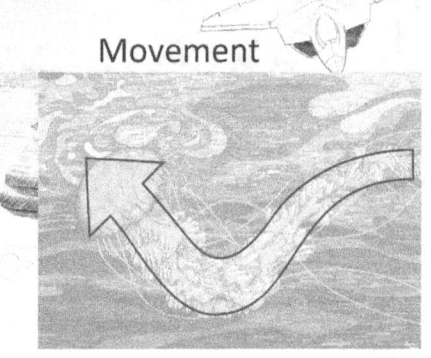

Introduction

» In the draft we witness the talent, but in the execution we witness the art. «

- Marie von Ebner-Eschenbach -

Introduction

Finding the Right Composition

The success of a painting depends on more than just artistic and technical skills. Right from the start, you should pay close attention to the harmonious design of the picture. The more thought the artist invests prior to the first stroke on the paper or canvas, the more beautiful their picture can be.

The depiction of a natural scene on flat paper is subject to the laws of drawing and painting. So, once you have selected your motif, it is worth thinking carefully about how you are going to depict it on the canvas or drawing surface.

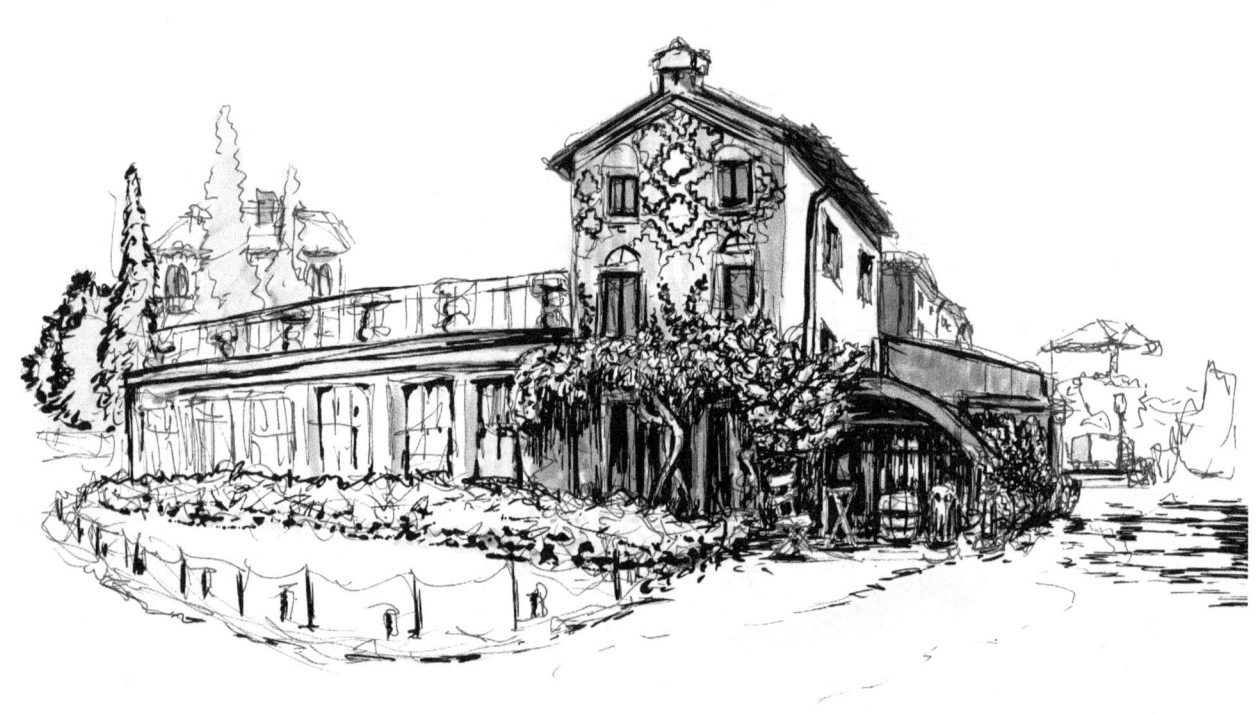

Ink drawing of a building

From my own experience, I can confirm that a picture can be improved considerably with a certain amount of planning. From a relatively static and unexciting starting point, you can develop your picture into an interesting and dynamic work of art. In retrospect, I am always glad that I did not spontaneously start my final picture with the first idea I had, but rather gave the composition the chance to really develop. Small tricks and improvements can greatly increase the impact of the picture, and sketches are always very helpful.

Whether you are drawing or painting, spontaneous sketches are a legitimate foundation for any artistic endeavor. While sketching, you can immediately discern the shortcomings of any specific format. On your second attempt, however, you can turn a meaningless sketch into a minor masterpiece. For example, when comparing your initial sketch with reality, discrepancies between the multidimensionality of nature and the flat sheet of paper become obvious. This is the stage to focus on each and every weak point and consider the proper usage of pictorial composition. For every dimension in nature or space, there is an appropriate drawing technique. With proper planning, any picture can become as lively as reality.

In the following series of images, you can see how, with the aid of a few sketches, a composition for an image can be worked out step by step.

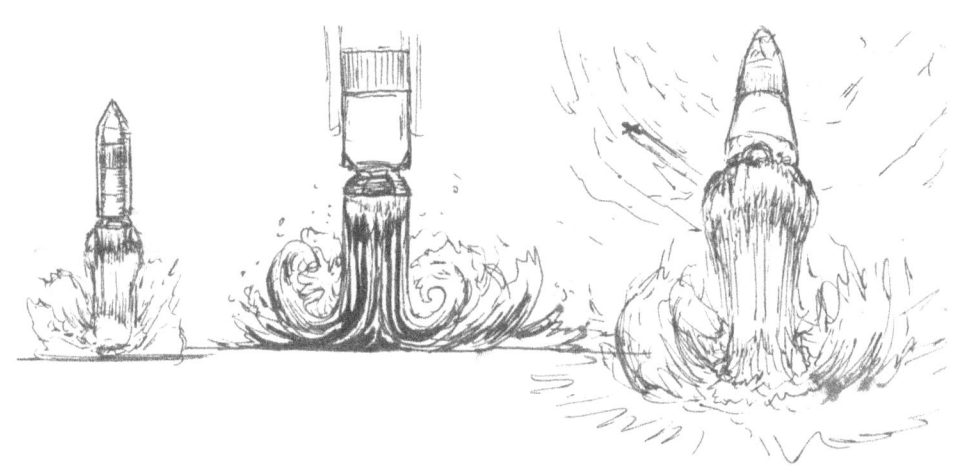

Sketches of a rocket taking off

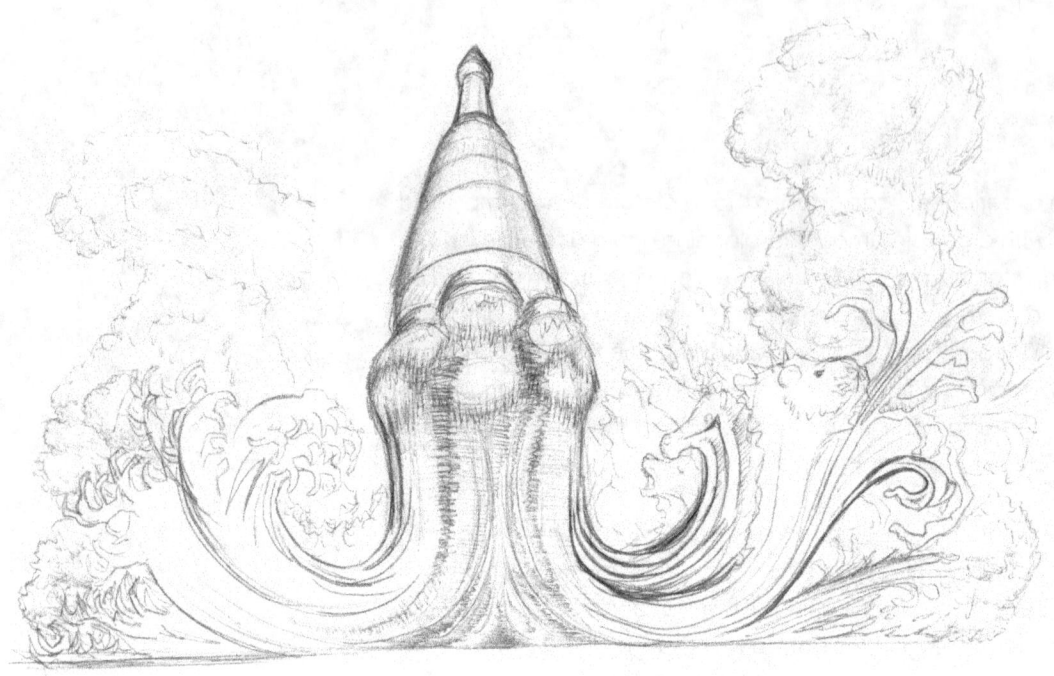
Experiments with perspective, fire, and smoke

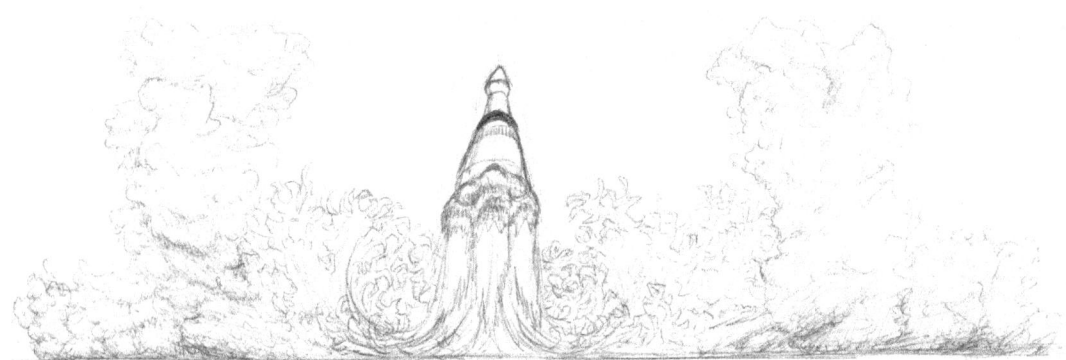
Further development of the composition

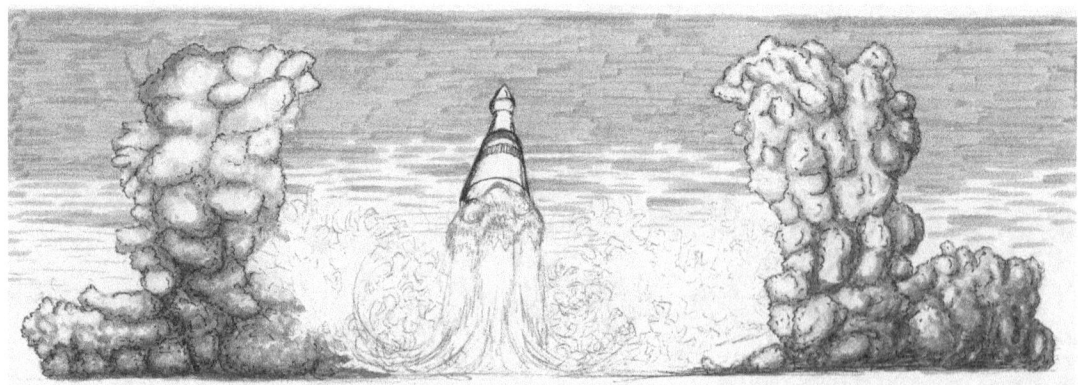
Experiments with the background design

12 INTRODUCTION

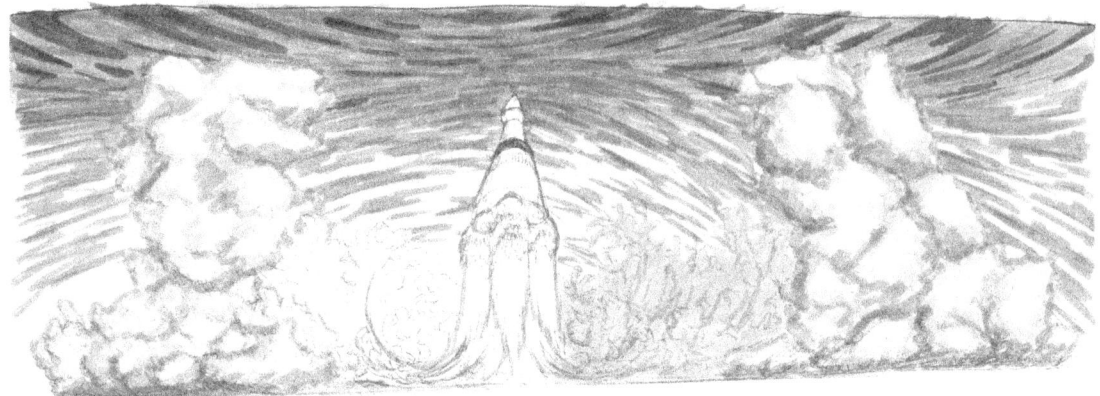
Making the background more dynamic

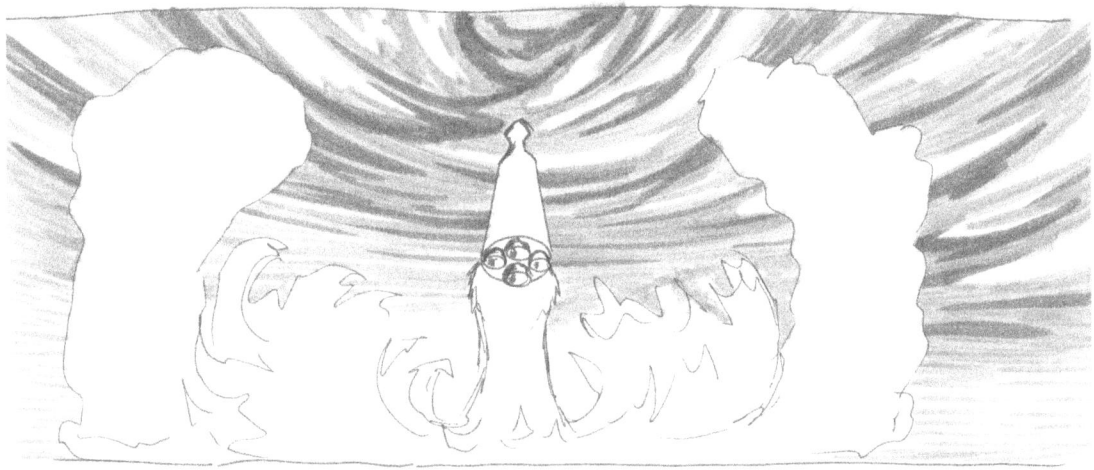
Final design for the background

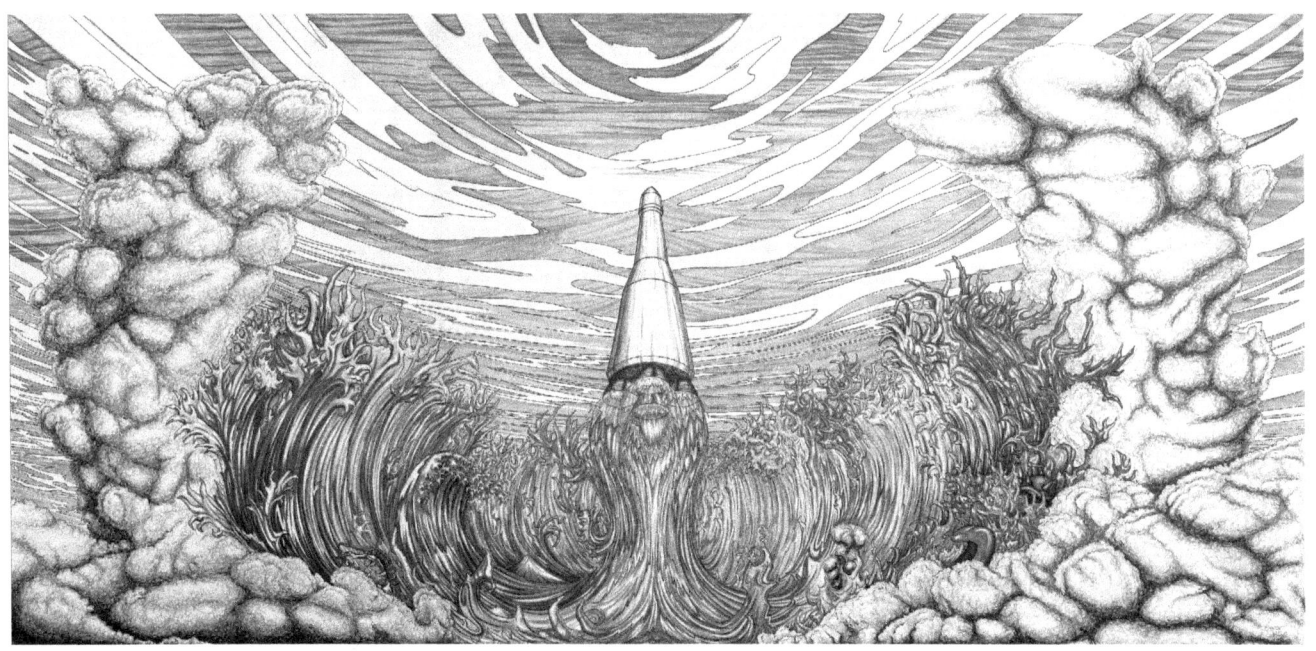
Completed image

What Does Composition Mean?

When we speak of image design or pictorial composition, we are referring to the formal structure of works of art – be they paintings, graphics, reliefs, or sculptures. Composition can be thought of as the technical side of creating a work of art. It is one of those artistic skills that can be learned, no matter what level of personal talent you possess. The first steps of composing an image include selecting the motif and deciding how to crop the image. However, color, light, perspective, and proportions are also elements of pictorial composition.

Now, you may think that binding rules cannot actually be applied and are therefore superfluous. Especially since modern art, as is generally assumed, has broken with traditional rules. But beware: Picasso is said to have once claimed that there is nothing artistic about simply painting an exact copy of a table. When asked what he would recommend for an artistic interpretation, he is said to have replied: "Measure it." And with this paradox, he succinctly and aptly made the necessity of certain rules clear.

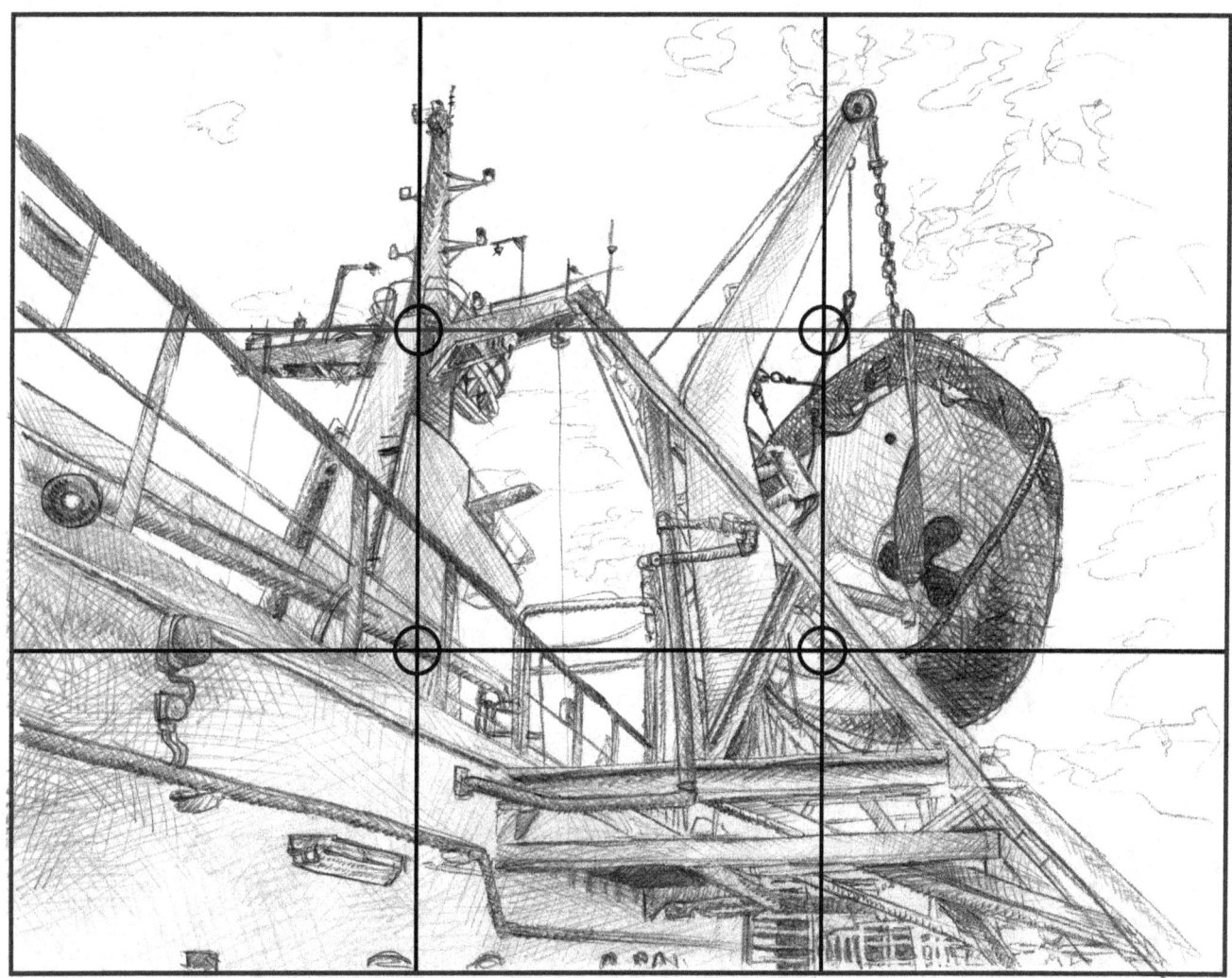

Image composition with the aid of the rule of thirds

In order to discover our own form of artistic expression, we need certain knowledge and rules. They form an arsenal that we can use in different ways. When making art, rules help us to find our way. They form a framework within.

which we can move. However, rules also encourage us to approach them creatively, play with them or, if we dare, simply to break them. But breaking rules is not an artistic achievement in and of itself. You can only reject or flexibly adapt those skills that you have truly mastered. This is especially true in the visual arts, which can look back on a long, living tradition of rules and extremely well-thought-out "rule-breaking."

In this respect, the knowledge and skill required to recognize the rules of composition and, in particular, be able to apply them are indispensable for real artistic creation. The way in which we configure these rules for ourselves is always the second step.

The Motif - Basic Principles

Pictures aim to captivate the viewer and have an impact on them. It is quite irrelevant whether the image is a drawing, painting, or photograph. A good picture has a message that can be interpreted in different ways, and the center of attention is the motif.

Some pictures have one central motif, known as the main motif. Other images contain two or more motifs that are related to each other. Usually, one motif is subordinate to the other(s), and we can then speak of a main motif and a secondary motif or several secondary motifs.

However, a good picture does not necessarily have to have a motif. It can also do without one completely. In images like these, the viewer's gaze will take in the whole image. They can tell a story or draw attention to a problem. Sometimes they represent beautiful memories; other times they tell the story of a special experience.

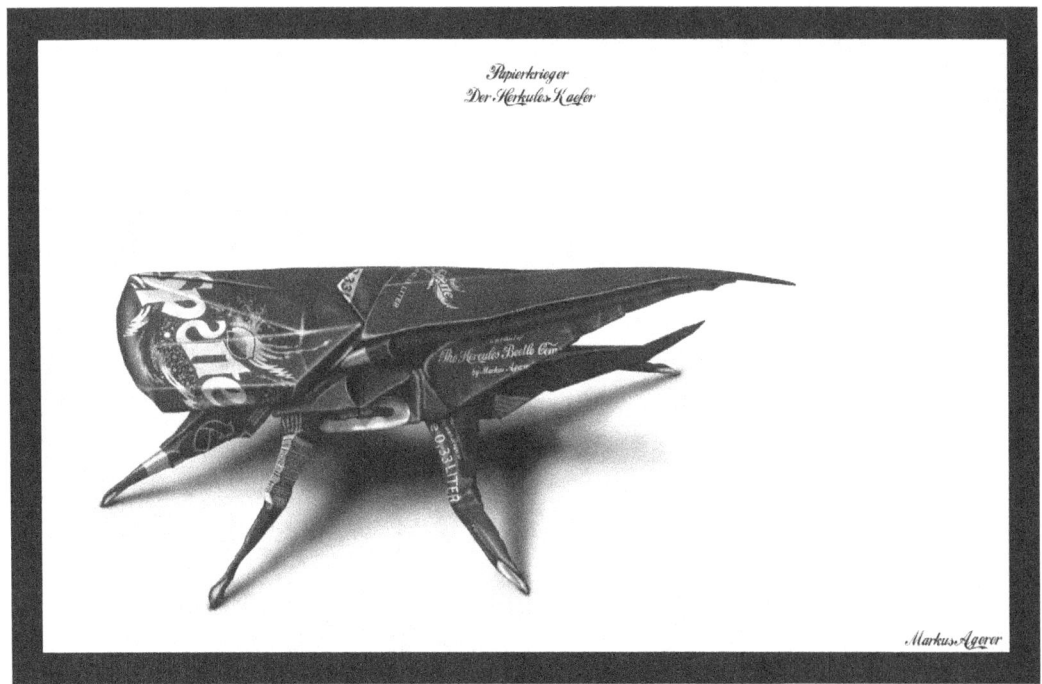

Illustration with a clear motif: The Hercules Beetle

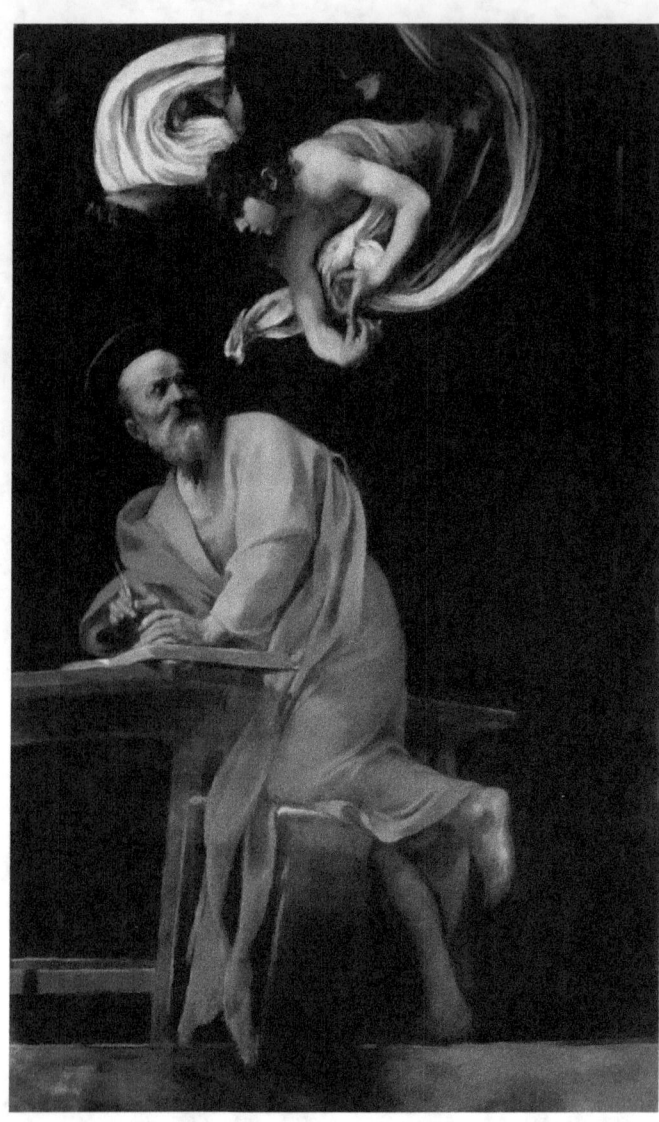

Painting with a main and secondary motif
(Copy – original: Michelangelo Merisi da Caravaggio, 1602)

Painting with no motif
(Copy – original: Pieter Claesz, 1660)

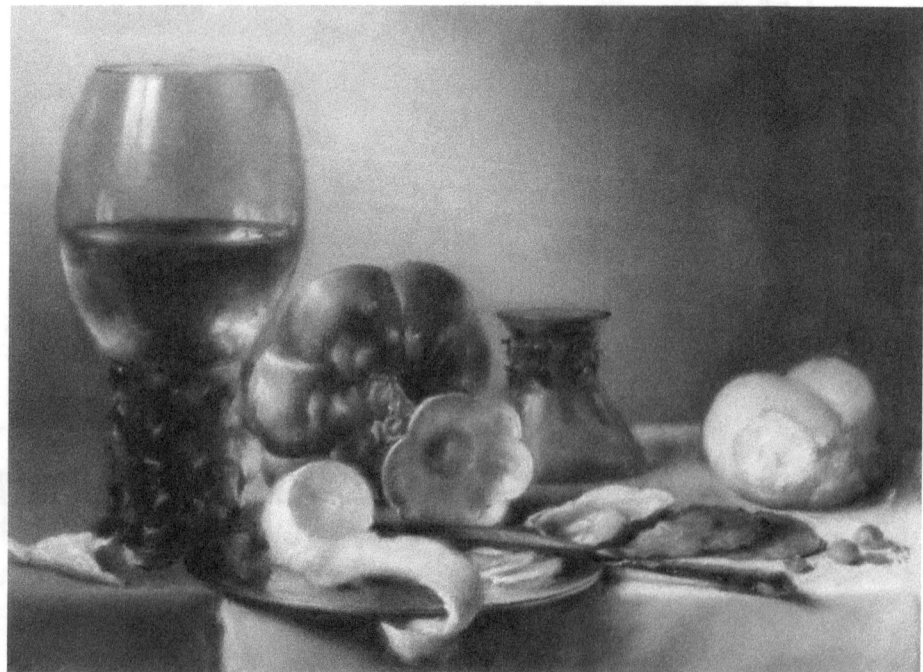

16 INTRODUCTION

The Organizing Principles

The organizing principles underlying formal image composition are quite simple, and they determine the relationships of the various elements in the picture to each other. However, these pictorial elements do not appear in isolation. In most paintings they appear in a very complex form, which can lead to confusion.

The organizing principles are:

Sequence

A sequence is the repetition of pictorial elements of a similar nature. Their distance from each other is uniform in order to make them appear aligned.

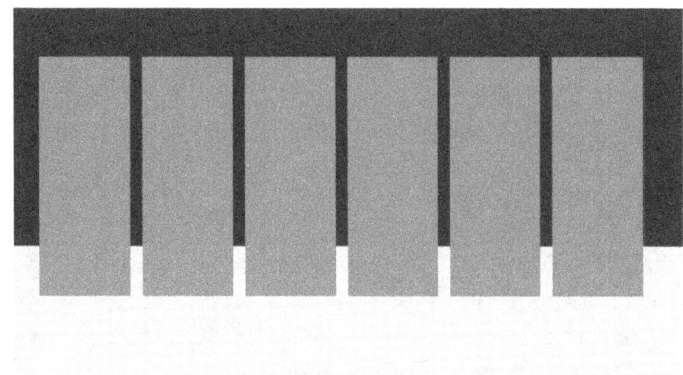

Rhythm

Similar or different pictorial elements are repeated at least once in the form of a sequence or appear in some other type of rhythm.

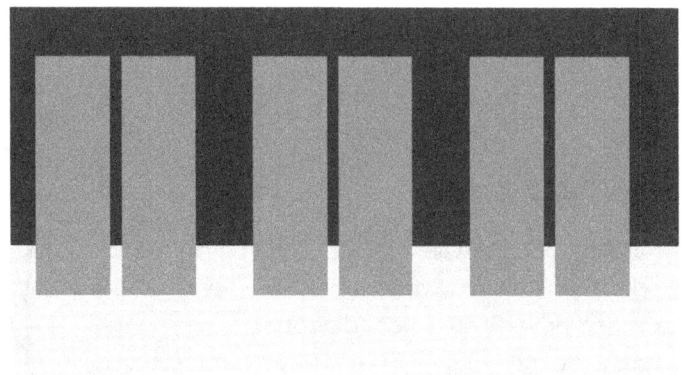

Aggregation

A group or several groups of similar pictorial elements are positioned on the picture plane in whatever way is required. The proportion of the arrangement appears balanced, and each group is recognizable as a kind of unit.

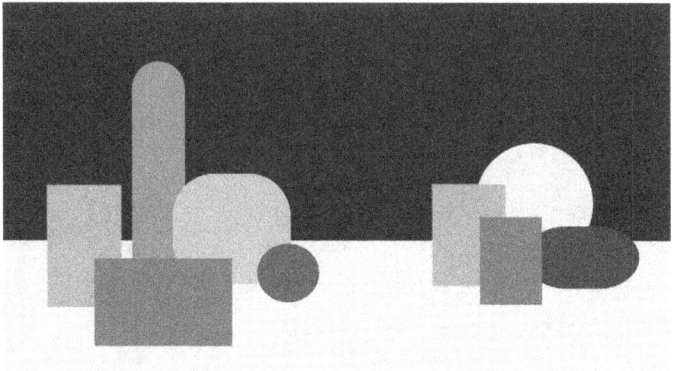

Accumulation

Identical or similar pictorial elements are concentrated in one part of the image area. They are close to each other and can partially overlap.

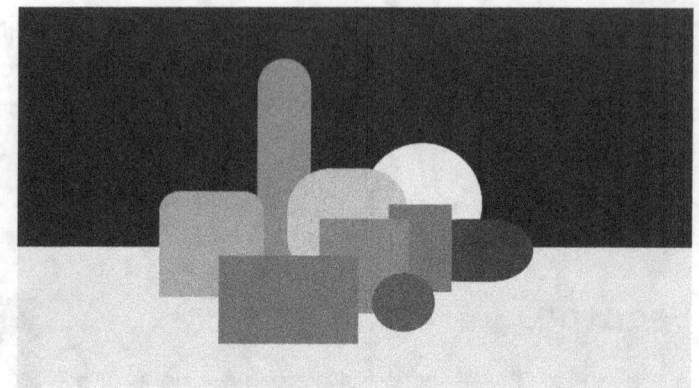

Dispersion

Different individual pictorial elements are arranged at regular or seemingly random intervals on the picture plane. A regular arrangement creates a static, inactive effect, while an irregular arrangement is dynamic and lively.

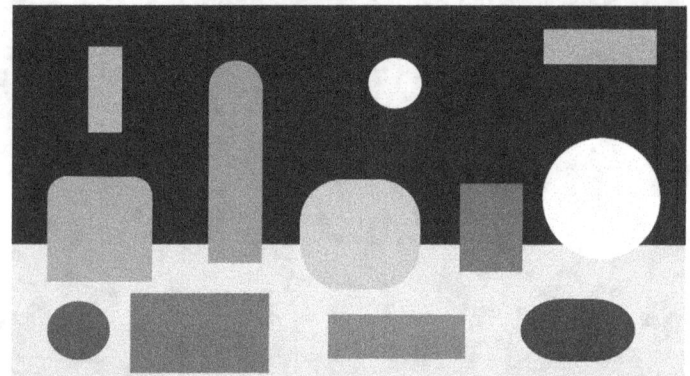

Symmetry

Symmetry occurs when pictorial elements are arranged symmetrically on an axis. This axis could be horizontal or vertical, or slant diagonally at any angle across the picture plane. This creates the impression of a reflection of the elements and thus a certain order.

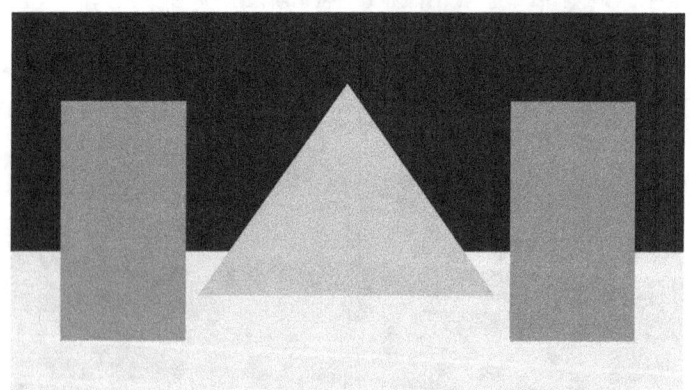

Asymmetry

The various elements of the image are deliberately positioned irregularly, so that no symmetry is created. Asymmetry can generate the impression of liveliness and tension.

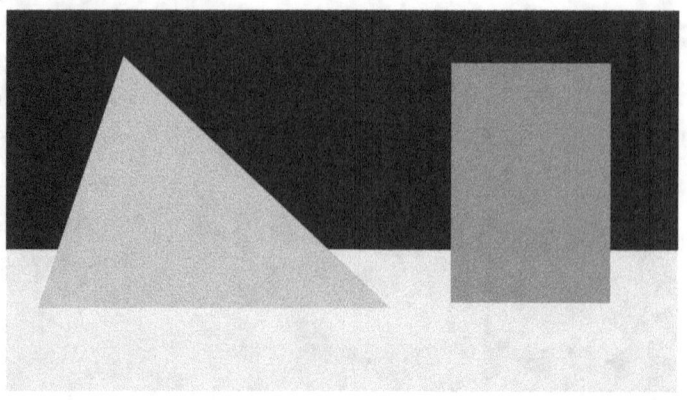

Structure

The structure (not to be confused with the structure of the surface or structure in the sense of the context of the work) is created by a sequence of similar elements, which, depending on the arrangement, can have a restless but also severe effect. Structure-giving elements are usually dots, lines, or other geometric patterns.

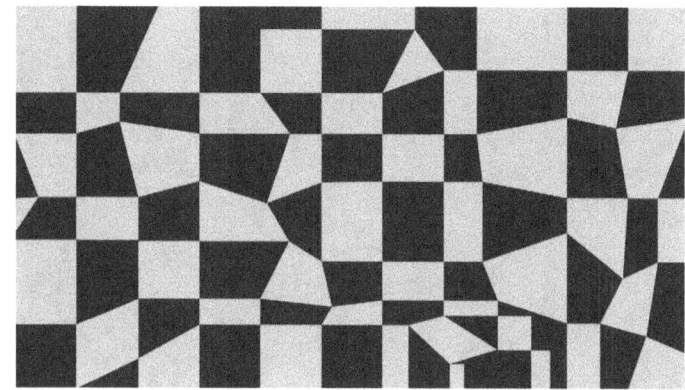

Grid

The grid is a special type of structure whose surface is divided up in a standardized way. Dots or lines are distributed in a strictly geometric or rhythmic manner and create a restless effect as they increase in number.

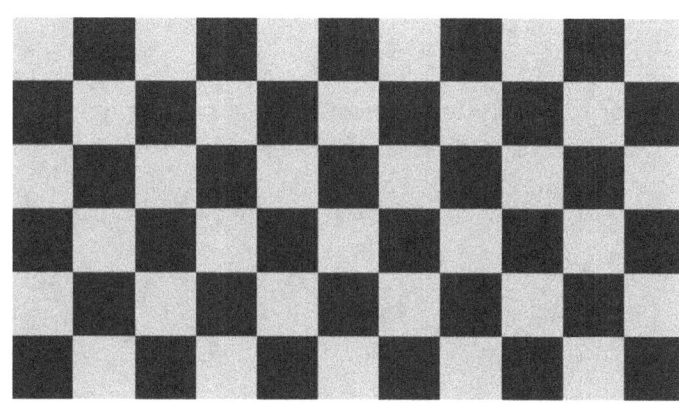

Focal point

An individual pictorial element or several pictorial elements are emphasized by color or concentration and thus form the focal point of the image. Depending on the position of the focal point, different effects can be created. Positioning the focal point centrally reduces tension. However, if the focal point is shifted to one side, the picture appears less balanced but oftentimes more interesting for the viewer.

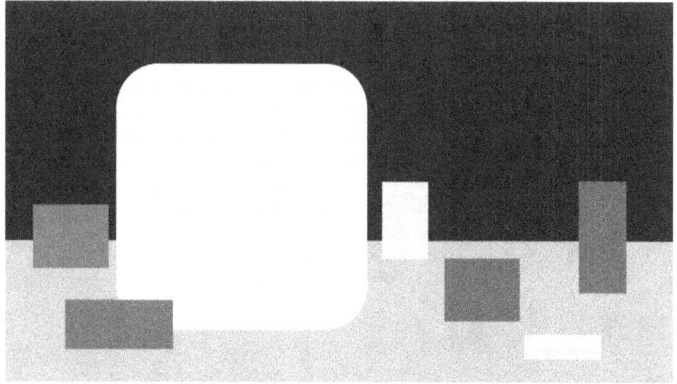

Contrasts

Contrasts can be generated through opposing elements, thus creating tension. Contrasts can result from form itself but also from quantity, quality, or orientation.

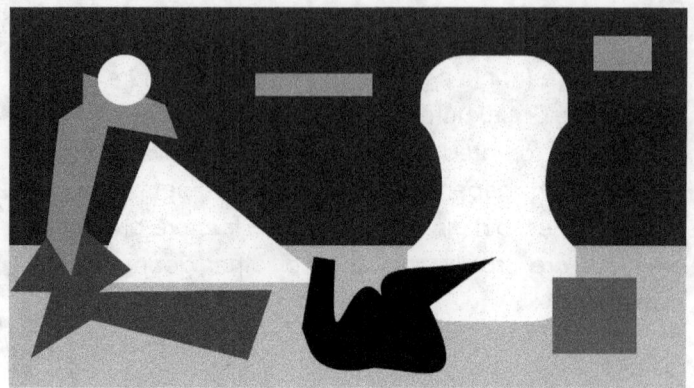

Dynamic compositions

Through expanding, concentrated forms and elements, an impression of restlessness can be generated in a picture. A special dynamic can often be achieved by creating diagonal and wavy lines that are positioned asymmetrically and involve strong contrasts.

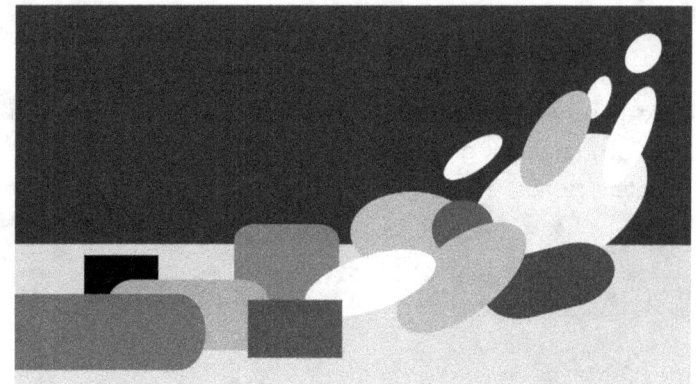

Static compositions

In contrast to dynamic compositions, static compositions involve closed elements and clear shapes. Here, straight, vertical, or horizontal lines stand out, which conveys calm and motionlessness.

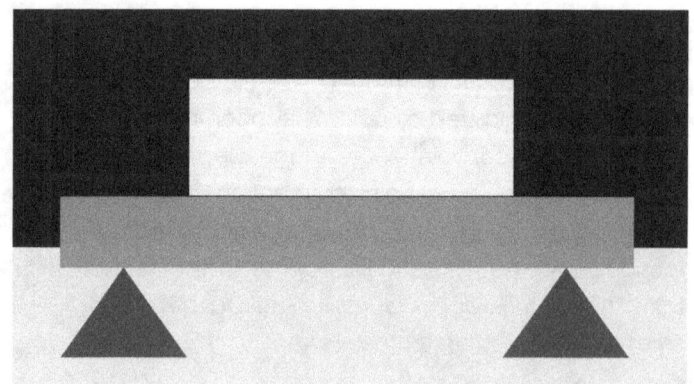

Perception and Psychology

» Simplicity is the highest form of sophistication. «

- Leonardo da Vinci -

Perception and Psychology

Why we like one picture rather than another is due to the way our brain processes what we perceive. Our mind invariably attempts to perceive some kind of figure standing out from the background; this function has always been essential for our survival. Under certain conditions, particular things attract our attention and are then focused on by the eye. This quickly separates the important from the unimportant. Artists can make use of perception and psychology in their image creation and composition. Those who understand how the brain works can use this to create better pictures. Therefore, in this chapter we will first take a look at the topics of perception and psychology and then turn to the actual design of the image.

Basic Psychological Principles

The focus of our vision will form the psychological basis for our pictorial composition. In general terms, this is the attention that a person can focus on a certain thing; the section of the picture that the viewer focuses on is perceived much more sharply and more consciously than the rest. The reason for this is not only the structure of the eye but also the cognitive processes that take place in our brain: The viewer initially allocates their attention to the potentially interesting elements of a picture.

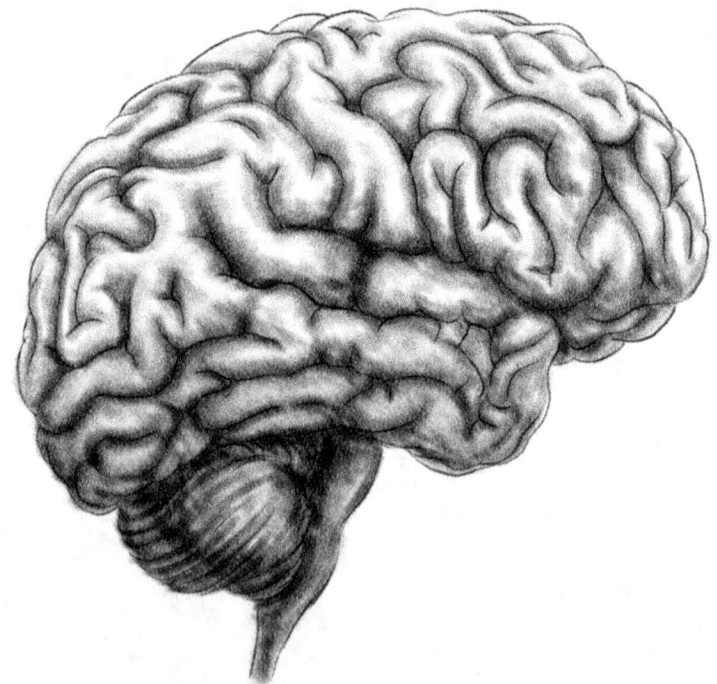

Thus, everything that is non-existent, extraordinary, or uncommon in the real world attracts the attention of the viewer. Bright, unnatural colors will have this effect. In addition, any pictorial elements that stand out from the rest of the picture attract our attention. What makes an element stand out can vary considerably. For example, we notice bright objects very quickly – especially if they are in front of a dark background. Color contrasts also attract attention. And if clear lines can be seen in a picture, the viewer is inclined to follow them with their gaze.

A completely different method of guiding the focus of the viewer is to include elements that encourage them to form an emotional connection. For example, depicting people or faces works particularly well. They draw the viewer's gaze extremely strongly.

The above examples are just a few simple methods of how the artist can control the attention of the viewer in the picture. In the following chapters, you will learn many more techniques.

Figure-Ground Relationship

The figure-ground relationship describes the distinction between foreground (figure) and background (ground) in our perception of our surroundings. This human ability is essential for survival on earth as it is the only way we can recognize and understand our world and what is happening at any given time. The relevant information is quickly filtered out of a multitude of impressions, which enables a person to judge a situation and react accordingly.

In visual perception, the human being always makes the distinction between "figure" and "ground": That which is recognized as important crystallizes as a figure distinct from the spatial or planar environment – the ground – and stands out from it. The figure-ground relationship is thus derived from the human brain's efforts to assign meaning to certain forms or objects.

This basic knowledge of Gestalt psychology helps us in the creation of images. If you understand the figure-ground relationship, then you also know when a central motif will be recognized as such and how to make objects disappear into the background.

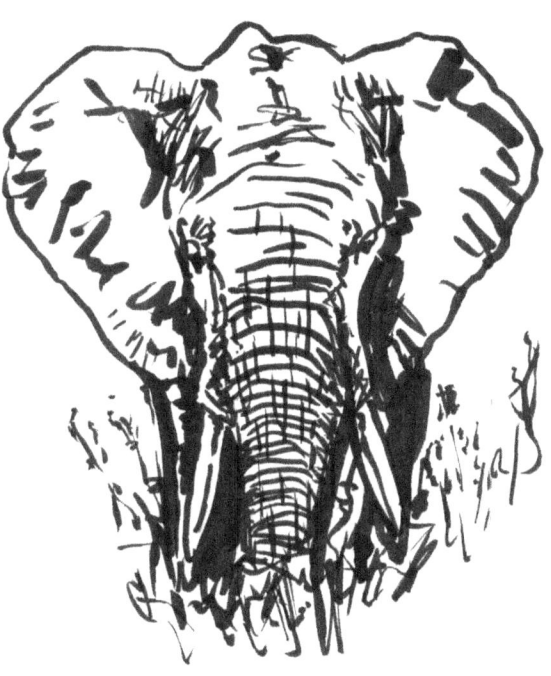

The figure in front of the background in this drawing can be clearly recognized

Criteria for Perception

If the brightness values of the highlighted figure and the surrounding background are considerably different, it is easier to extract the relevant image content. The figure then represents a striking positive form and the background a negative form within the overall composition.

If, however, there is a certain balance between the pictorial elements of the figure (foreground) and the ground (background), the viewer will be unable to weight them clearly: What one person recognizes as a figure, another may see as background. Or the same person may find their perception switching back and forth, seeing a pictorial element sometimes as ground and sometimes as figure. This is the case with the well-known "Rubin's vase" image: Depending on whether you focus on the inner form – a white goblet – or the framing picture elements – two black profiles facing each other – each is alternately recognized as figure or background.

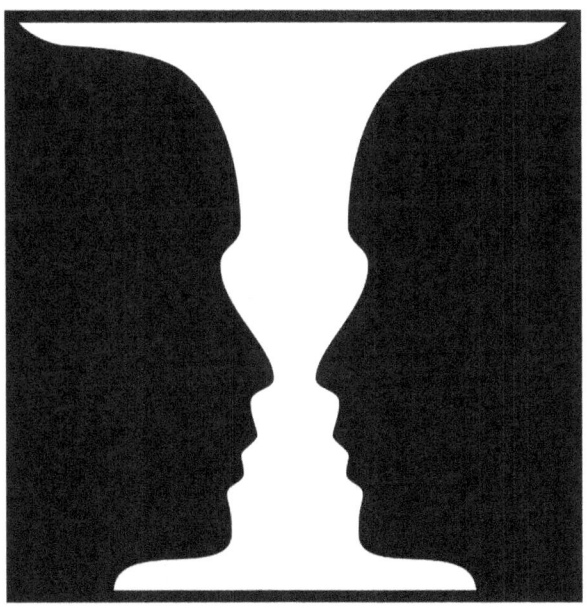

Rubin's vase

For hobby and professional artists, this phenomenon is the source of some important design criteria, which are as relevant to painting, drawing, and photography as they are to sculpture, handcrafted objects, and interior design. If you want to convey a very clear pictorial message, you should establish strong contrasts in terms of figure and background. To the viewer, bright, optically lifting (convex) and smaller forms are more likely to be perceived as figures, as are symmetrical picture elements. Darker and larger areas, however, usually appear as background or ground. When asymmetrical forms are present, the viewer is also more likely to associate these with the background.

With some experience, you will succeed in putting these principles into practice and what you are trying to convey in your image will be clear to the viewer at first glance.

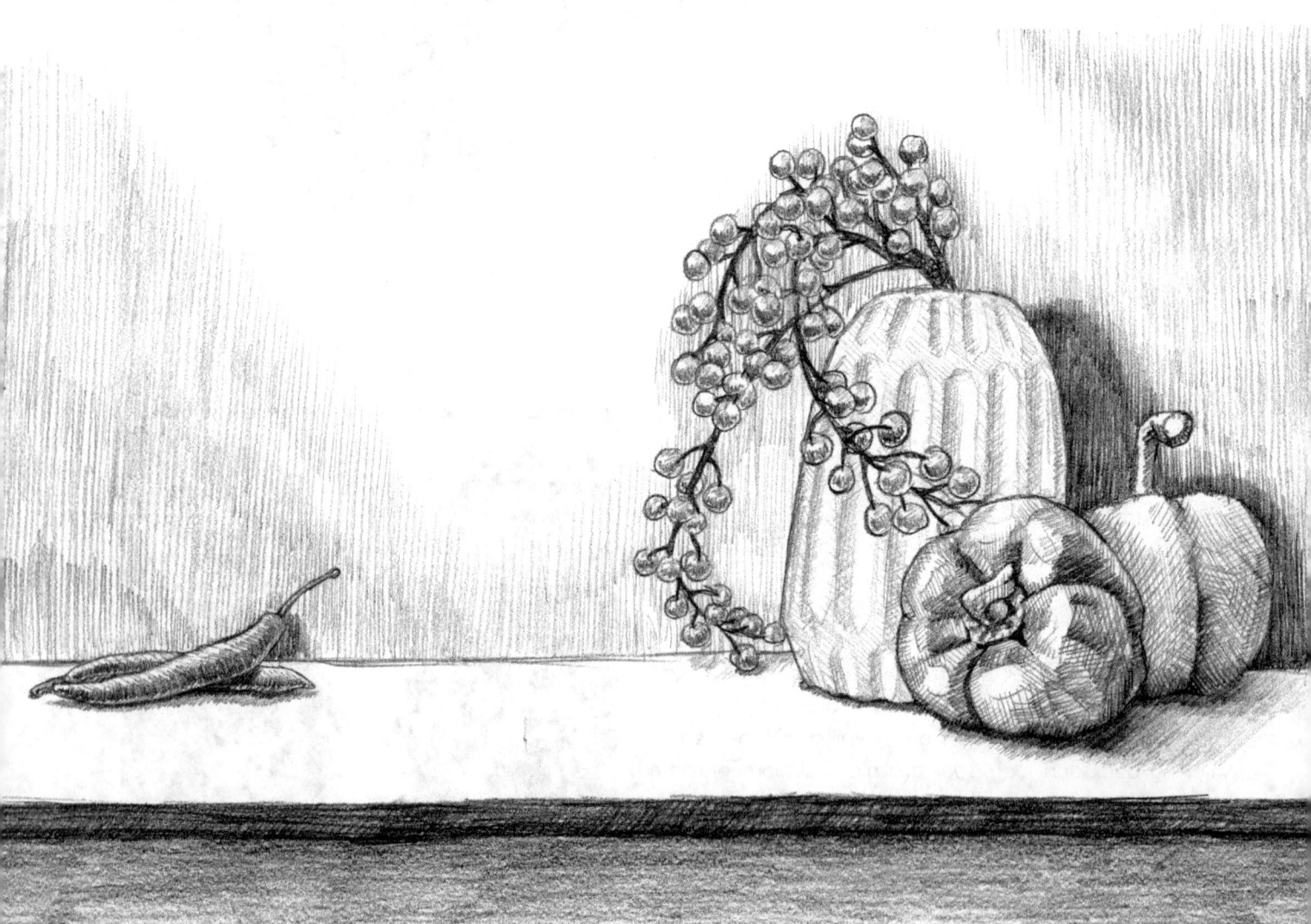

Objects emerge clearly from the background because of the value contrast and clear shapes

Design Principles

The way we perceive anything is fundamentally very individual. If you look at a picture together with your partner or a friend, it is possible that it will have a completely different effect on each of you, as you will notice if you then discuss the image. Despite these very individual perceptions, there are certain design principles that concern form and how to build up elements within a picture.

These principles are laid down in the psychology of design. Each one can have a very different effect on the elements within a picture. At the same time, without them it would be difficult to build up the elements within a picture at all.

The Law of Proximity

This law states that two or more elements that are very close together are often perceived as one element. You should take this into account when composing a picture.

Often, it is very important to include some empty space if you want to create an appealing pictorial element; filling the whole picture with different elements is often counterproductive since it blocks the view of the most essential elements. Instead, reduce the composition to just a few elements, which you bring closer together by creating proximity.

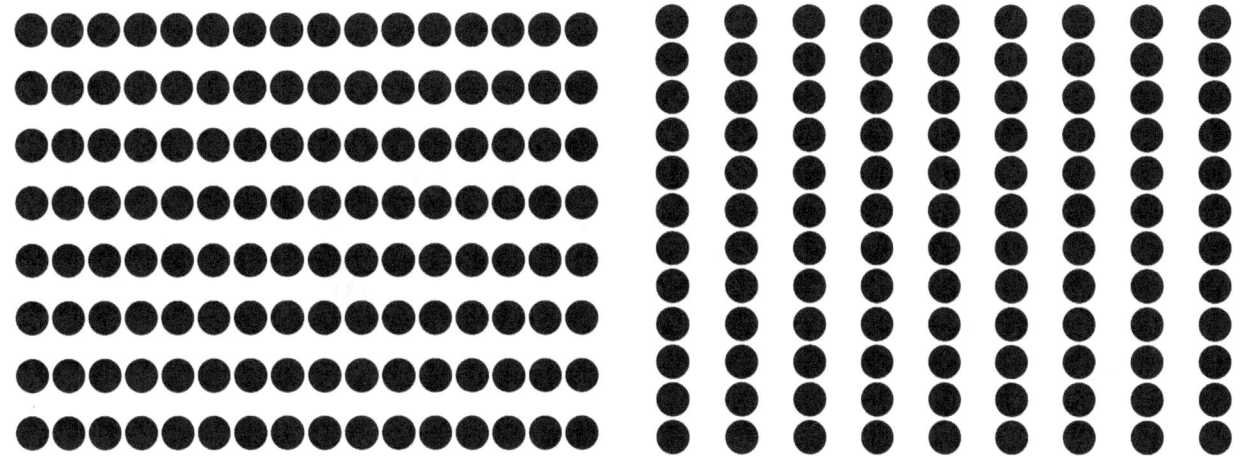

Dots that are located close together are perceived as belonging together

The Law of Similarity

There are many different types of similarity. Elements are similar if they have the same color, shape, or size. Similarities can also arise in terms of materials or surfaces. The more similar the objects are, the stronger the inclination to group them. Contrary to the law of proximity, however, grouping by similarity also occurs over greater distances. In this regard, it is also important that the image or space is not unnecessarily overloaded. This would distract the viewer from the most essential elements and could distort the message of the picture.

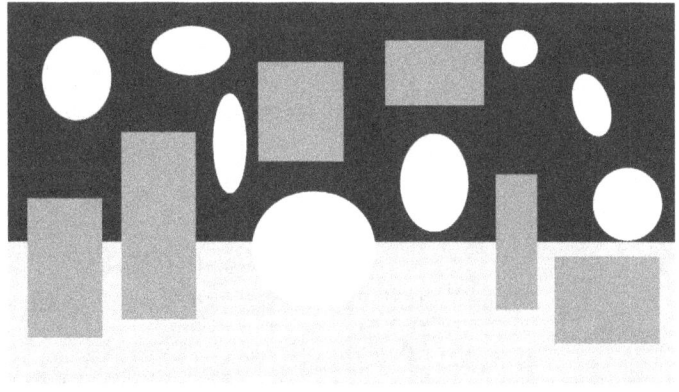

Objects that are similar to one another in form and color will be perceived as a group

The Law of Good Form

The law of good form seeks to express that simplicity is always preferable to a complex structure. For this reason, the law is often called the "law of simplicity" or the "law of conciseness." If you shape elements and connect them in a special way, you should always make sure that they produce memorable forms and are not too complex. You should therefore design elements whose structures are known to the viewer so they can identify with them more easily. Many viewers first perceive structures in their simple form and thus see them as making a particular statement. You should take this into account when creating the elements of a picture.

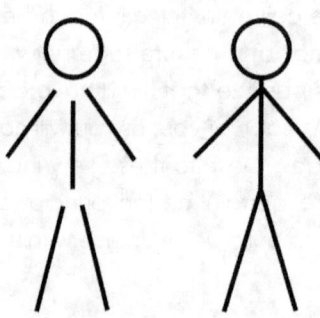

The figure on the left is recognized as a form less frequently than the figure on the right

The Law of Closure

Closure occurs when an object has a closed outline or when several elements are enclosed by a line. This causes the objects to be visually grouped together, and they are perceived as belonging together even though they may be unrelated, visually dissimilar, or consist of other different elements. By framing the objects together, you are giving the viewer the very specific instruction that you want these things to be understood as one.

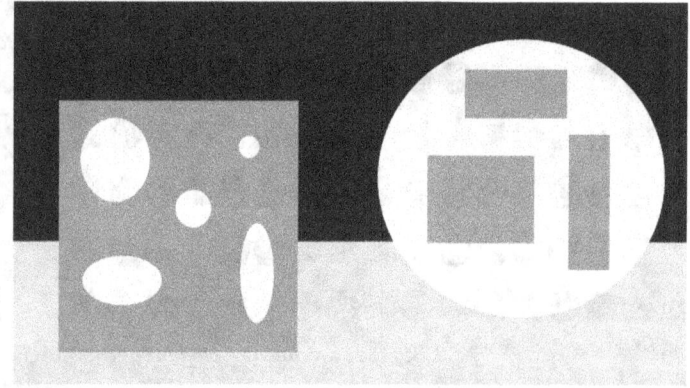

Objects are perceived as a group when they are framed by an outline

Even if, as can be seen in the example image, round forms are enclosed within an angular form or angular forms are enclosed within a round form, the law of closure takes precedence here. The round forms are much more strongly related to the angular form that is enclosing them, and the same applies to the angular forms that are enclosed by the round form. The law of similarity, which exists between the large round form and the small round forms, is much less noticeable in this composition.

Perception and Psychology

The Law of Continuity (Good Continuation)

If you include lines as elements in your design, you can assume that they will be perceived by the viewer as always following the simplest possible path. This also applies when two lines cross each other; in this case, the viewer will follow the straight path in one direction or the other. However, they will never assume that you intended to include a bend in the path.

In addition, lines do not have to be displayed in their entirety. The viewer will mentally fill in any short interruptions and follow an imaginary line until it restarts. A line can also emerge if you arrange a corresponding pattern of individual elements.

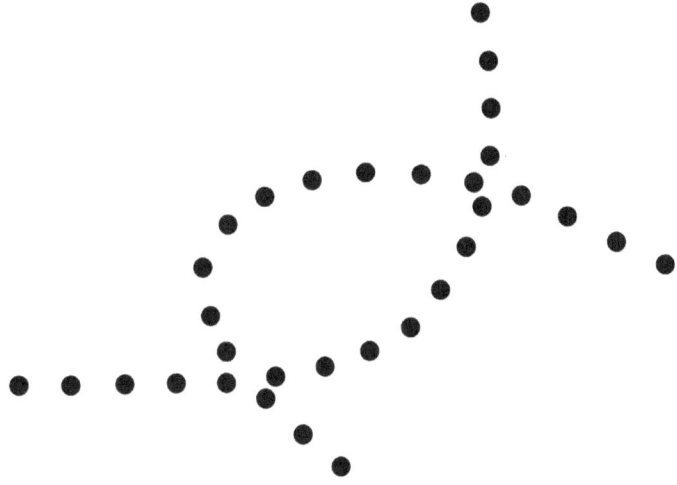

In our minds, a continuation of lines and line-like forms takes place

The Law of Common Fate

Elements exhibiting similar behavior are almost always perceived as belonging to the same group. This is the case when objects move or change in a uniform way. A good example is a group of dancers dancing together. The individual qualities of each member of the group recede, while their visual similarities come to the fore.

The law of common fate is particularly strong when the elements are moving in the same direction and are the same shape.

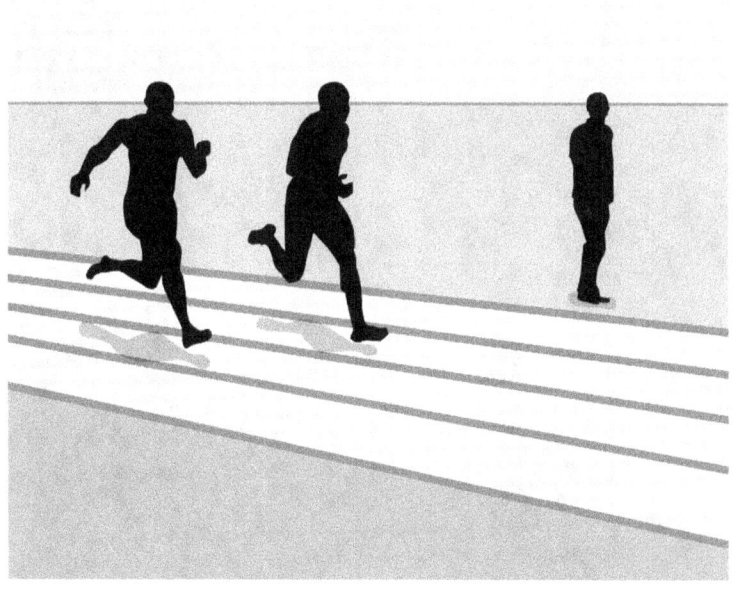

Two runners share the same fate and are perceived as belonging together, while the man at the edge is recognized as an outsider.

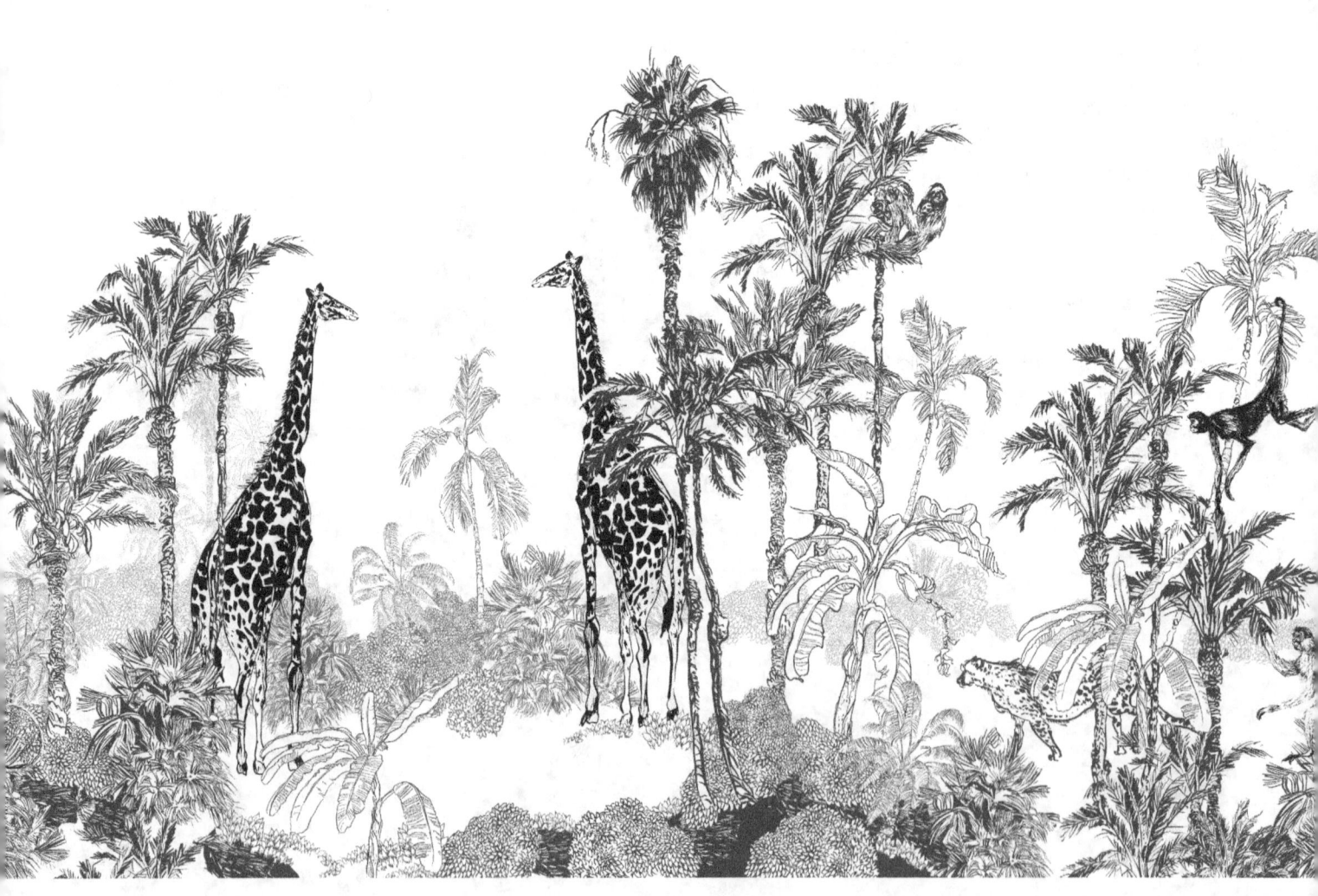

Methods for Subdividing an Image

*» It is significant that painters comprehend
nature and teach us how to see her. «*

- Vincent van Gogh-

Methods for Subdividing an Image

In this chapter, we deal with methods of image subdivision. This is one of the most important compositional techniques because subdividing a picture is an enormous help for us in the creative process. By subdividing the basic image, we can in principle determine the basic structure of the work. The methods presented here will help the artist to create a successful composition that can appear balanced or even exciting. However, you should always be aware that the techniques described here are only orientation aids. They are neither a panacea nor a guarantee that you will create an accomplished picture.

Symmetry

In image compositions using central axes, the image is divided into two halves of equal size. The center axes can be used individually or together. The diagonals extend from one corner of the image to the other. This method can be used repeatedly in landscape pictures.

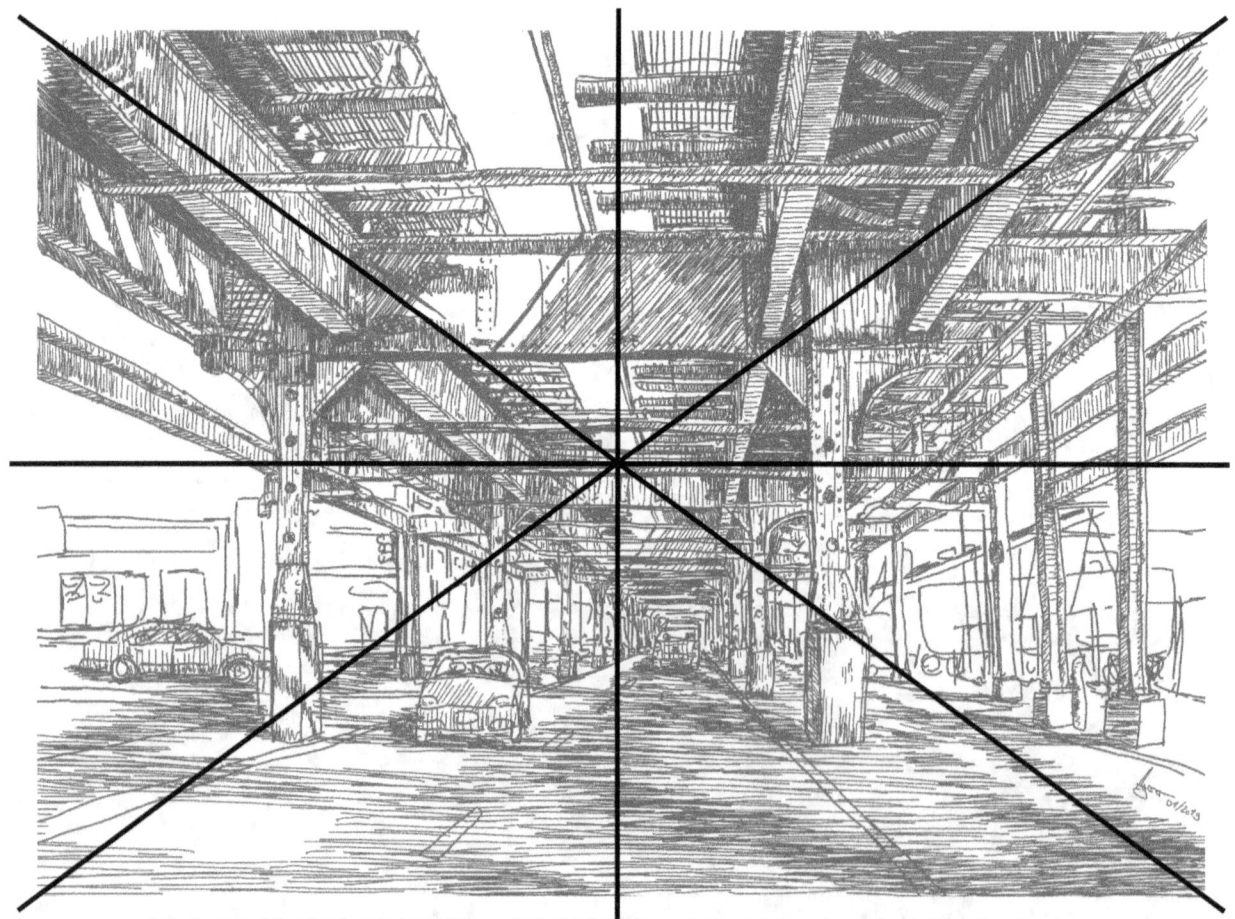

Roadway with steel construction – designed with an approximately symmetrical structure

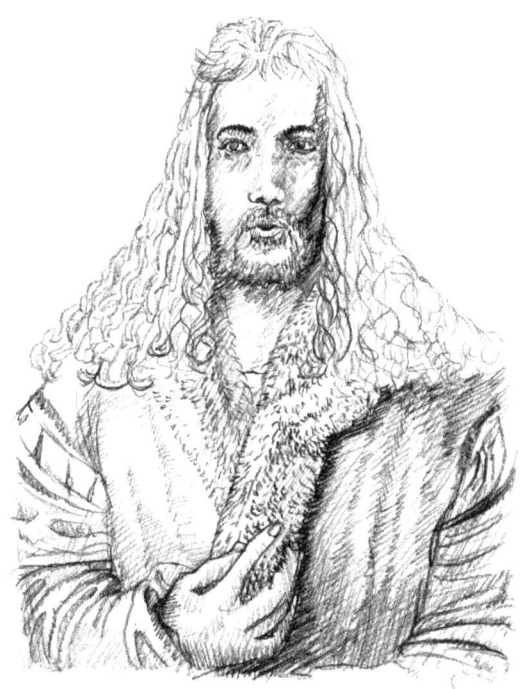

Portrait with symmetry – self-portrait of Albrecht Dürer
(drawing/copy)

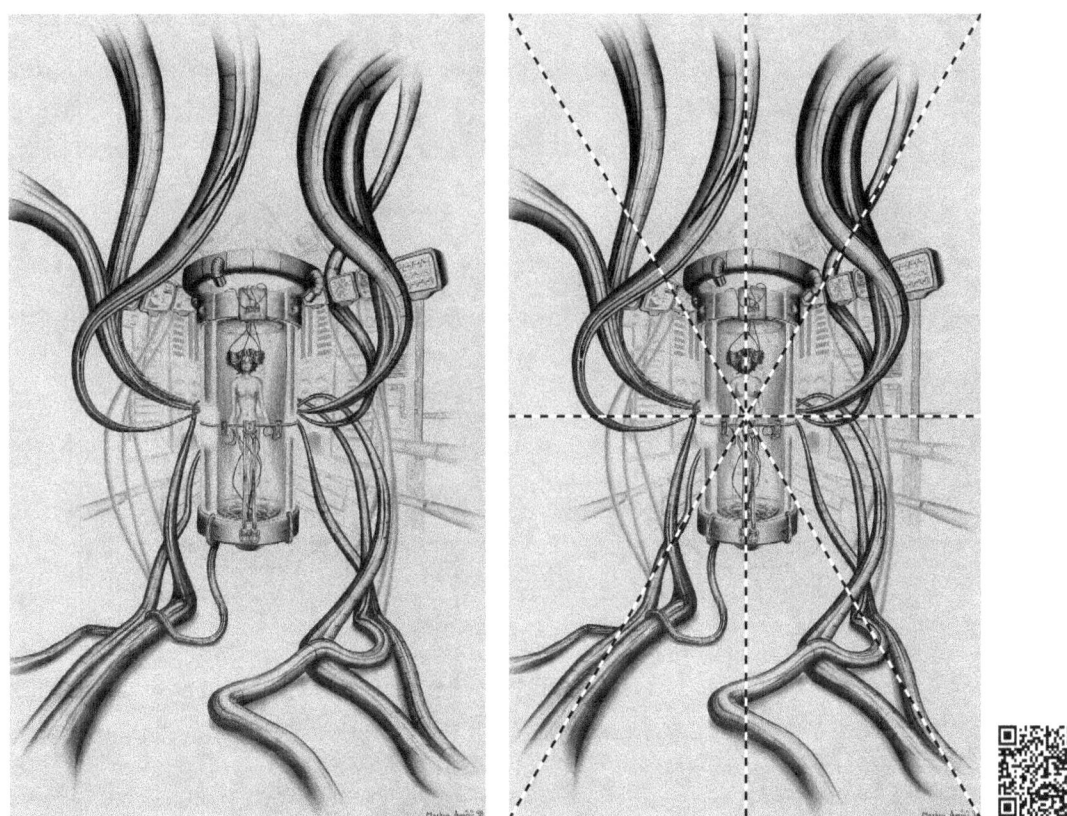

Pictorial composition of the picture "Human & Machine," created using center line and picture diagonals

The composition of pictures based on central axes and diagonals was common in the Renaissance since paintings in this period were often constructed symmetrically. Nowadays, this method is rarely used as the opinion that the main motif should not be centrally positioned has prevailed.

The Golden Ratio

The golden ratio is an aid for subdividing images according to a defined ratio. The resulting lines can be used to align image objects. The subdivision can be used both vertically and horizontally. In addition, the subdivision can be made in such a way that the entire image is subdivided into nine rectangles.

The intersection points that result can also be used to align image objects. The golden ratio is one of the best known design techniques and is very often used for landscape motifs.

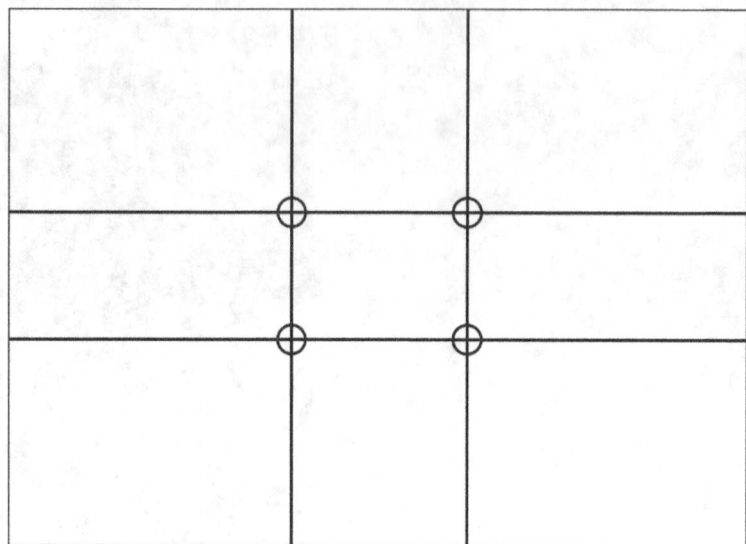

Golden ratio with intersections

Orientation according to these lines and intersections can help to create a harmonious image composition. However, the golden ratio is never a guarantee for the creation of a good image. It is – among many other design techniques – purely an aid, the use of which also requires experience.

Applying the Golden Ratio

You can use the following formula to subdivide your image according to the principle of the golden ratio:

$$\frac{a+b}{a} = \frac{a}{b} \quad or \quad \frac{a}{a+b} = \frac{b}{a}$$

If we consider the overall length of a side to be 100%, then the individual lengths of a=61.8% and b=38.2% are what emerge.

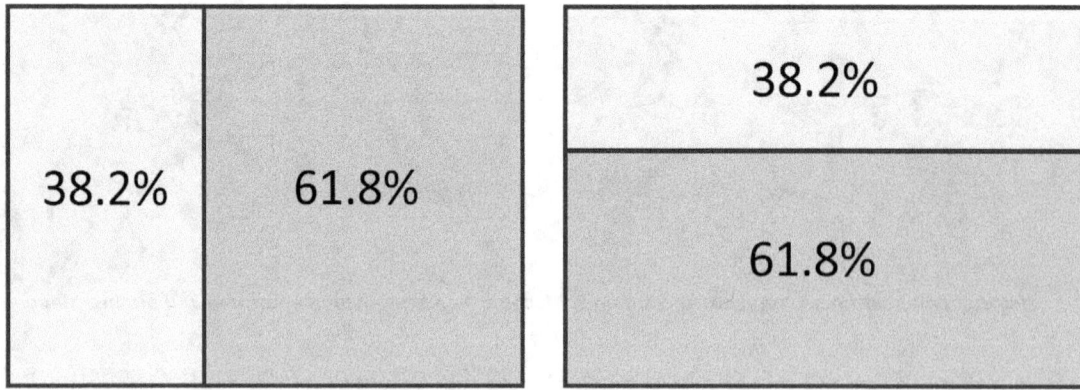

Segmentation according to the golden ratio

Methods for Subdividing an Image

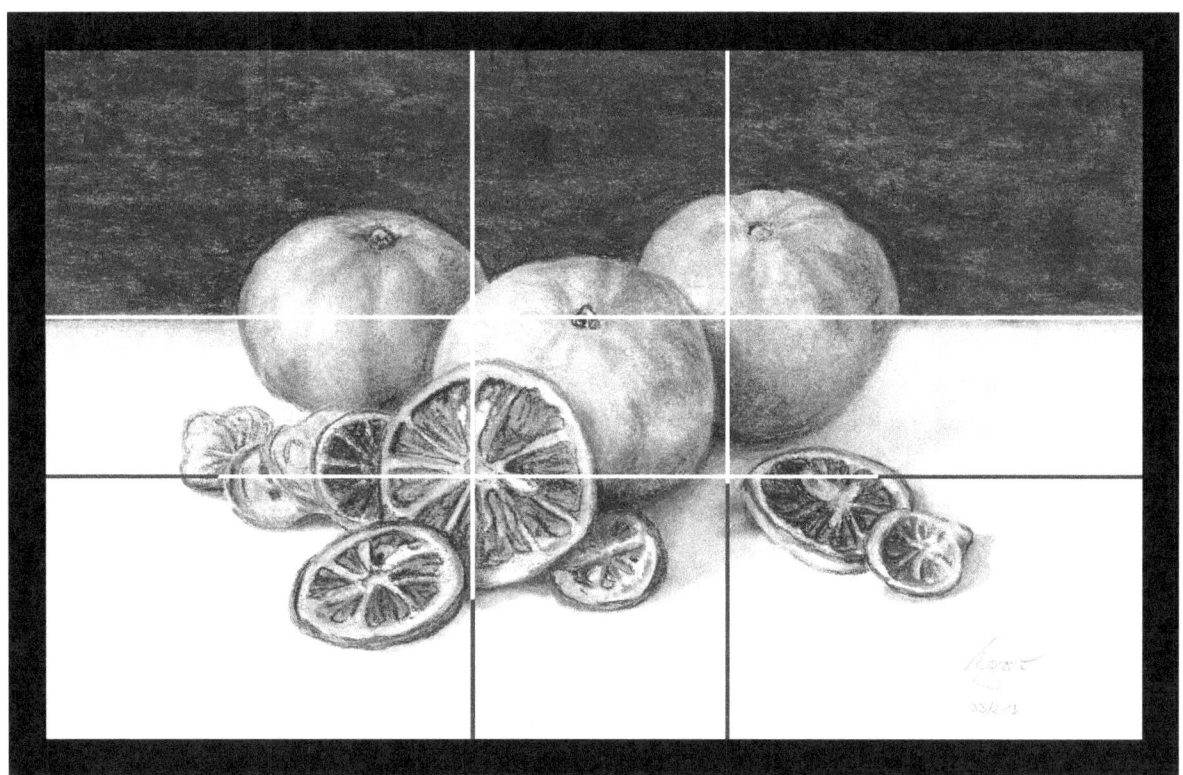

Still life based on the golden ratio

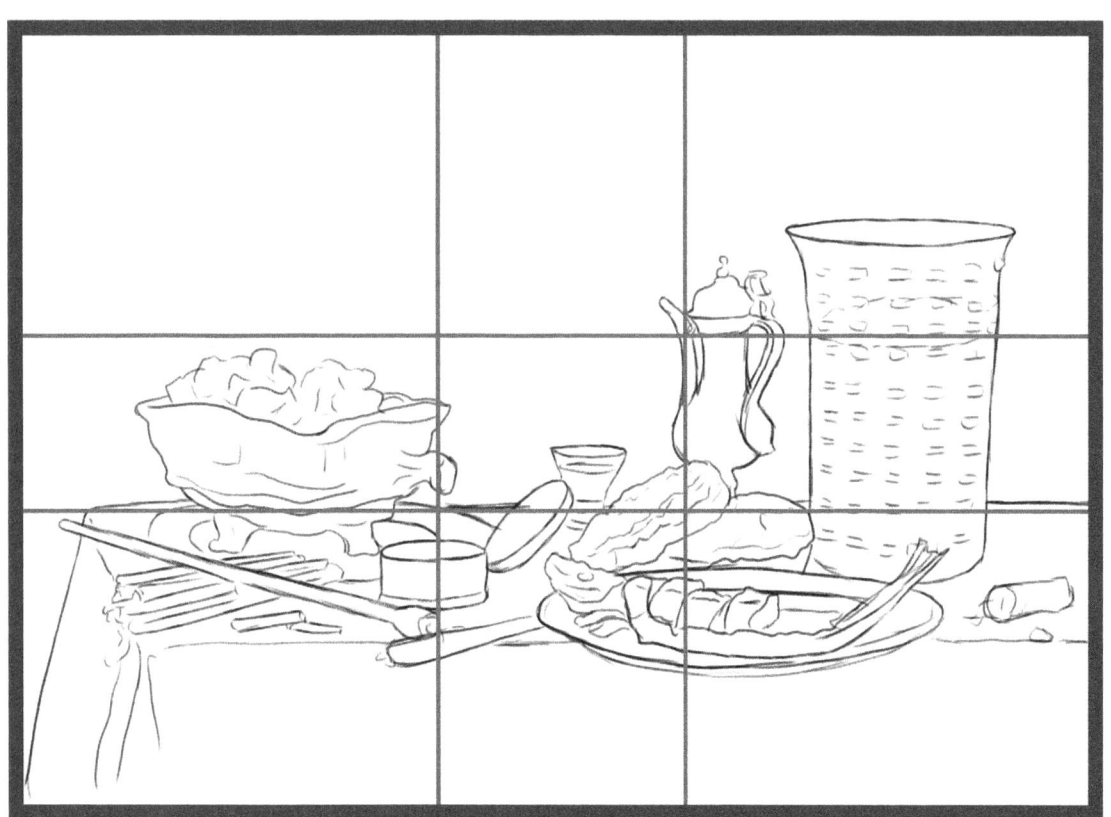

Picture objects and table edge are based on the golden ratio
Sketch of a still life painting by Pieter Soutman

It is noteworthy that the proportions of the golden ratio come from nature and can be found again and again in natural forms. This is probably the reason why division according to the golden ratio is perceived as particularly harmonious by humans.

Examples of the occurrence of the golden ratio in nature include the dimensions of an ivy leaf or the arrangement of leaves in various plants. This is also referred to as the golden angle, which is approximately 137.5°.

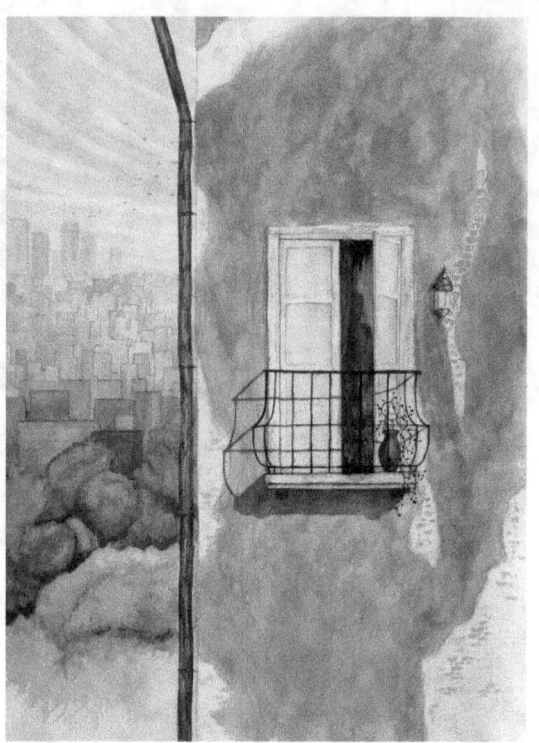

Pictorial composition with the aid of the golden ratio

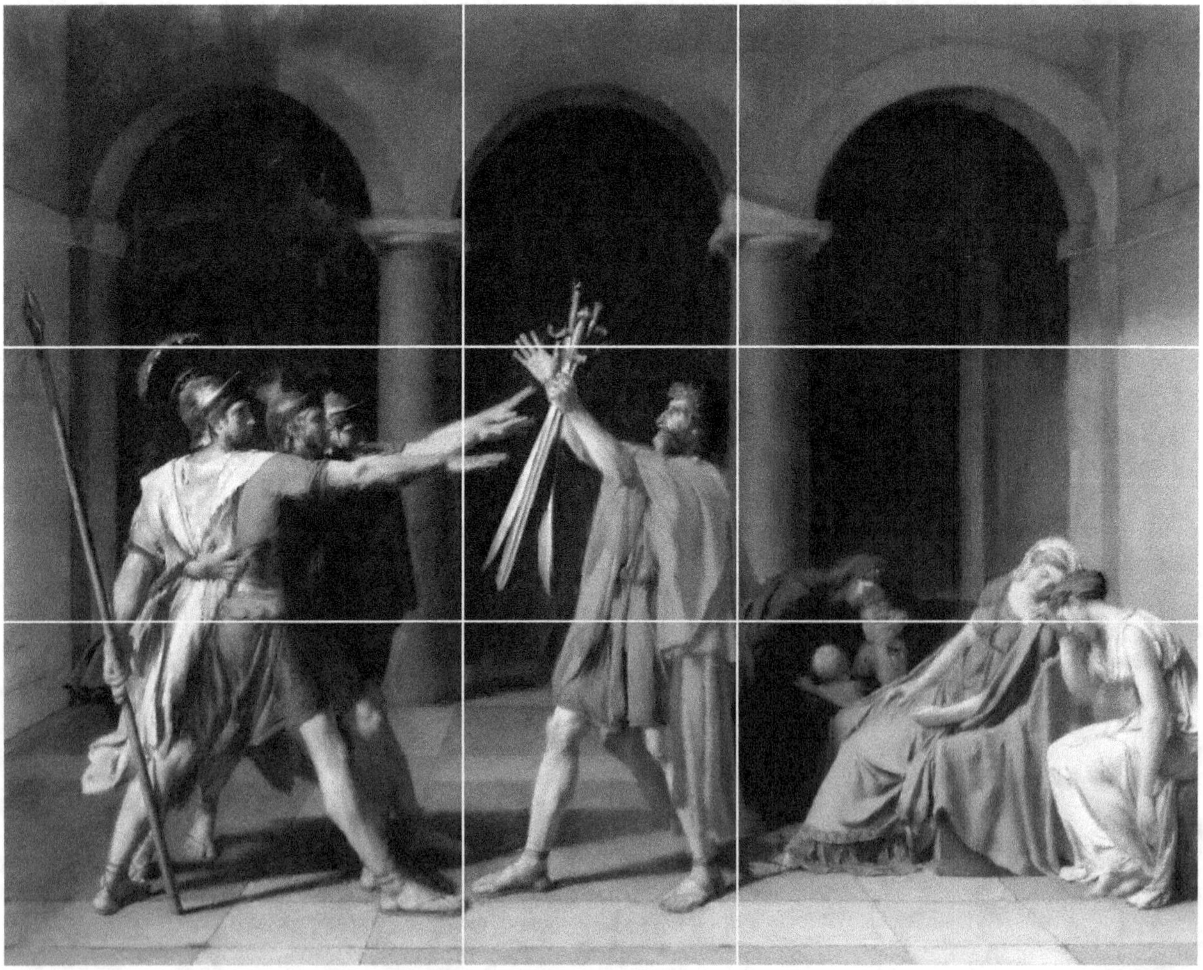

Obvious usage of the golden ratio in the painting "Oath of the Horatii" (copy)
Original: Jacques-Louis David, 1784

Methods for Subdividing an Image

The Golden Spiral

The golden spiral is a term we often hear, and the "Fibonacci sequence" is often mentioned in the same context. The Fibonacci sequence is an infinite sequence of numbers in which each number is the sum of the two numbers preceding it (0, 1, 1, 2, 3, 5, 8, 13, 21, and so on).

The golden spiral is formed when squares whose sides correspond to the numbers of the Fibonacci sequence are lined up. A quarter circle is then drawn in each of these squares, resulting in a spiral. The resulting rectangles are subdivided according to the golden ratio. Thus, the Fibonacci sequence is linked to the golden ratio.

This is demonstrated in the image below.

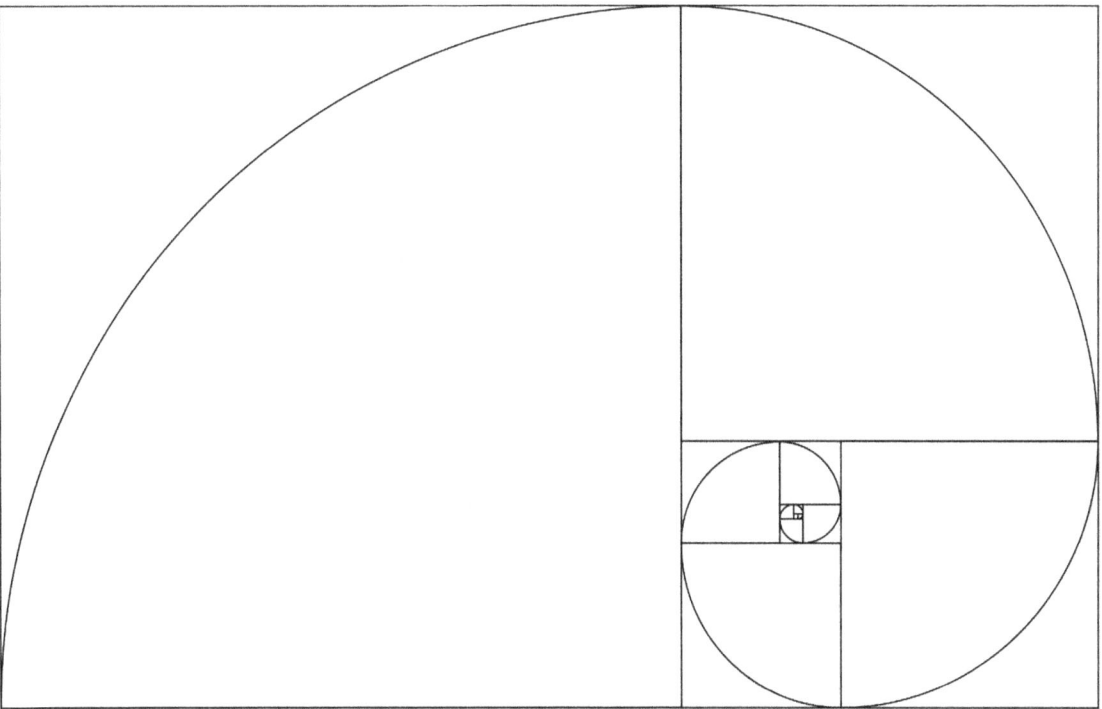

The golden spiral

The golden spiral can be used to aid harmonious image composition, for example by placing an important point in the center of the spiral. A typical example of this would be the eye of a person in the picture. However, as with the golden ratio, the golden spiral can never serve as a guarantee for a successful composition.

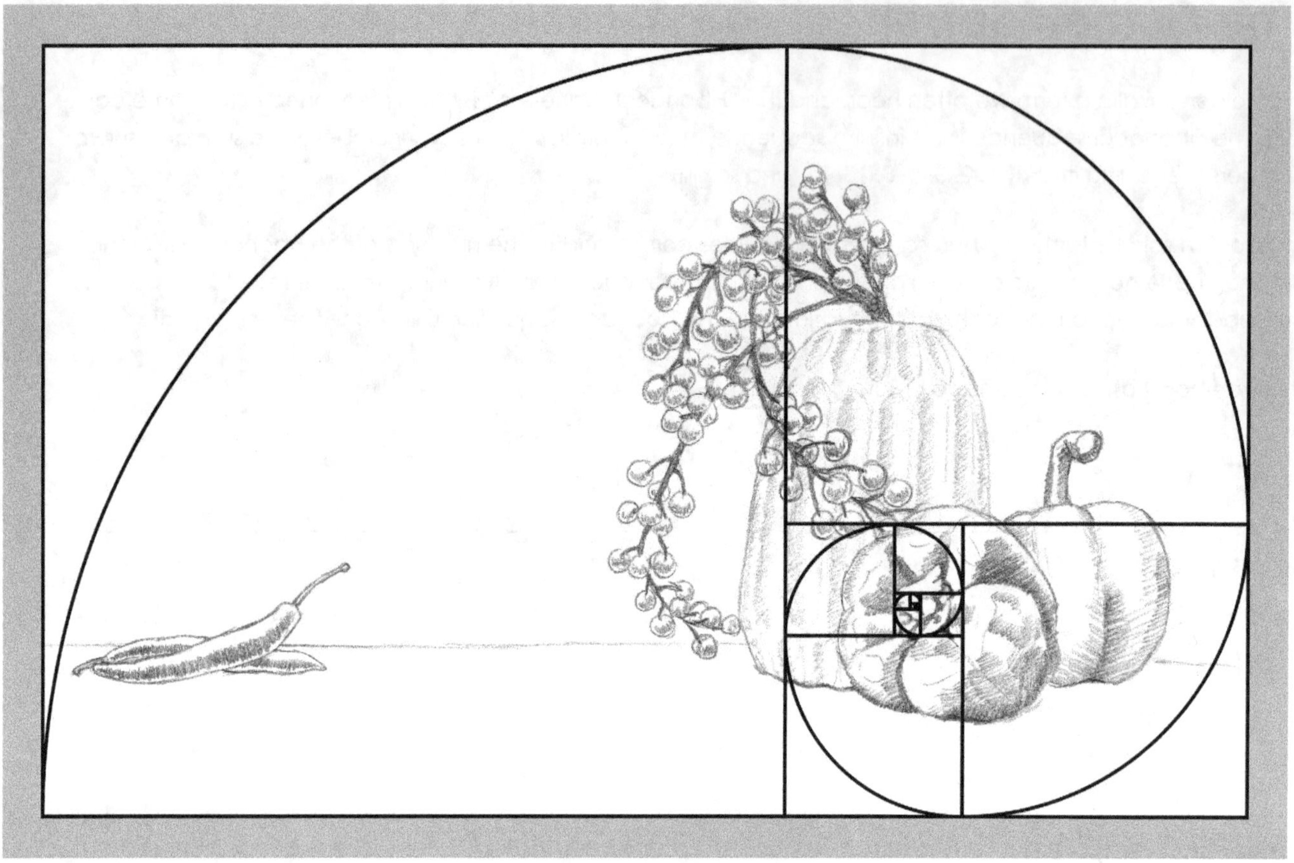

Use of the golden spiral in a still life

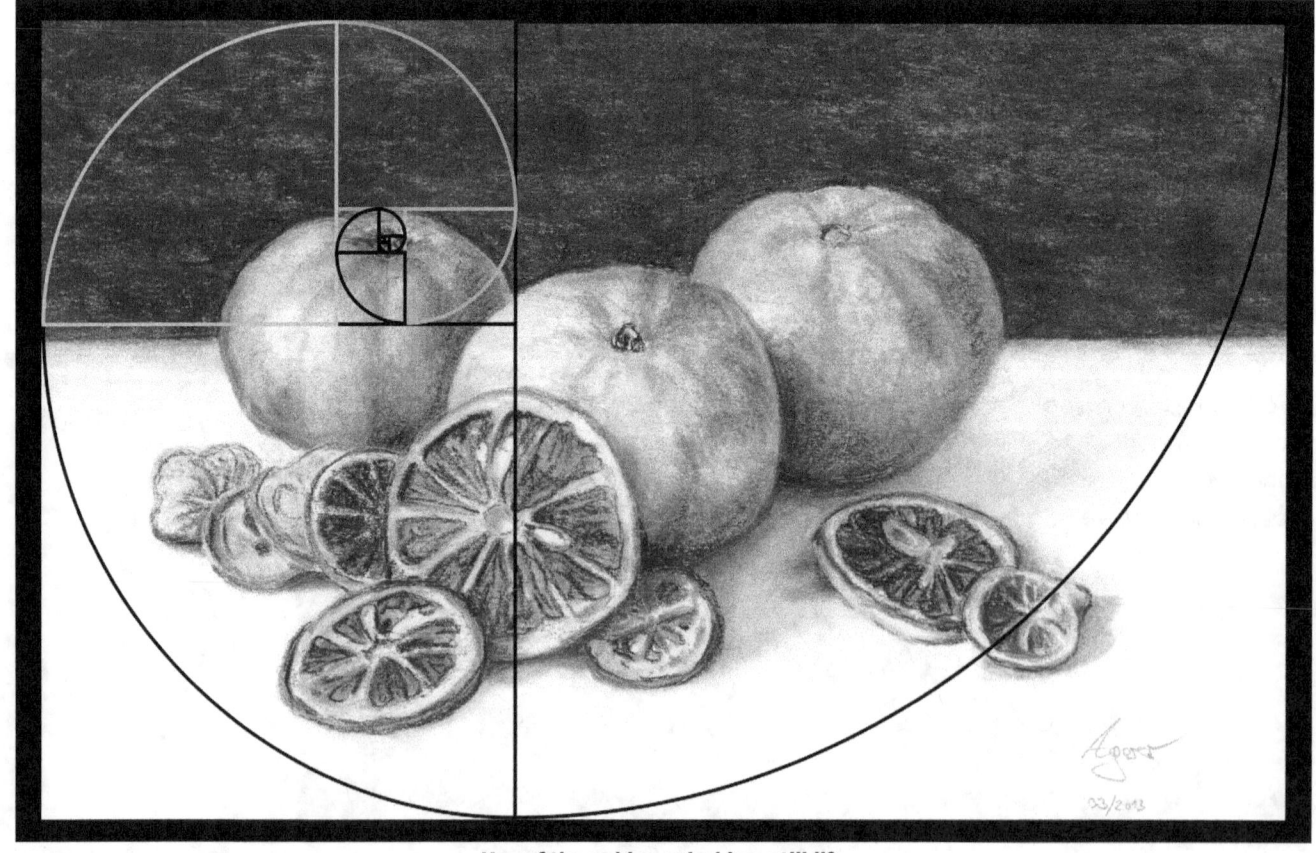

Use of the golden spiral in a still life

The Rule of Thirds

The "rule of thirds" is a composition aid based on the subdivision of pictures according to the rules of the golden ratio. The rule of thirds is mainly known from photography, but also plays an important role in other areas of the visual arts. Like the golden ratio, it is one of the most popular design methods.

As the name suggests, the picture is imaginarily divided into three equal parts. This division into thirds can take place both horizontally and vertically. Alternatively, it is usual to divide the picture directly into nine equal fields, which are very helpful for the design.

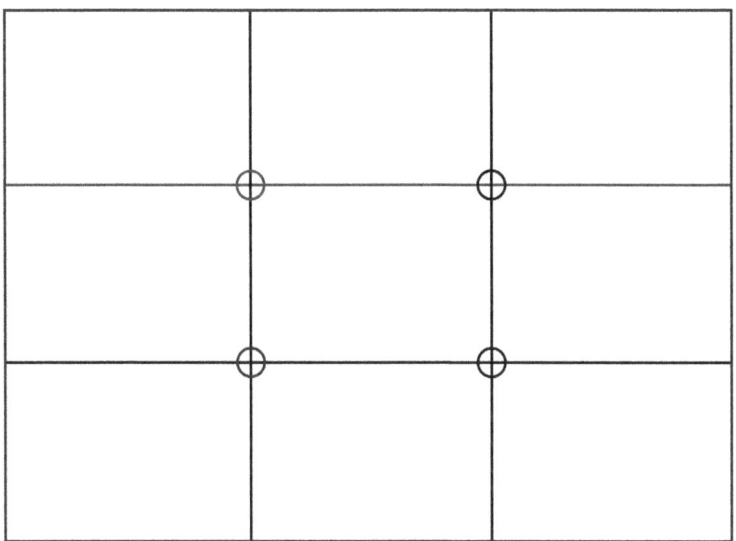

Subdividing into thirds with intersections

The intersections between the subdivision lines can also be used as compositional aids. Often, good images are created by placing the main motif on one of these intersections. With these aids, it is possible to create harmonious compositions and attract the viewer to the visual layout.

When applying the rule of thirds, however, be aware that it is – contrary to what the name may suggest – not a fixed rule but rather a design aid. The use of this method does not guarantee an appealing composition. The primary aim of the rule of thirds is to prevent the main motif from being placed in the center of the image, as this usually creates a boring and static composition.

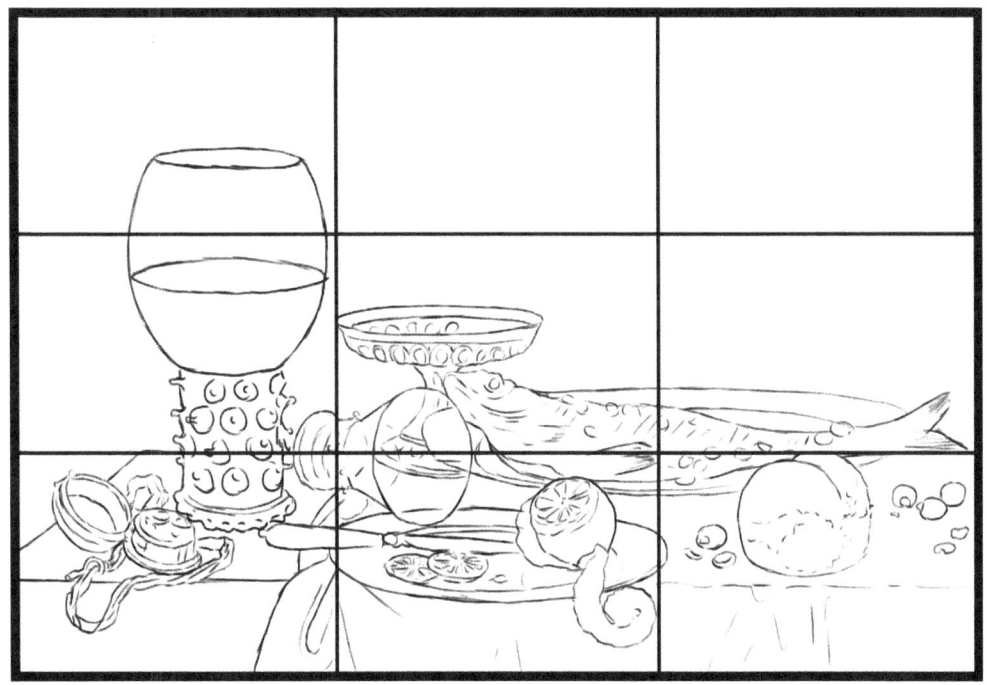

Example of the use of the rule of thirds – sketch of a still life painting
Original: Willem Claesz Heda, "Still Life with Roemer and Watch," 1629

You can use the rule of thirds without any other compositional aids. If you like, you could also sketch the subdivision lines on the paper before you start. However, the image is usually divided into nine parts rather than three. Using this method, you can orient yourself to the subdivision lines when positioning your motif. You can leave the center empty, or place elements there that do not flow, or only subordinately flow, into the picture design.

Make sure that you move the most important design elements to the side. However, it is important not to push them too far to the edge. As already mentioned, you can also use the four intersection points to compose the picture. Often, it is very appealing if striking elements of the pictorial composition are positioned at these points.

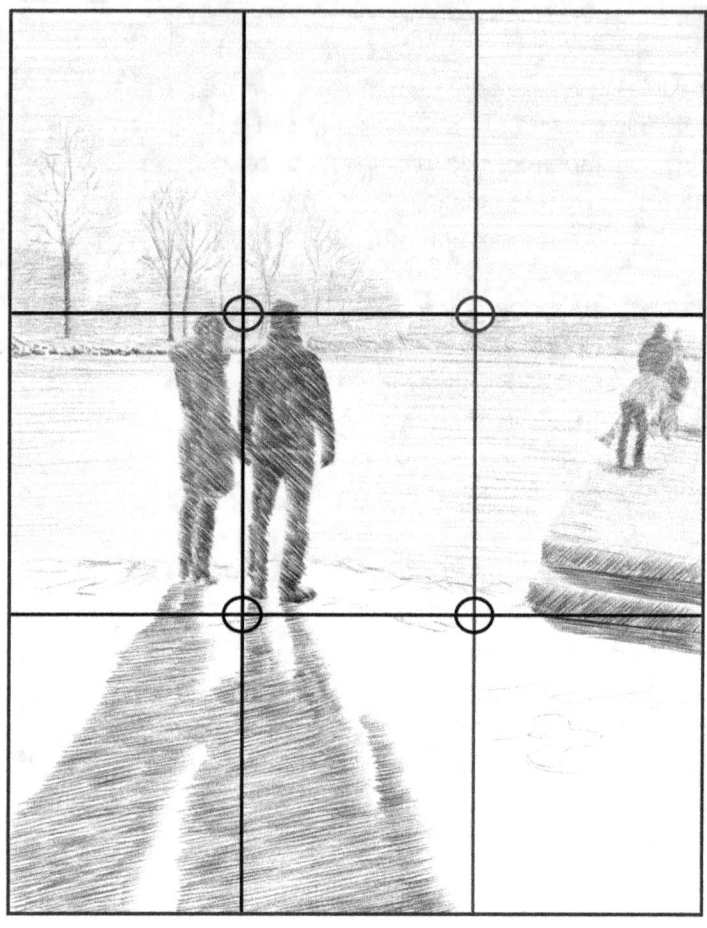
The main visual focus of the picture is at the top-left intersection

Subdivision of Image Levels

The rule of thirds is often used to divide the composition into three picture levels: foreground, midground, and background. This compositional technique is therefore an ideal method of creating landscapes.

The three levels represent what is close by, the more distant area, and the sky. In landscape paintings, for example, you will often see a subdivision in which either two thirds of the image is landscape and one third is sky, or vice versa. The pictures in this chapter are very good examples of this.

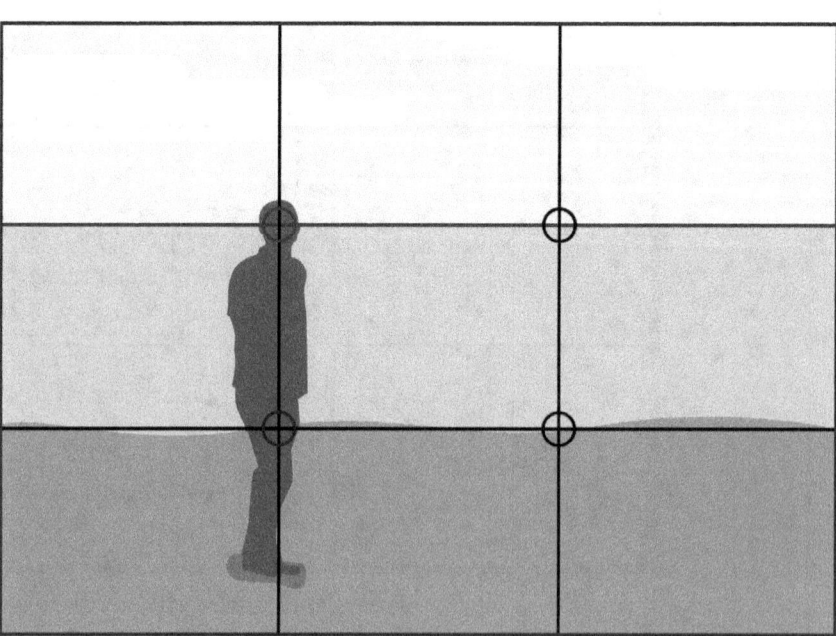
Subdivision into thirds: fore-, mid-, and background

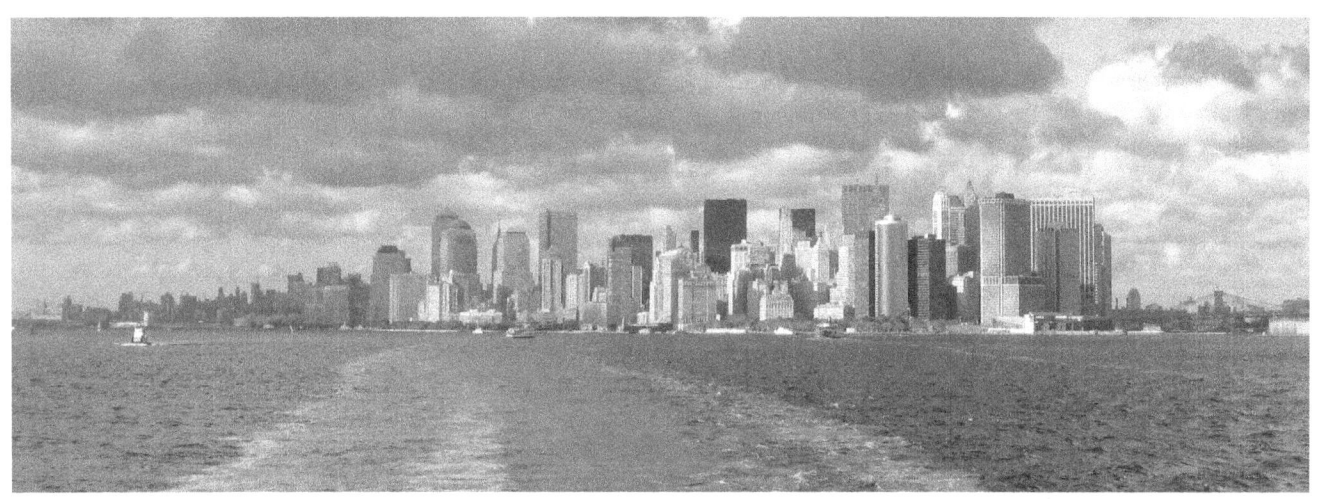

Landscape picture – skyline of New York

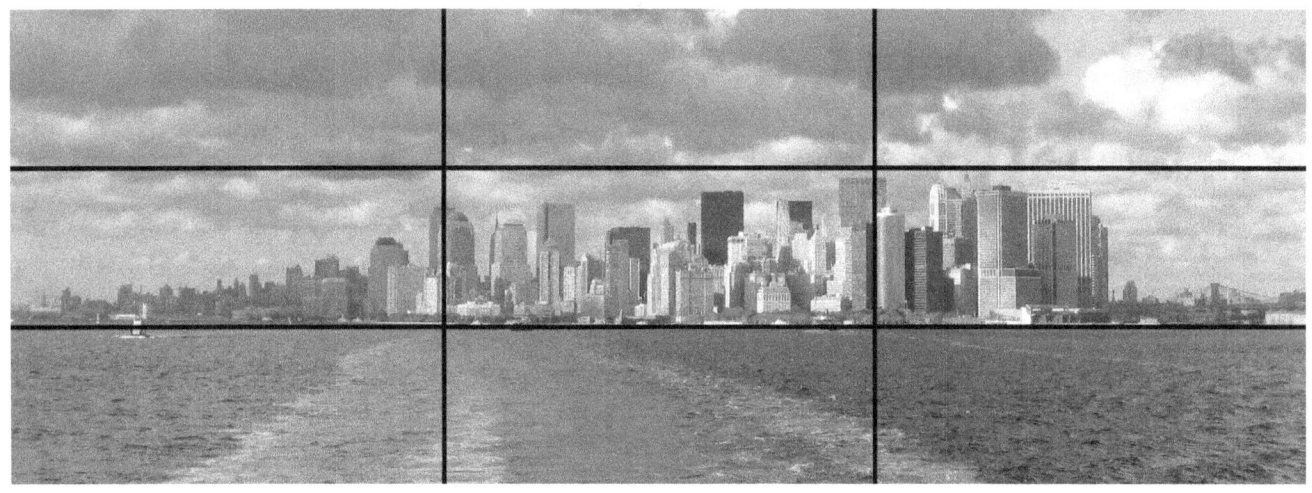

The same image subdivided into thirds

Image Selection and Optimization - Example

In the following example, we want to compose a cityscape. Before we start painting, we have to choose the ideal photograph to use as a template. We have two different photographs of the same city scene to choose from. Compare the two images and think about which one is better suited from a design perspective.

Photograph 1:

The large building is not the main focus in the first photograph. Thus, the scene in the square to the right of the building becomes the center of attention. However, there is no particular motif to be seen here. The composition of the picture therefore seems a bit unbalanced and lacking in content.

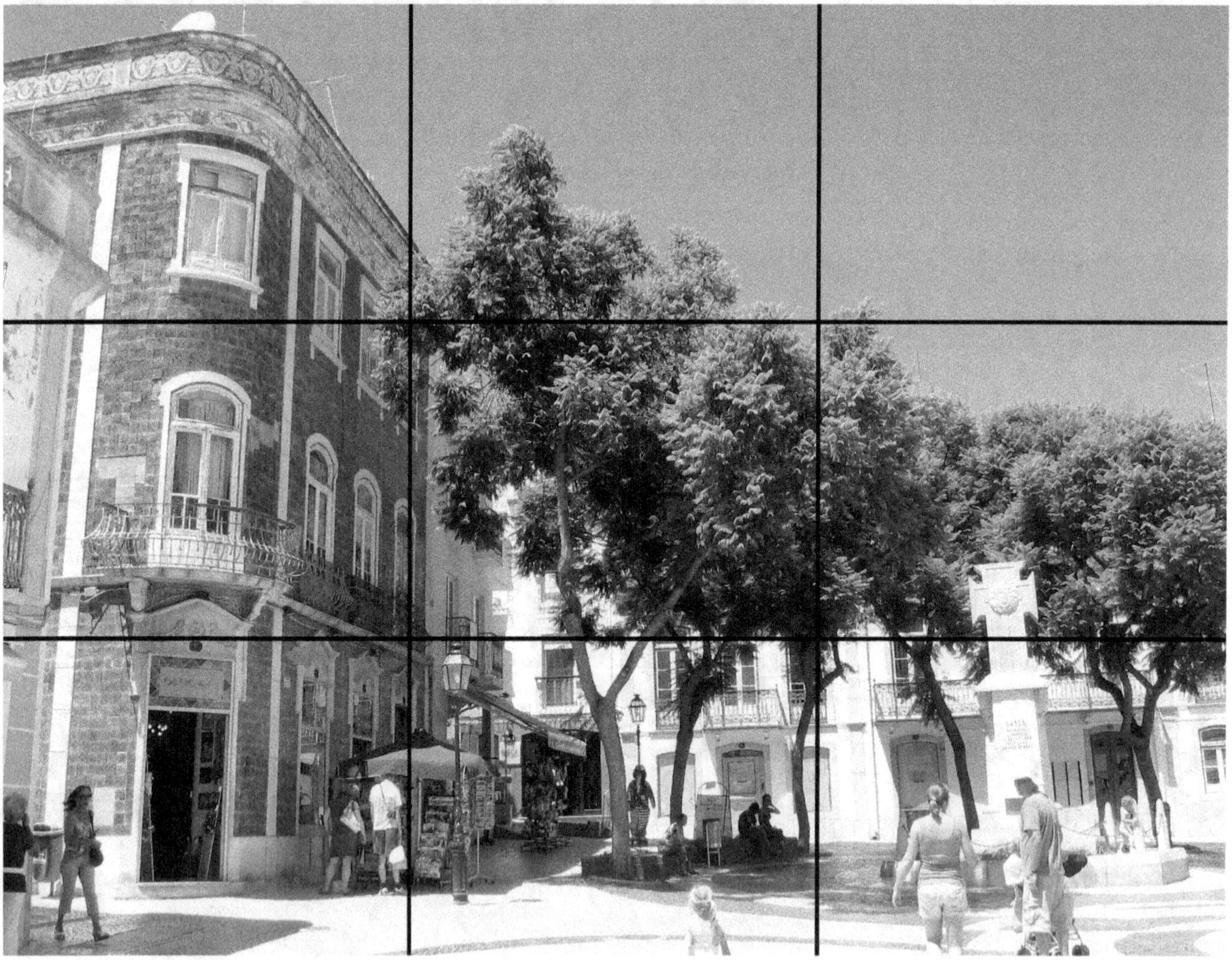

Photograph template 1

Photograph 2:

In the second photograph, the building has moved further toward the center of the picture. This makes it stand out as the actual motif or eye-catcher. In the square in the foreground, there are several people spread out, which makes the picture even more interesting. All in all, the composition of the second picture seems more coherent and balanced; therefore, this photograph was selected as the basis for an oil painting.

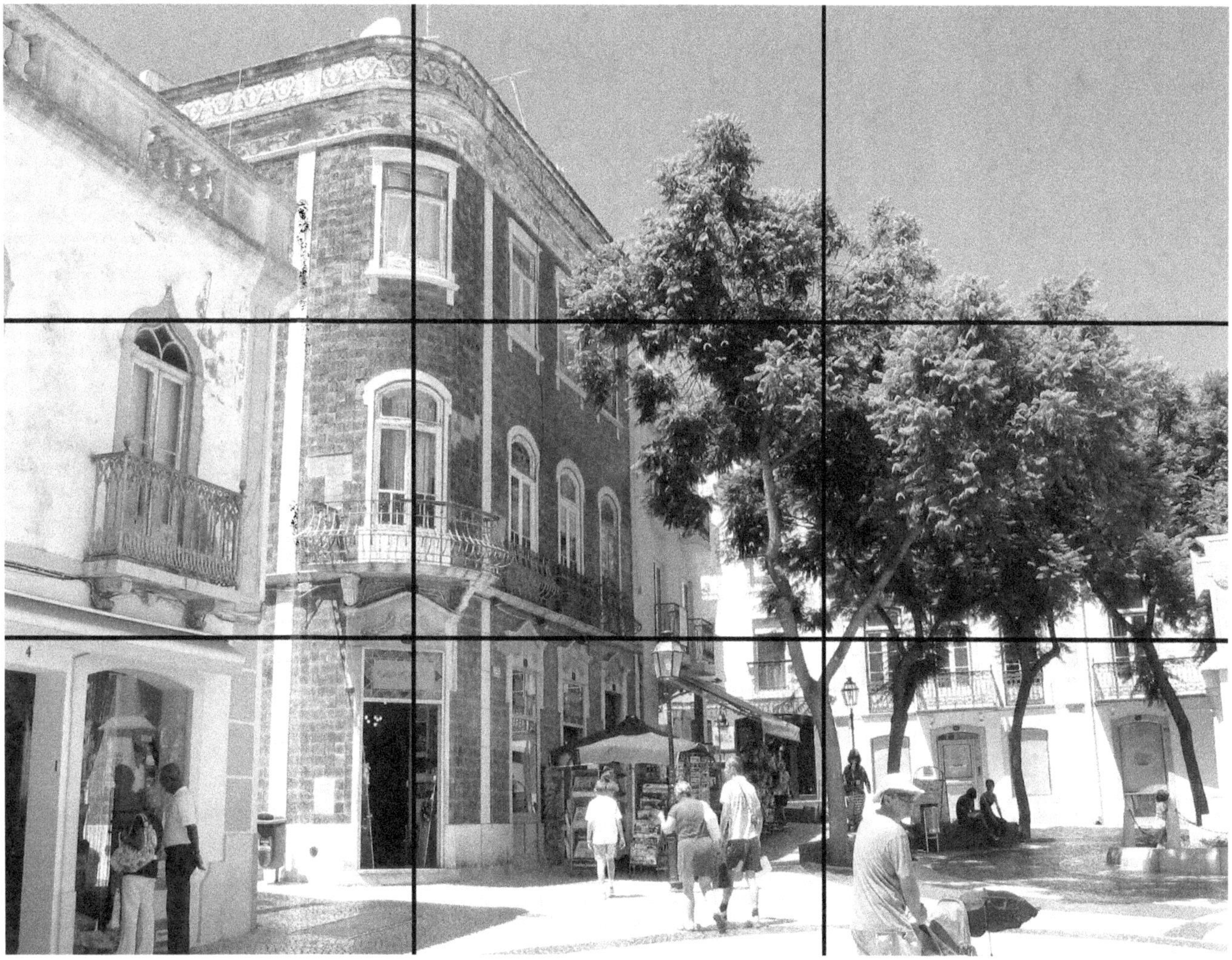

Photograph template 2

When composing photographs, you have the disadvantage of having to work with what you have in front of the lens. However, the advantage is that you can take many shots and then select the best one. In this case, the favored photograph was then used as a photograph template for an oil painting. A few details were changed to achieve an even better composition.

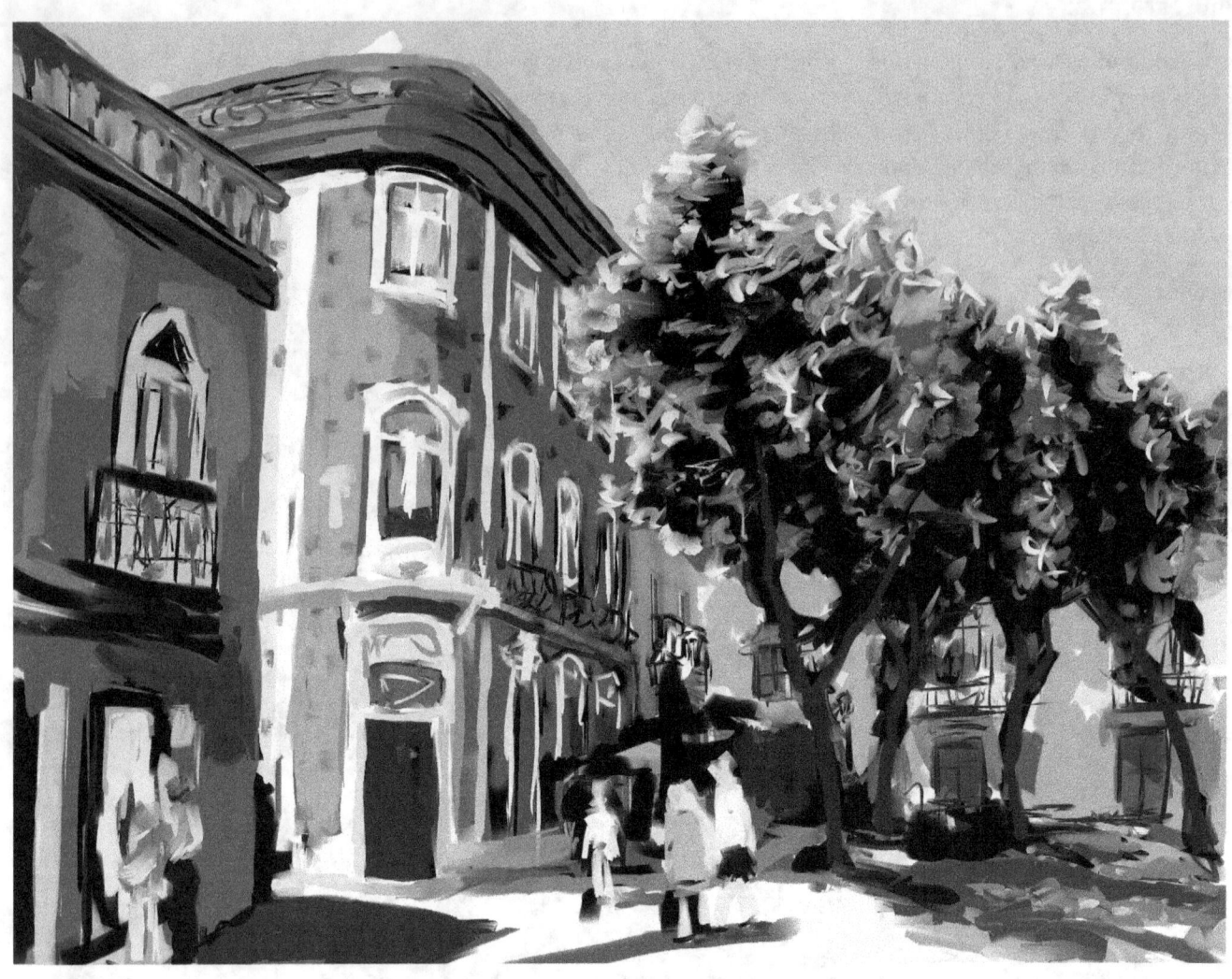
Conversion of the photograph template to an oil painting

A small flaw that is noticeable in both photograph templates is the position of the horizon. When applying the rule of thirds, you can see that the horizon is not on a third line, which makes the bottom of the image look a bit squat. However, this is not a catastrophe and was used as an opportunity to expand the painting downwards to optimize the composition.

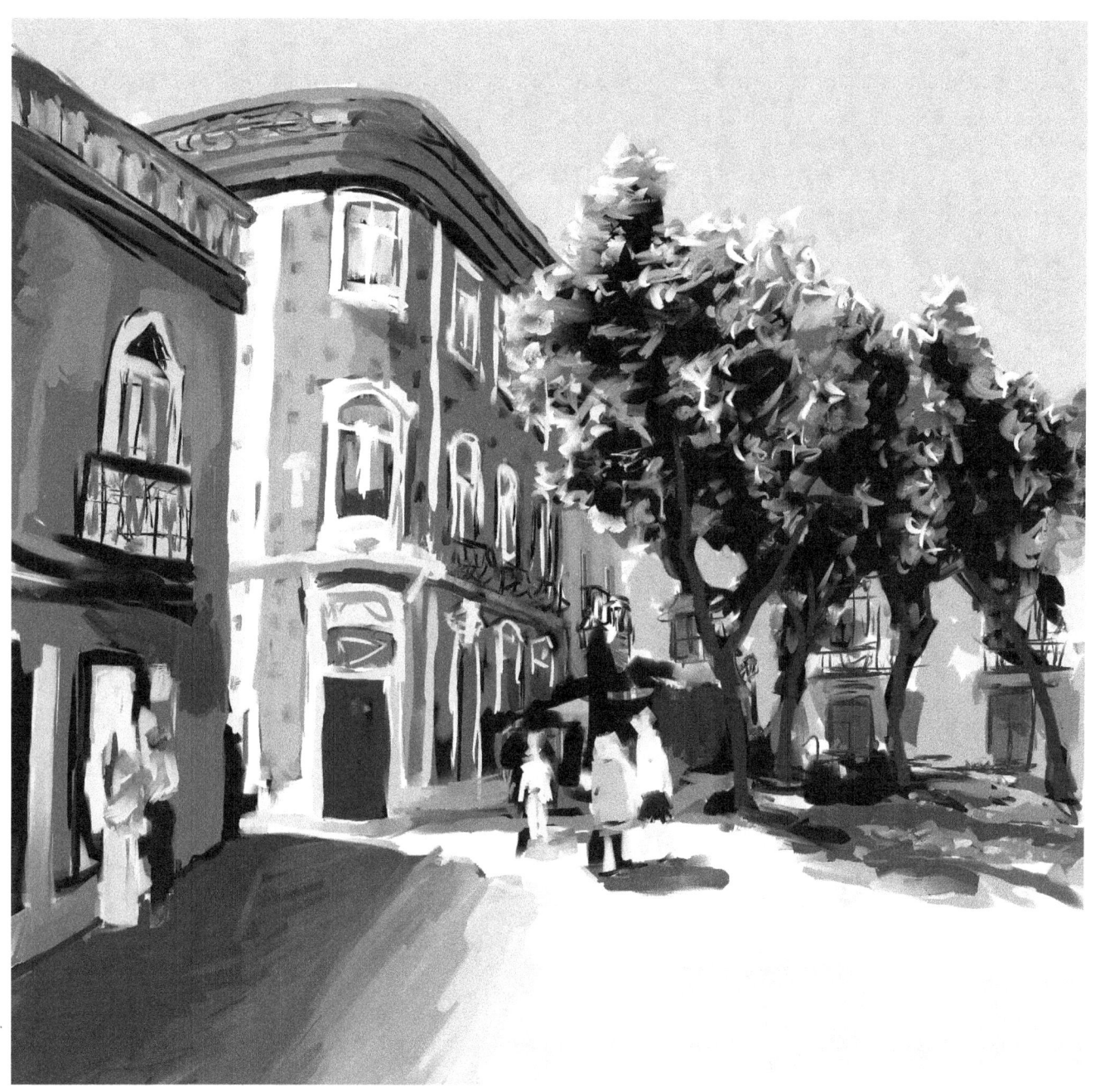

Optimized painting composition with expansion downwards

Which pictorial composition makes a better impression is a matter of taste. Compare the two options and form your own opinion.

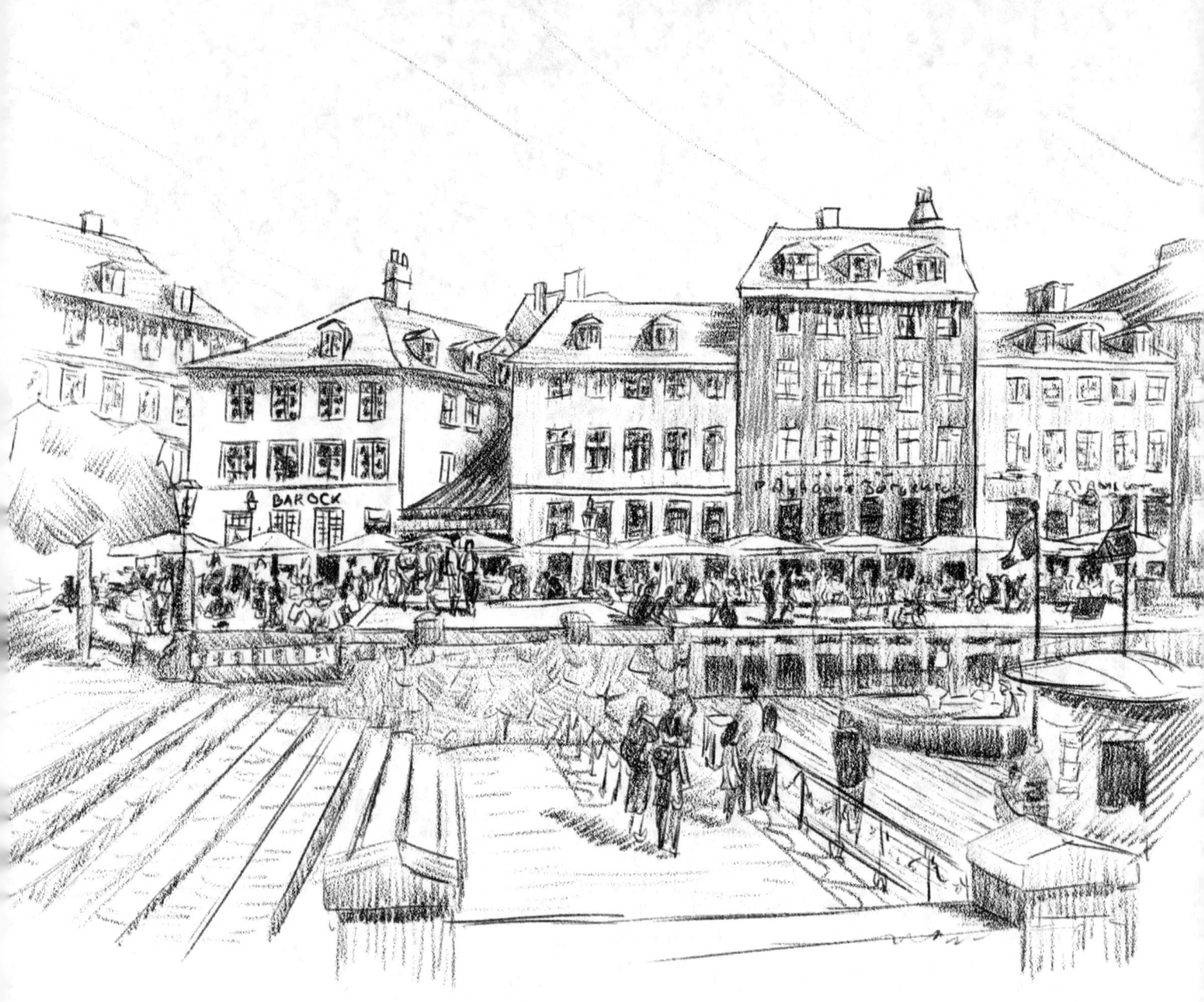
Pencil drawing of the harbor of Copenhagen with the help of methods for subdividing an image

Graphic Design Elements

» Art does not reproduce what is visible, rather it makes it visible. «

- Paul Klee -

Graphic Design Elements

Graphic design elements are elements such as the point, line, contour, shape, surface, or structure. They are the typical means of representation in drawing and also occur in painting and photography. The graphic design elements are basic techniques with which pictorial compositions can be created very easily.

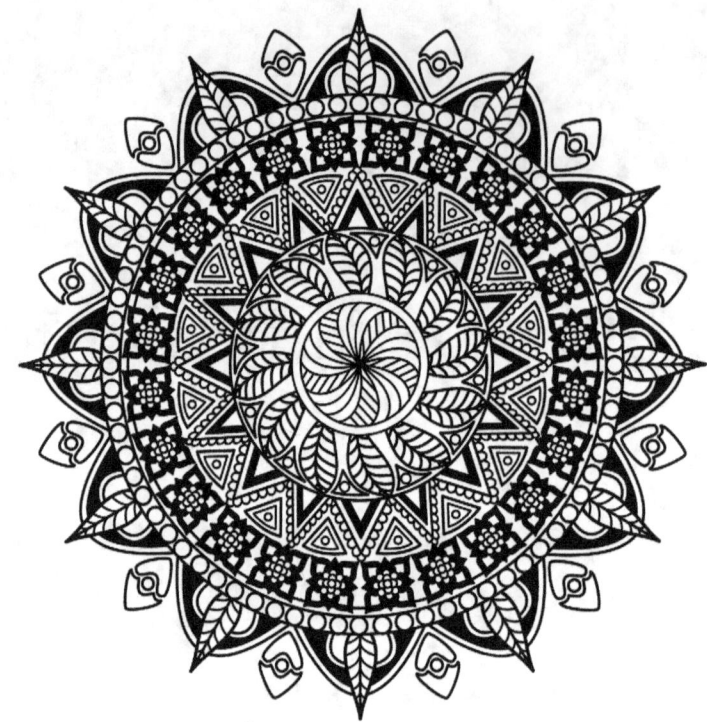

Mandala based on graphic elements

Points

The point is the smallest possible element in a drawing and the basic graphic design element. If you are painting or drawing abstract images, as in the style of Wassily Kandinsky, you can also include points that are nothing more than points. In a work that shows real objects, however, this is not so easy. Here, we benefit from the fact that very small objects that catch the eye are also perceived as points. The easiest way to take advantage of this is when a small or distant isolated object is placed in front of a uniform background and has a strong contrast to its surroundings. The contrast can be found in the tonal value (brightness) or in the color (color contrasts).

For a pleasant and interesting pictorial effect, skillful positioning is important. As is always the case with composition, if the image is placed centrally, you run the risk of making it look too rigid and boring. Successful positioning is achieved through compositional techniques such as the rule of thirds, which are also described in this book.

In the following pictures, you will find several variations of the same motif. It involves a boat which can be interpreted as a point due to its distance from the viewer.

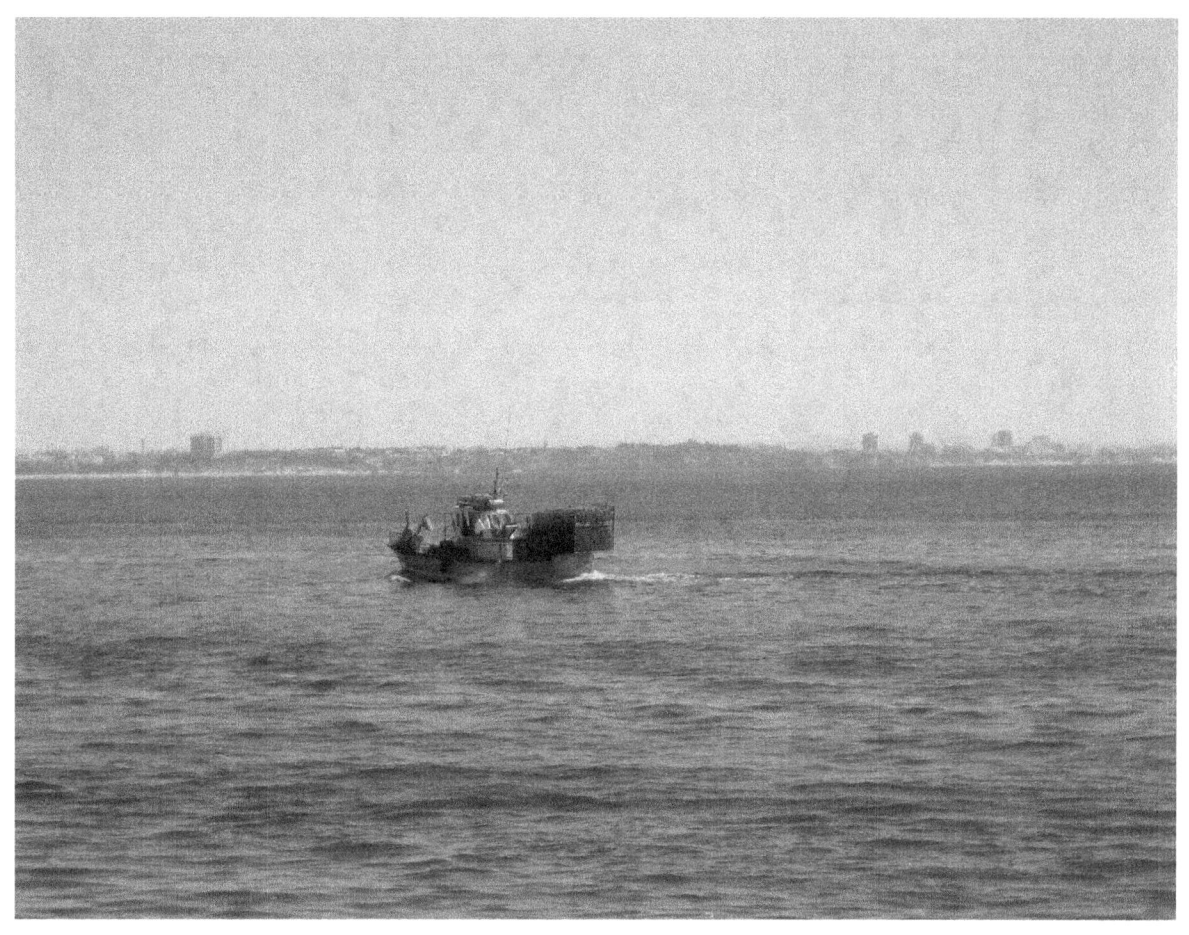
Positioning of the boat a bit too far to the left

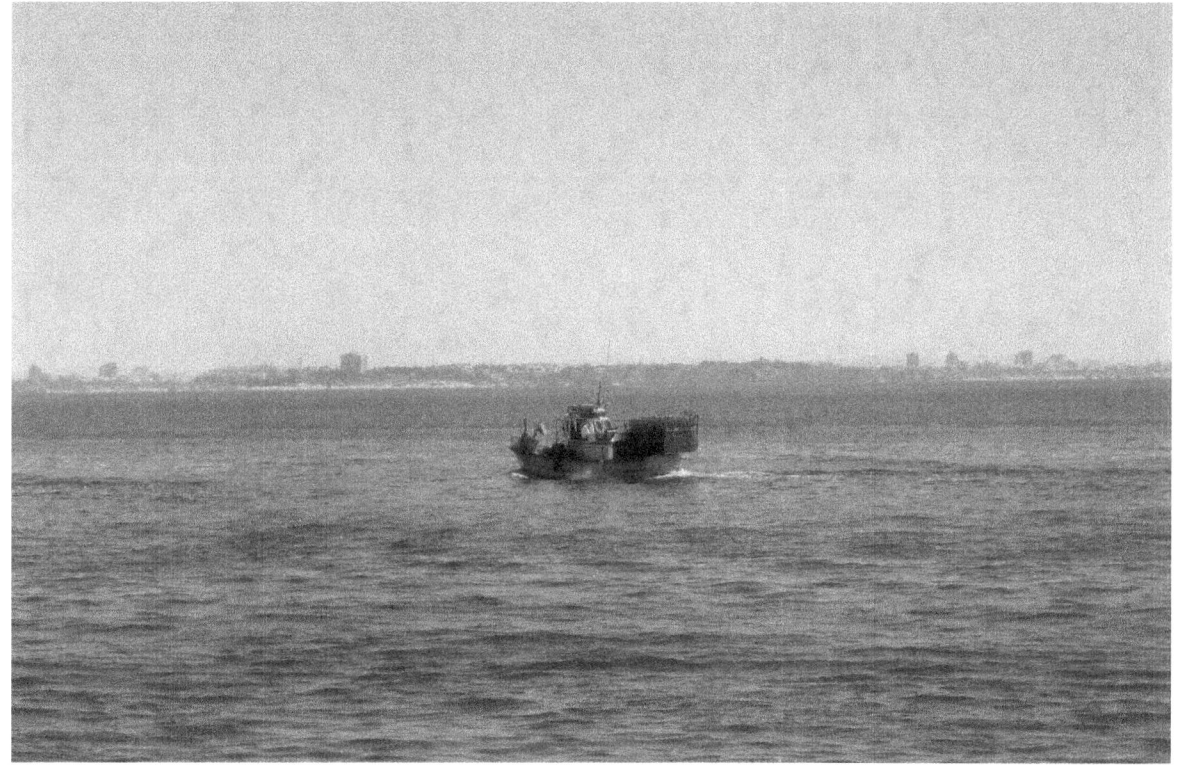
Central positioning in the middle of the photograph

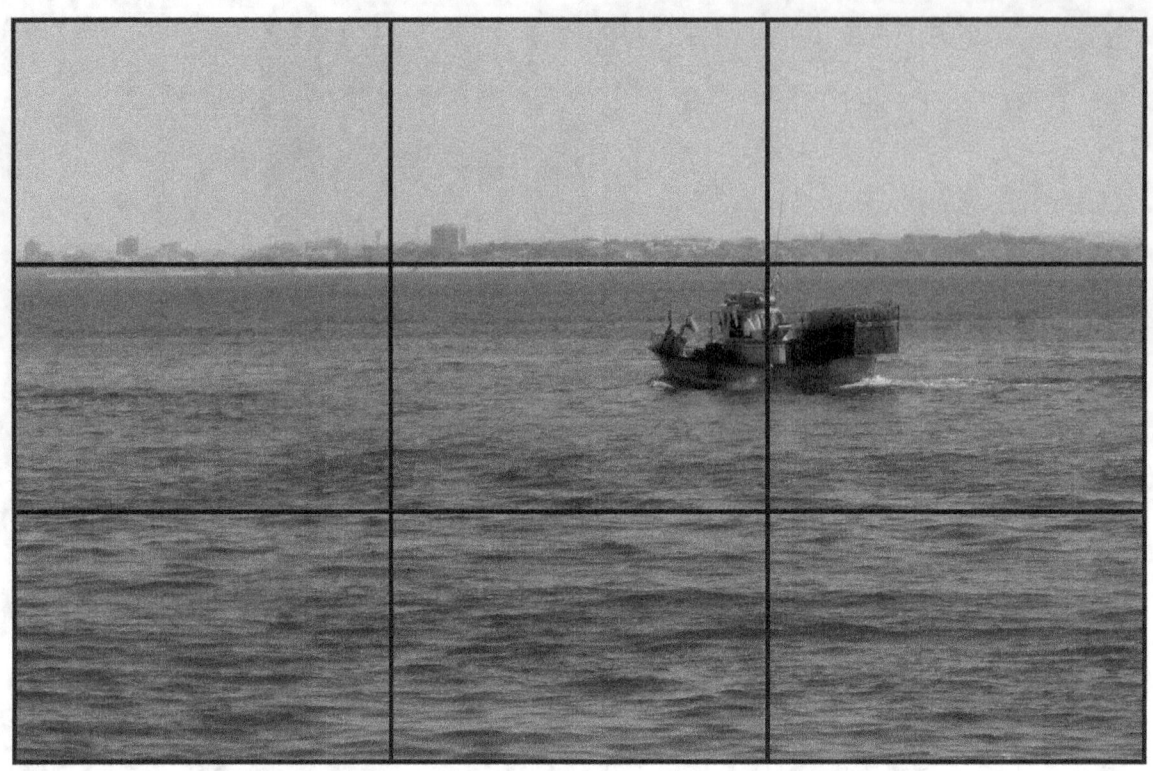
Positioning based on the rule of thirds with the horizon on the line of the upper third

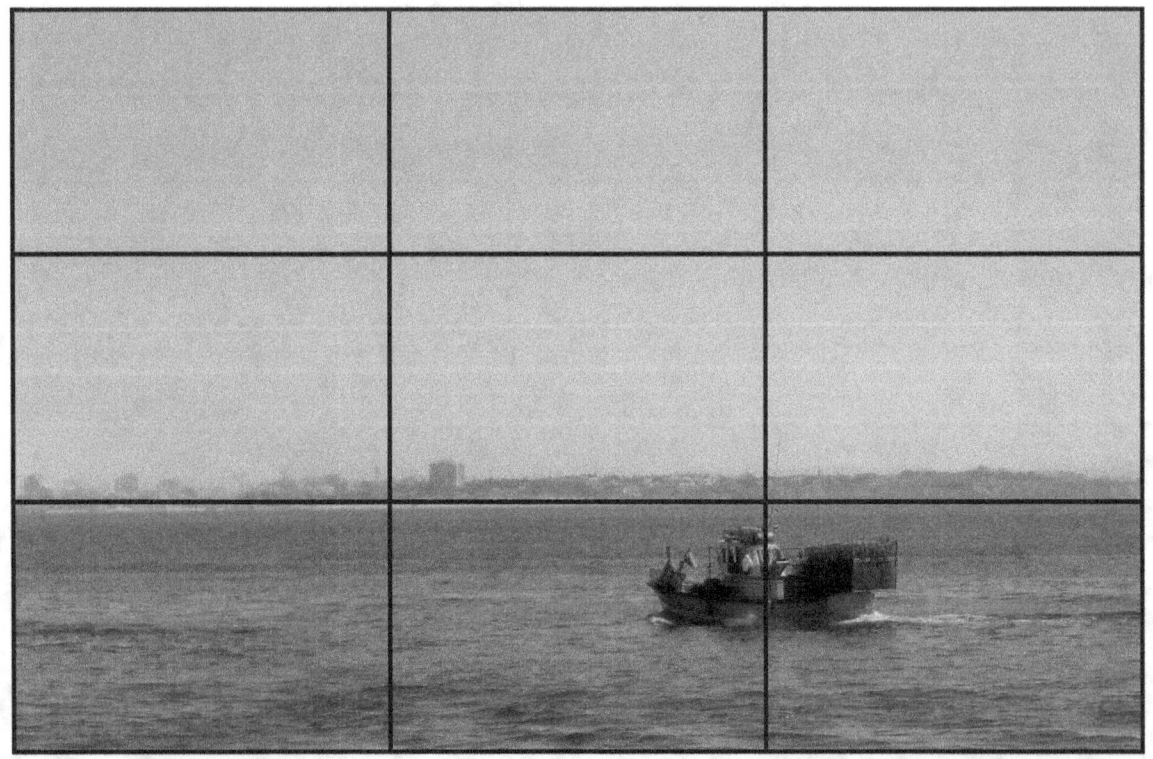
Positioning based on the rule of thirds with the horizon on the line of the lower third

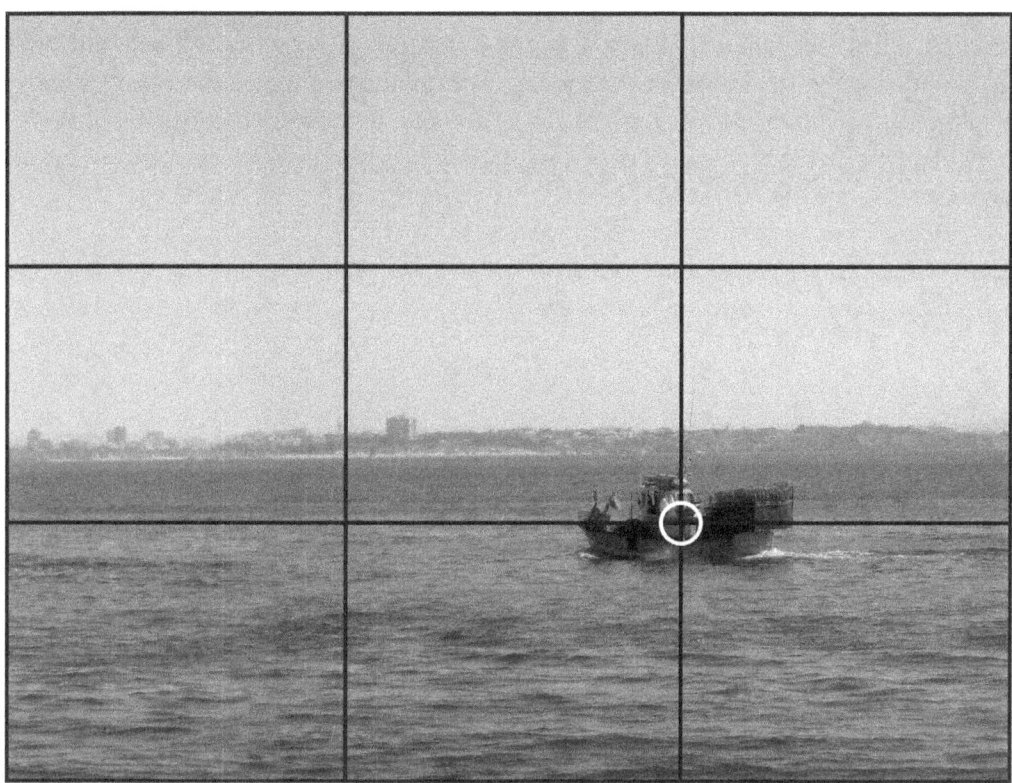
Positioning based on the rule of thirds with the boat on the intersection point

When comparing the different variants, with the point motif in different positions, differences become clear. In the end, the position on the lower right intersection of the third lines was chosen as this makes the composition appear most balanced.

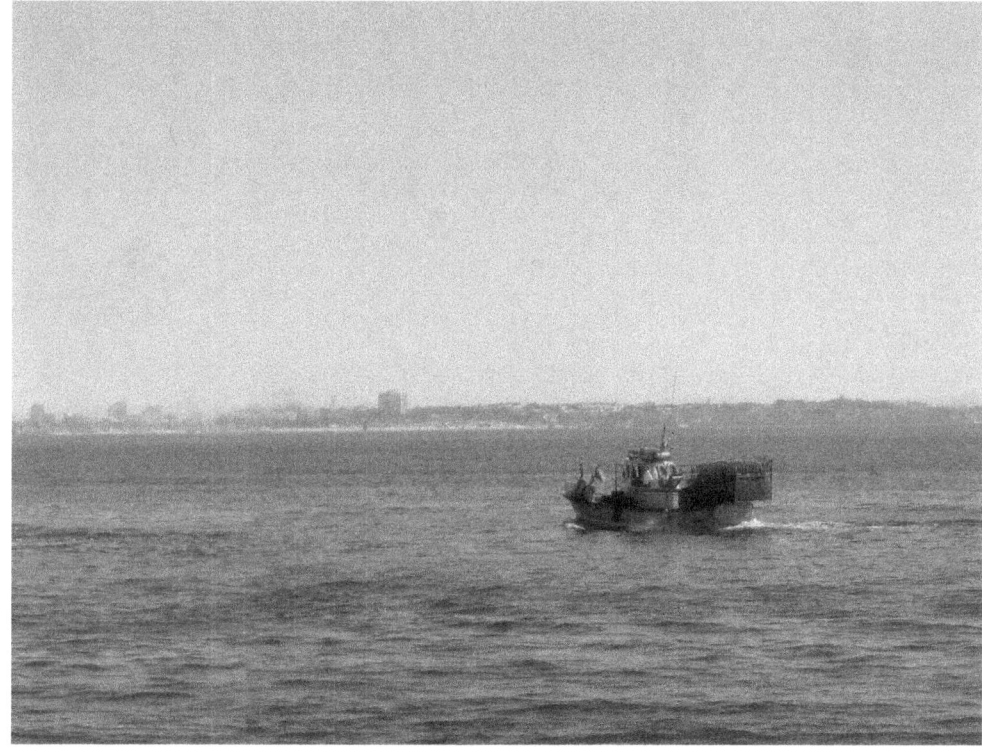
Final selection

If you include two or more points, more complex compositions can be created. The rules described above will also apply, but what is added is the dimension of distance. Two points within an image will automatically interact. An invisible line connecting the two points is inevitably created for the viewer. The strength of this mutual interaction is determined by factors such as the background and the conspicuousness of the points. If one element is too dominant, this can be loosened up by adding further elements to the picture.

Several points can also form a line or a curve. Here we are also dealing with a line that emerges only in our imagination. In addition, using several points can give the impression of a surface. Both effects are determined by Gestalt design principles such as the "law of proximity" or the "law of good continuation".

Example Image 1: Paper Warrior #3 – Tarantula

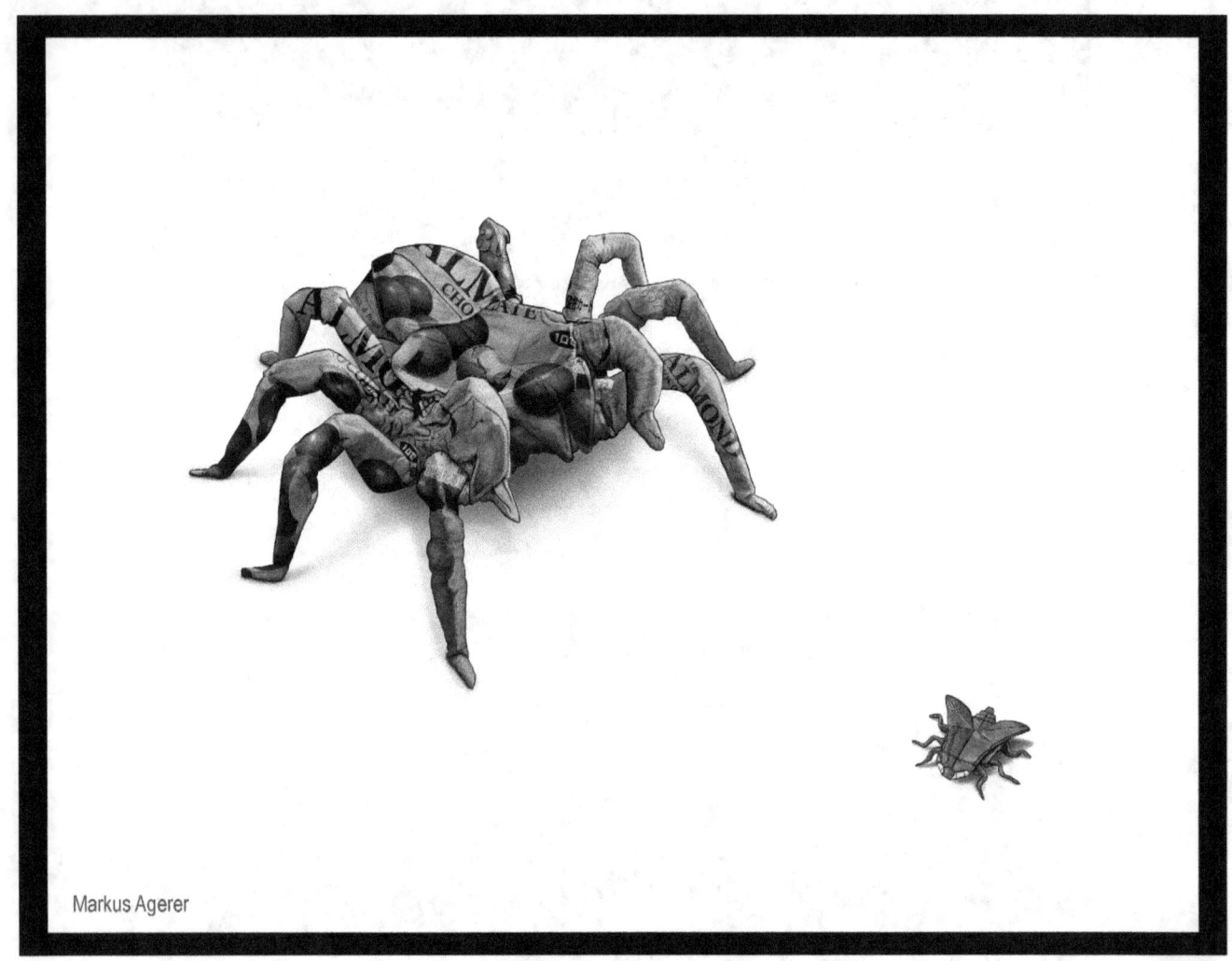

Paper Warrior #3 – Tarantula

The illustration with the origami figures shows not only the visually dominant tarantula but also a fly, which is so comparatively small that it is perceived as a dot. This dot automatically attracts the attention of the viewer and, in combination with the contrast between the hunter and the hunted, creates considerable tension in the picture.

Example Image 2: Poppy Field near Argenteuil

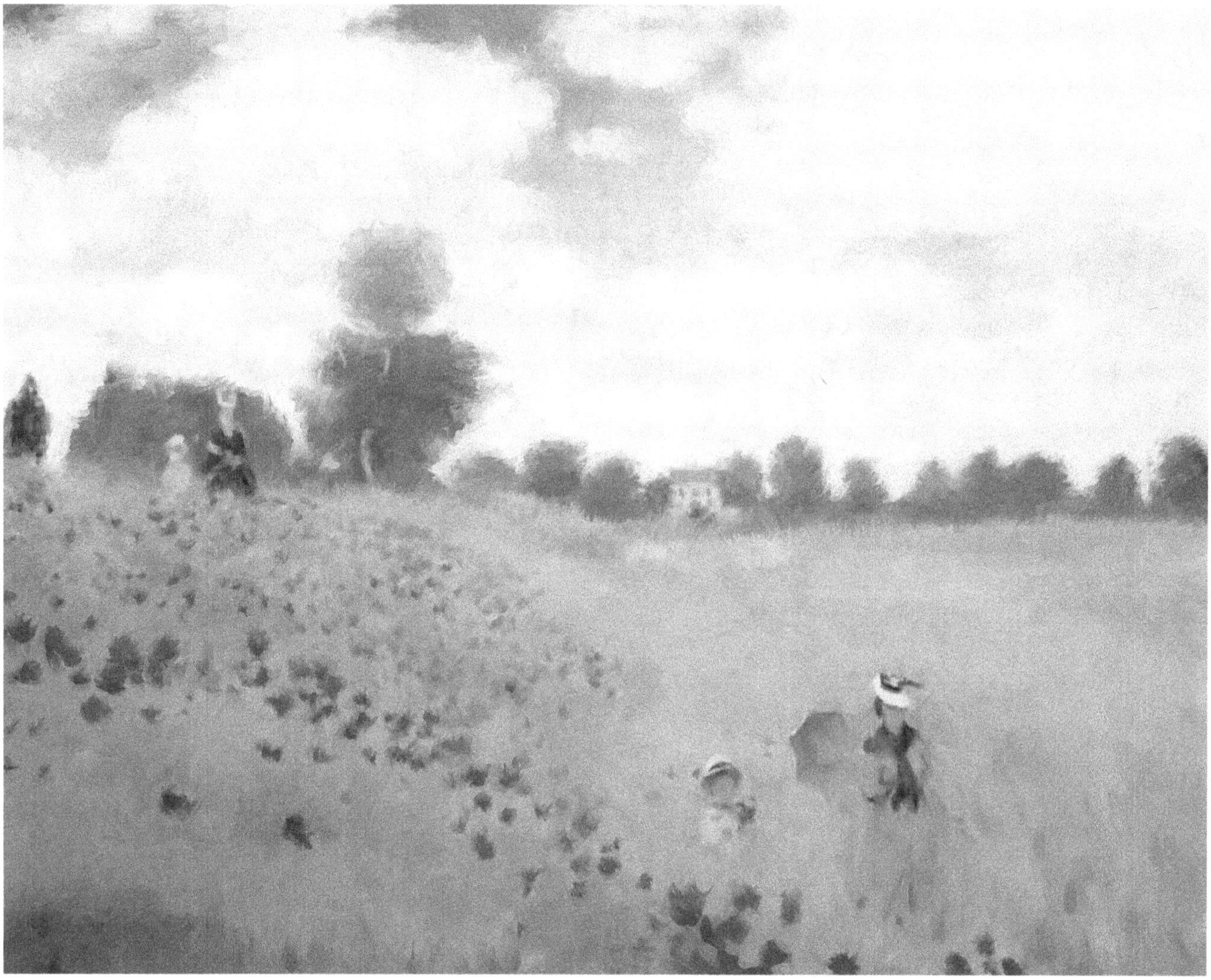

Poppy Field near Argenteuil – copy
Original: Claude Monet, 1873

In the example picture, "Poppy Field near Argenteuil" by Claude Monet, the blossoms of the poppies can be seen as dots. They create a certain structure, convey a feeling for the distance between the objects in the picture, and also form a visual bridge between the characters in the scene. Alternatively, on an abstract level the four people in the picture can be viewed as dots. An imaginary line is created between the two pairs.

Lines as Design Elements

When we speak of lines as a design element, we mean visible lines in an image. So here we are not talking about lines that serve to align objects, such as the golden ratio. Rather, we mean lines created by the objects themselves and the effect these lines have on the viewer.

On the one hand, this effect can be emotional, for example by conveying feelings such as stability, narrowness, or dynamism. Dynamic features, such as movement in a certain direction, can also be visualized by lines. On the other hand, lines often guide the viewer's gaze through the picture, which is of great importance for a successful pictorial composition.

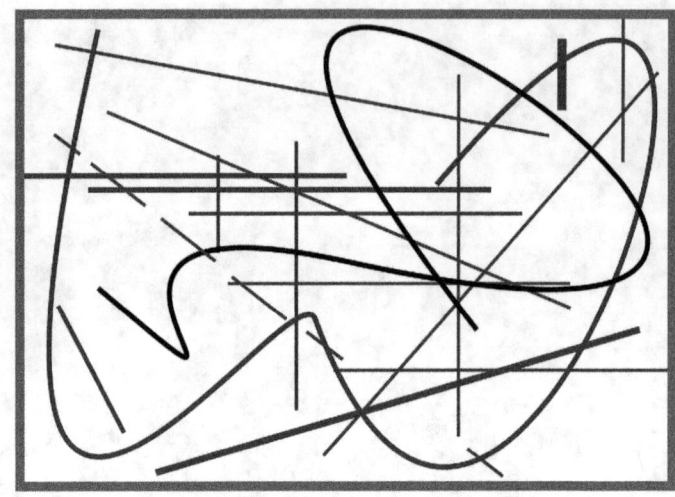
Lines going in different directions

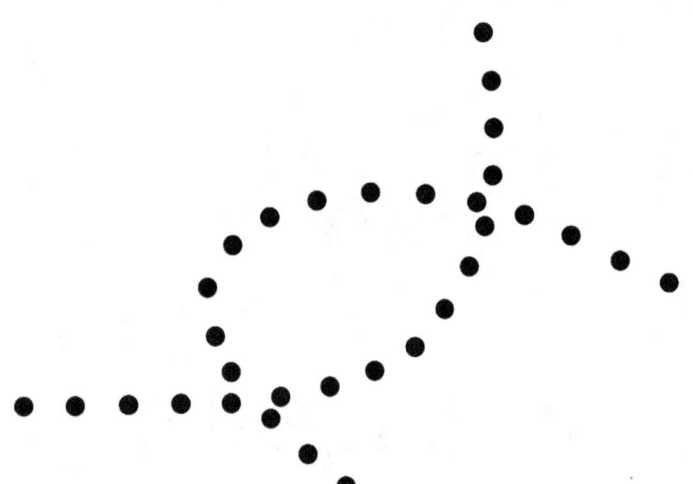
Dots become two lines

Lines can be created by copying a concrete line. This technique is often used in drawings and illustrations. On the other hand, lines can also be created by boundaries, for example in places where light and shadow separate, where surfaces with different tonal values adjoin each other, or where different patterns or structures meet. In particular, lines emerge in this way in paintings and photographs.

A series of dots can also be mentally completed by the viewer to form a line if the dots are close enough to each other and describe a continuous line. This is reminiscent of the Gestalt (form) principles of the law of proximity and the law of good continuation.

A distinction can be made between horizontal, vertical, and diagonal lines, as well as curves and lines of sight. We often refer to visible and invisible lines. For example, the line of sight of a person depicted in an image is an invisible line. Lines that are mentally created by an obvious movement of an object in the picture are also invisible lines.

The different types of lines in pictorial composition are described in detail below, as are the ways in which they can be used.

Different types of lines:

- Horizontal
- Vertical
- Diagonal
- Curves
- Lines of sight
- Visible lines
- Invisible lines

Graphic Design Elements

Horizontal Lines

A picture inevitably contains at least two horizontal lines: the upper and lower sides of the frame. The third horizontal line in many pictures is the horizon. In landscape paintings in particular, the horizon is the basis for the composition. It represents the reference line for all the objects in the picture and conveys the feeling of gravity in the pictorial world.

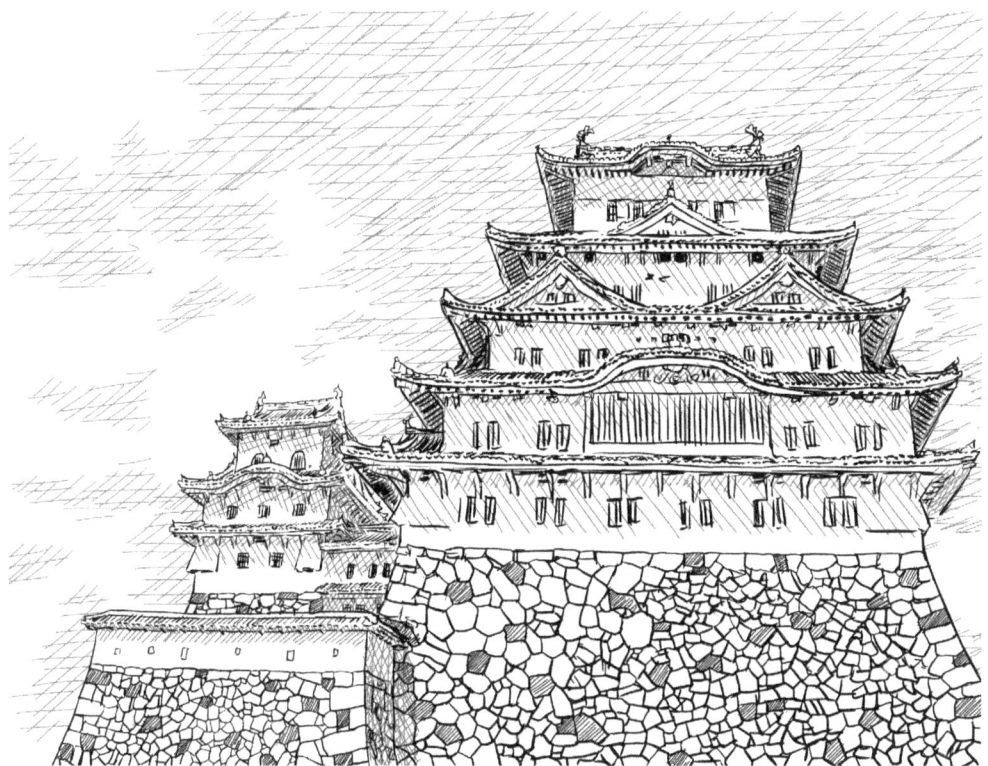

Drawing of Himeji Castle – roofs allow horizontal lines to emerge

What the viewer associates with horizontal lines are properties such as stability and tranquility. Our field of vision is aligned horizontally, so horizontal lines can be used to create the effect of space and depth. However, these lines are not very dynamic and bring little movement into the composition.

Vertical Lines

As with horizontal lines, there are automatically at least two vertical lines in an image, which are created by the image frame. If you allow more vertical lines to appear in the image, they can create a certain visual balance together with horizontal lines. With both line types, however, one should make sure that they actually run parallel to the picture frame, as angle deviations in comparison to the frame are very easily noticeable. Typical objects that correspond to vertical lines are trees, people, streetlamps, and the like.

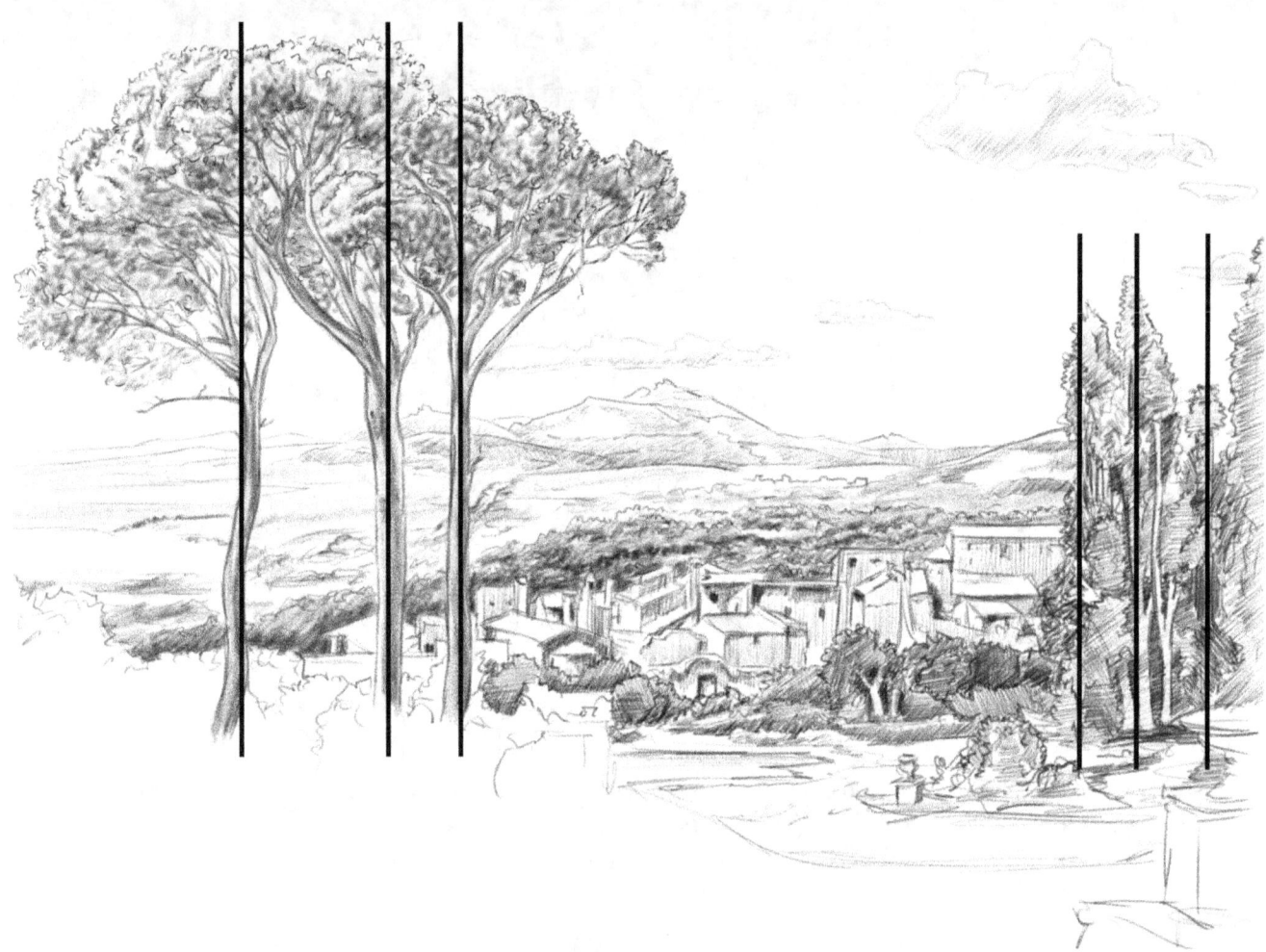

Trees in the foreground and middle ground correspond to vertical lines
Image: Drawing after the painting "Tivoli – View to the Villa d'Este" by Carl Rottmann, 1826

Vertical lines are more likely to represent speed and motion than horizontal lines. However, if used awkwardly, they can act as a barrier or grid. In addition, vertical lines can quickly lead the viewer's gaze out of the image if the gaze is not recaptured by other design elements.

At the edge of the picture, on the other hand, they can serve to keep the gaze within the picture. A portrait format is best for displaying a single vertical line in an image. Landscape format is ideal for compositions in which several vertical lines form a horizontal structure.

Diagonal Lines

The design of an image can be made more dynamic with diagonal lines, which can be very interesting and effective. While horizontal and vertical lines tend to appear rather static, diagonal lines are very dynamic. Diagonal lines suggest movement and speed to the viewer.

Additional tension can be created by displaying diagonals at different angles; the greater the difference in the angles of the various lines, the more contrast will result. A single diagonal is enough to create contrast since it will be at an angle to the vertical and horizontal lines of the picture frame. The maximum contrast is created by diagonals at a 45° angle.

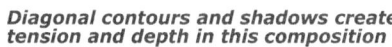

Diagonal contours and shadows create tension and depth in this composition

One example of how to create tension with diagonal lines is by tilting the horizon. This presents the viewer with a somewhat unfamiliar view, creating an unstable scene and maybe even a feeling of falling.

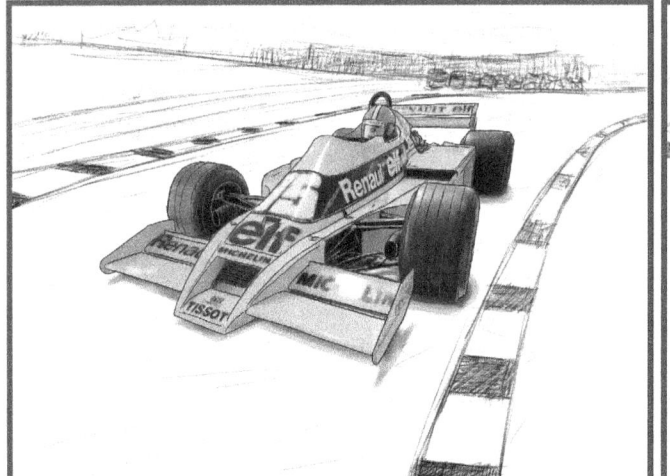 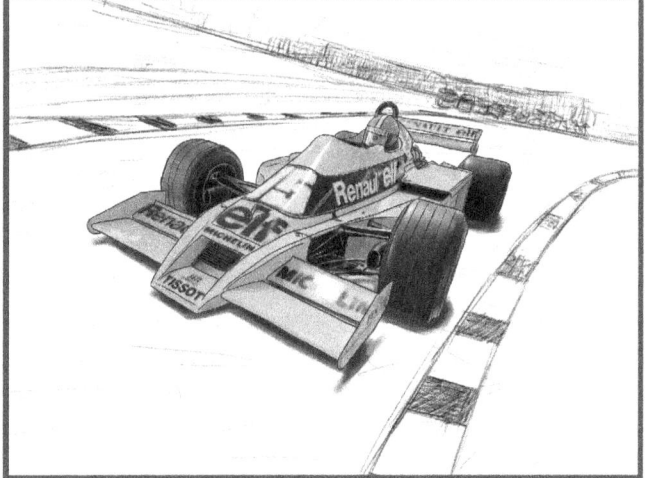

Comparison between horizontal horizon (left) and tilted horizon (right)

55

In the image comparison below using drawings of jets, you can see how the dynamics in the image change due to the incline of the objects in the image. The inclined position of the airplanes conveys movement and life in the drawing, while the horizontally flying jets appear comparatively static.

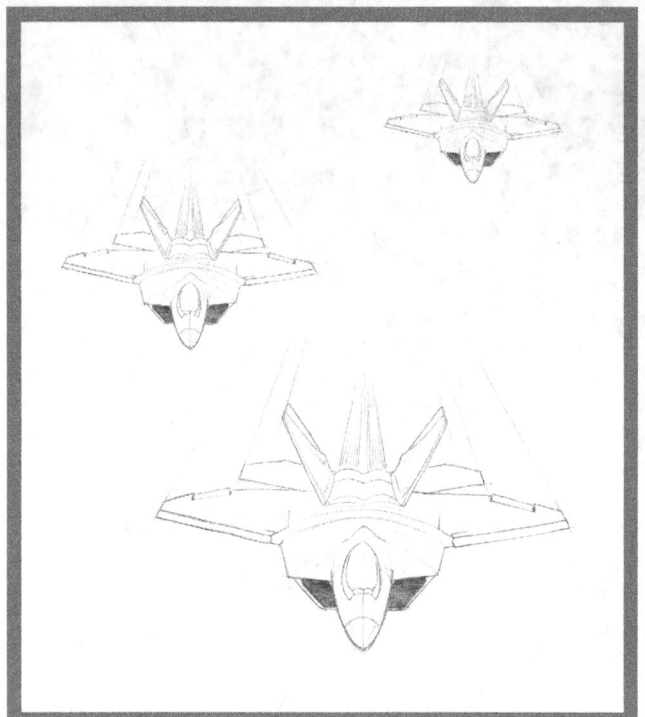
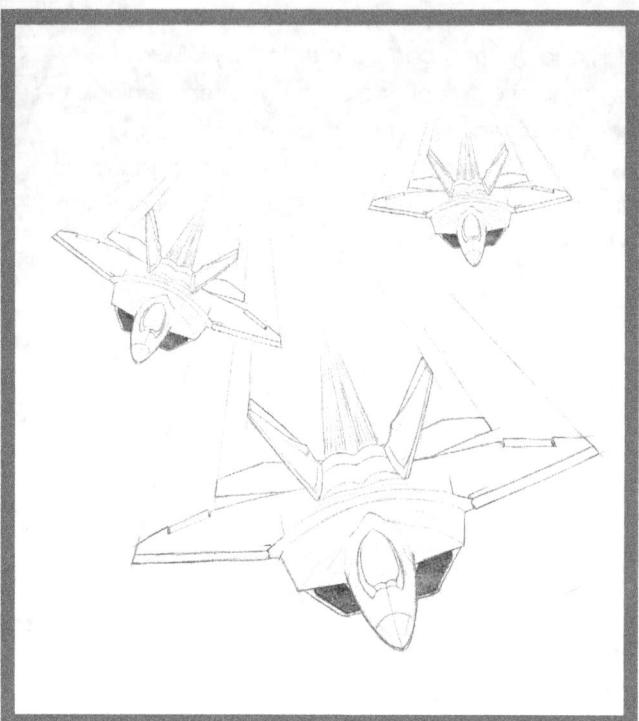

Drawings with jets in horizontal and inclined positions

Another special feature of diagonal lines is that they can convey an impression of space and depth. This makes them perfect for landscape drawings. Only diagonal lines can show the effect of perspective. The effect of depth can be particularly intensive if the objects in the picture are displayed from an oblique point of view.

In general, diagonals are often a product of the viewing angle since most scenes and objects actually consist primarily of horizontal and vertical lines. From a drawing point of view, the objects are then depicted in so-called two-point perspective.

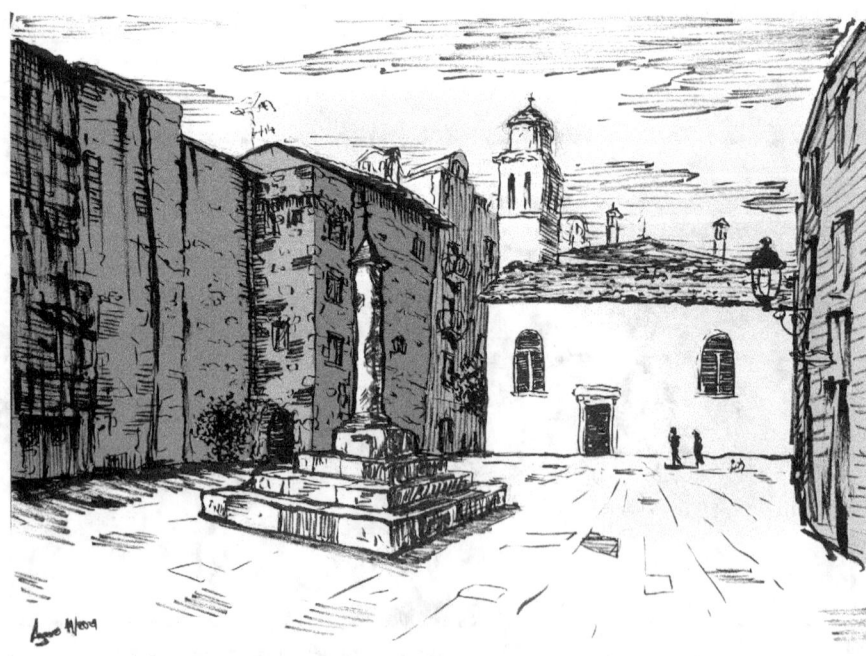

Lines help to create tension and depth in this pictorial composition

56 Graphic Design Elements

Example Image: Kajikazawa in Kai Province

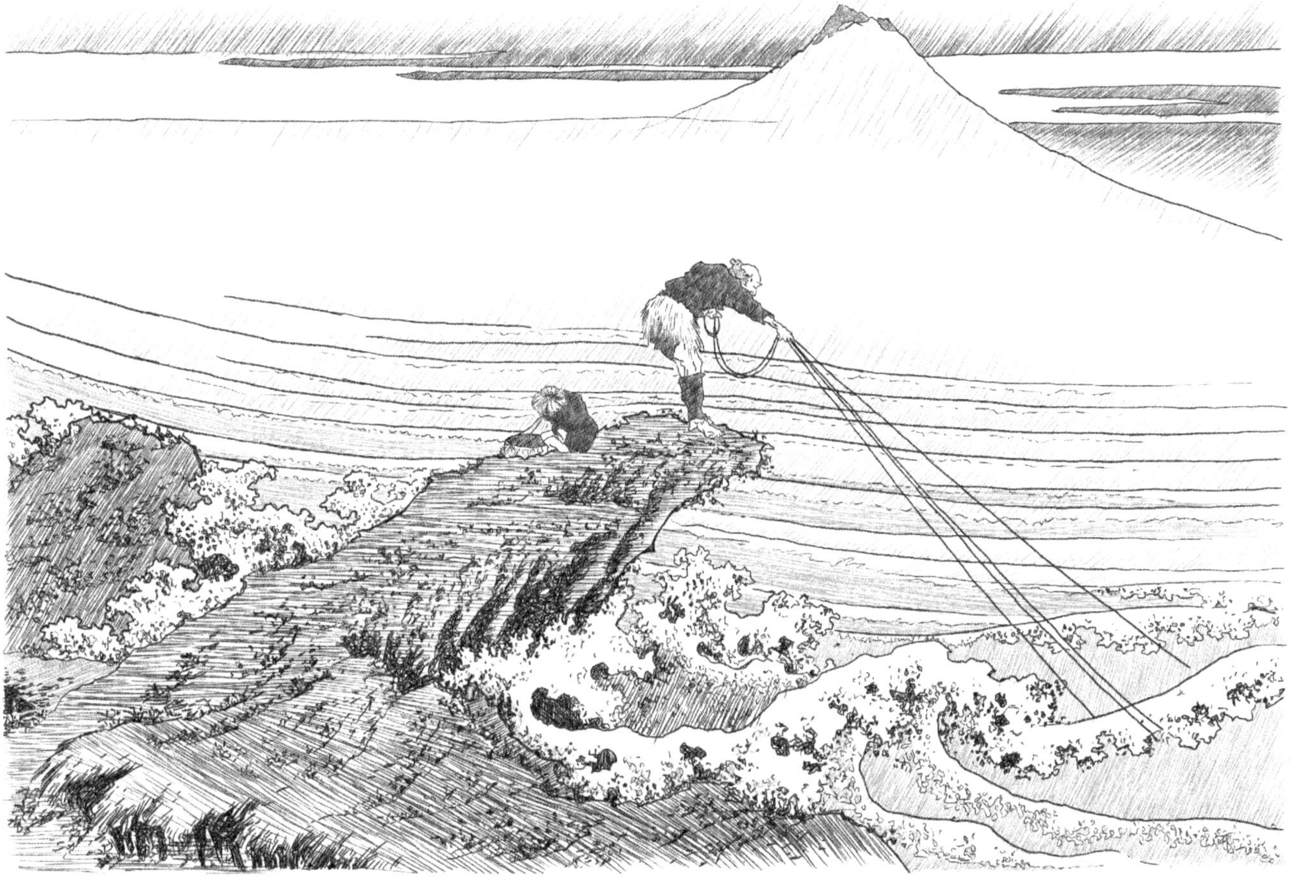

Kajikazawa in Kai Province
Drawing after the colored woodcut by Katsushika Hokusai, 1831

In the drawing, which was drawn from a woodblock print by the artist Katsushika Hokusai, we can see diagonal lines spreading out like a fan. In contrast to this, further diagonals spread out in the opposite direction and intersect with the other lines.

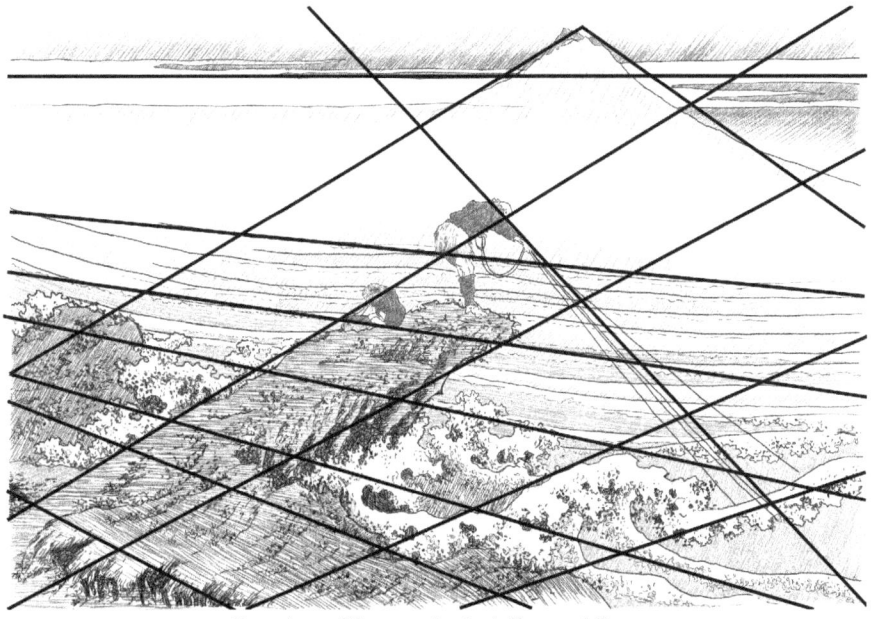

Drawing with accentuated diagonal lines

Several More Tricks Using Diagonals

Diagonal lines can help the viewer's gaze stay in the picture. While vertical lines can cause the viewer's gaze to move out of the image, oblique lines can lead the viewer's gaze from one side of the image to the other.

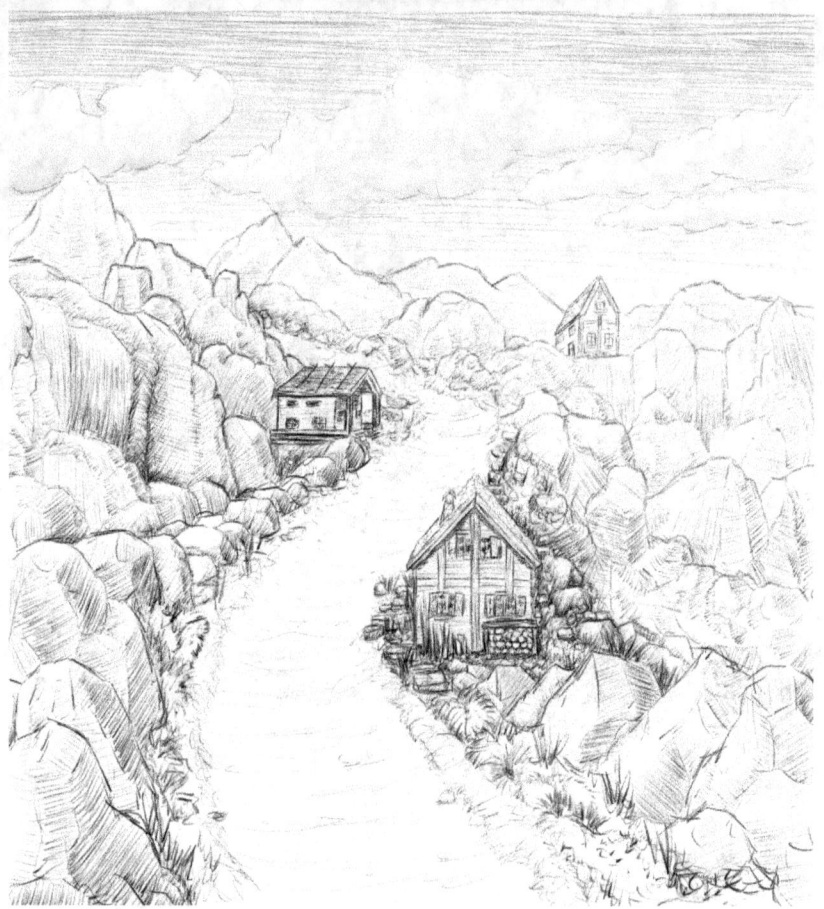

Zigzagging road guides the viewer's gaze through the picture

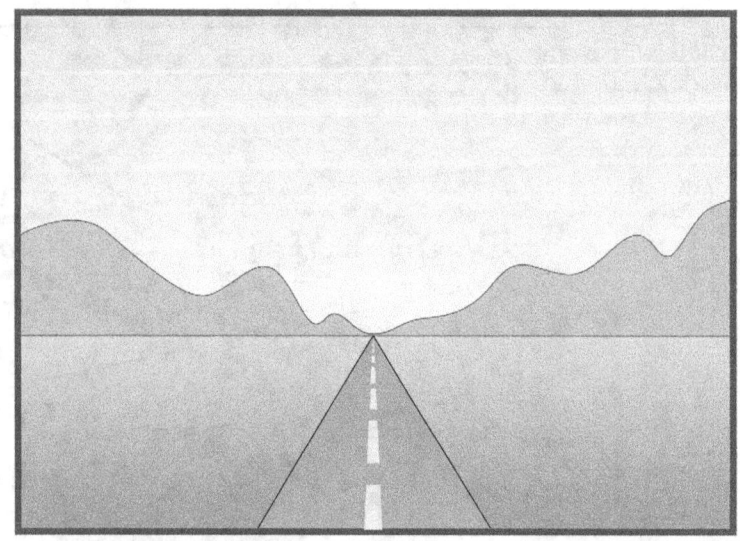

A vertically positioned road quickly guides our gaze out of the picture

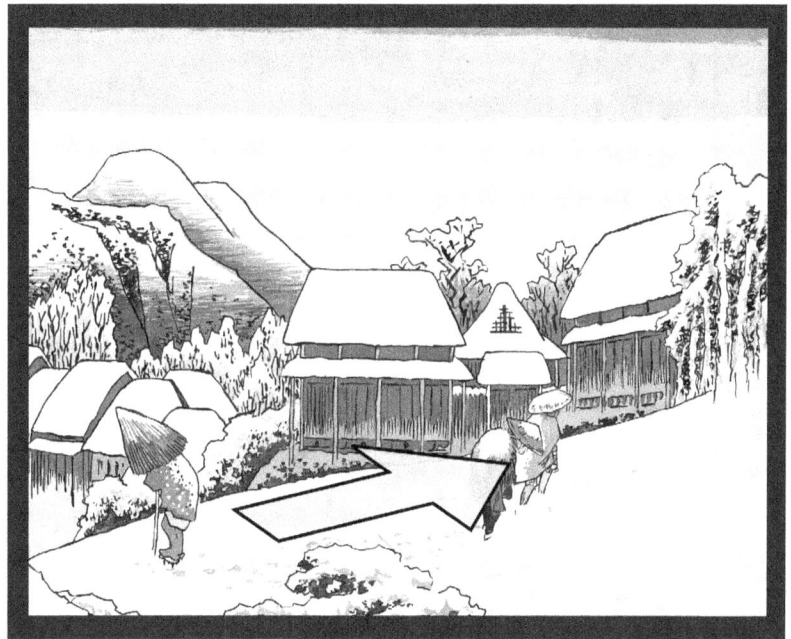

Ascending diagonals

Ascending and descending diagonals are often used to create certain image effects. They are called ascending diagonals if the line runs from the lower left to the upper right or descending diagonals if the line runs from the upper left to the lower right.

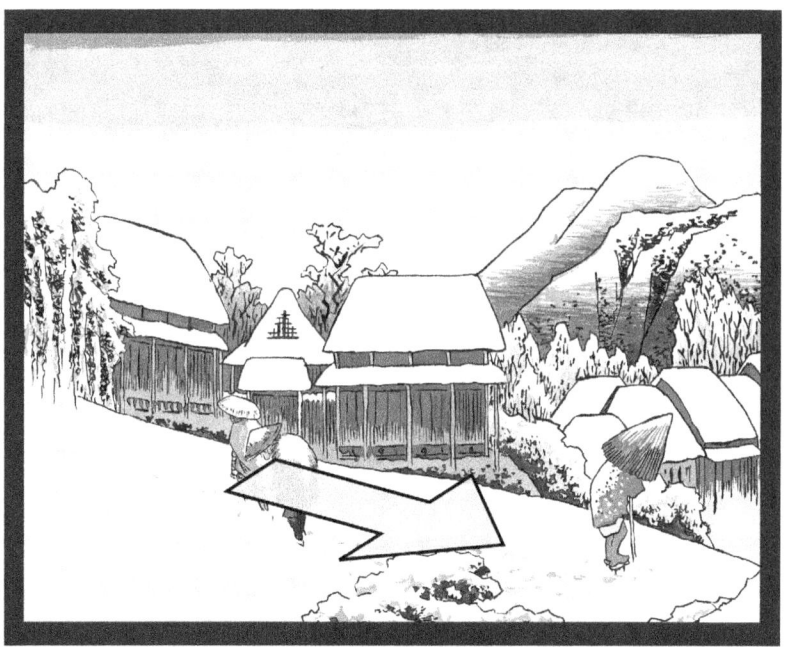

Descending diagonals

Descending lines tend to suggest negative feelings and can contribute to guiding the viewer's gaze out of the picture. In addition, the viewer spends less time with the details along the diagonals. In contrast, ascending diagonals are more associated with positive feelings and are more aesthetically pleasing for some people. The viewer's gaze is held in the picture for longer and lingers longer on the details that are near the diagonals.

Curves

Curves are lines that represent a particularly robust but also more difficult-to-master design element. Curves appear elegant and at the same time dynamic to the viewer. They convey an extremely bold feeling of movement and speed, which is a much stronger effect than diagonals are capable of creating. This is because curves are created by a continuous change of direction, which is typical of motion sequences.

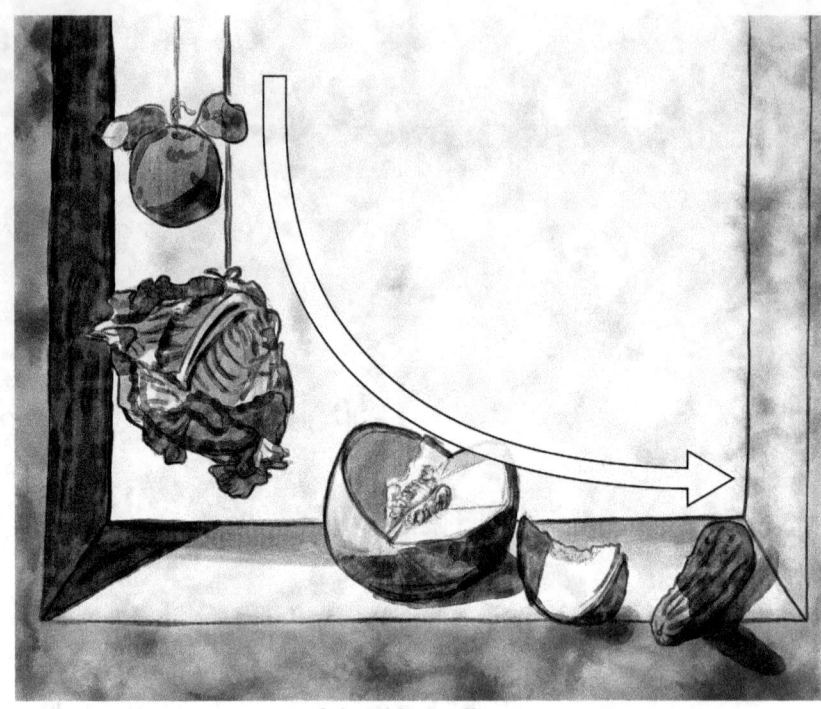

The arrangement of the objects allows a curve to emerge.
Drawing after a painting by J. S. Cotán

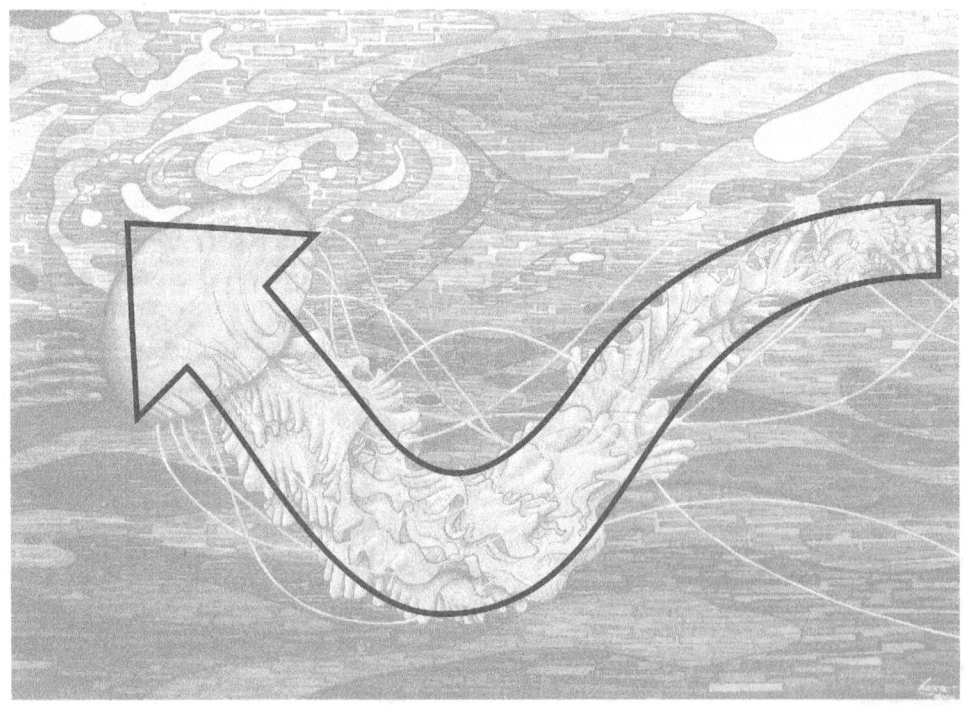

The curved shape of the jellyfish gives a sense of its movement

60   Graphic Design Elements

As is the case with diagonal lines, the eye of the viewer effortlessly follows any curve it finds in a picture. In this way, the eye can be guided through the picture.

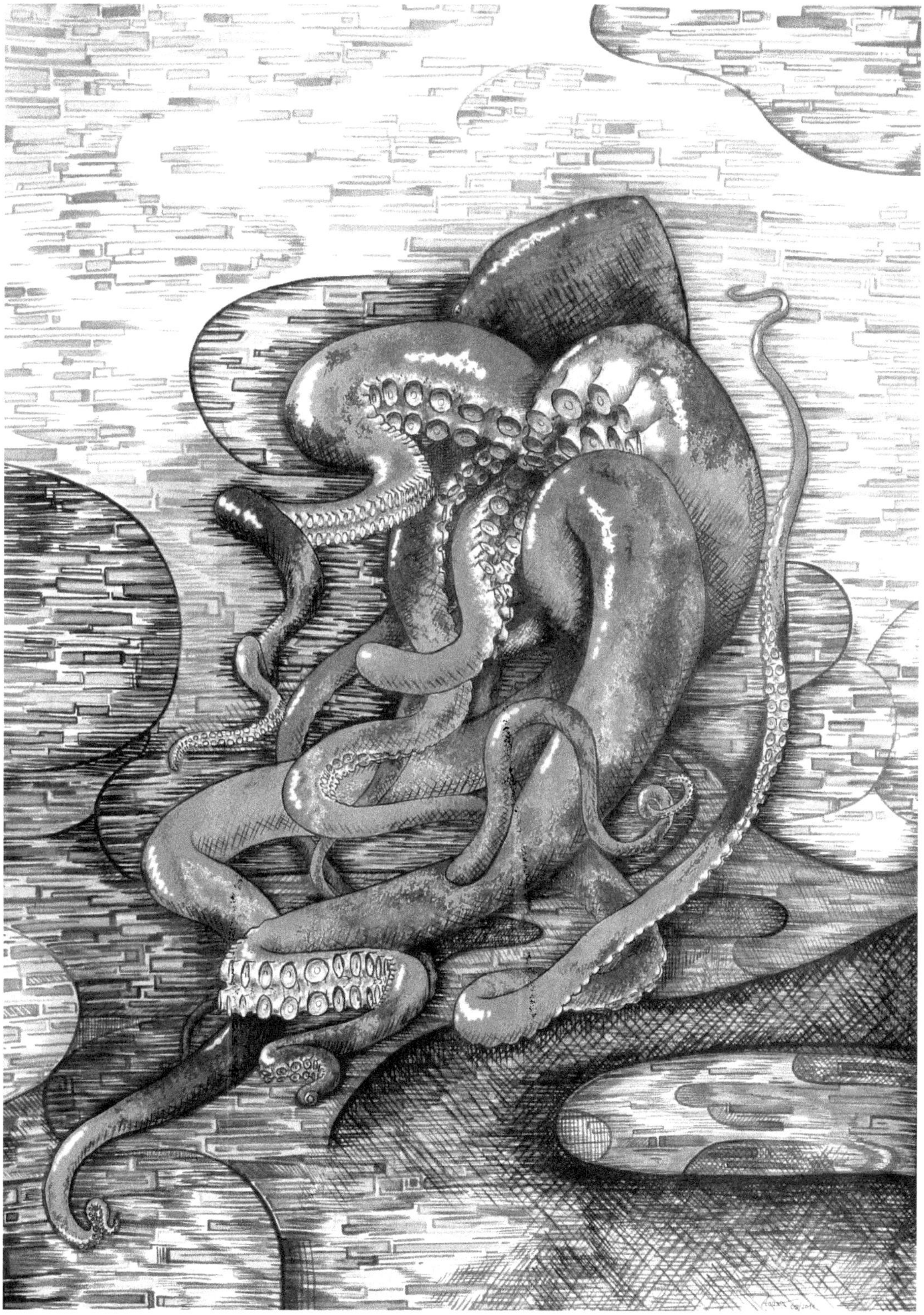

The winding tentacles of the octopus seem to set the illustration in motion

In terms of craftsmanship, curves present a problem in that they are more difficult to find. While diagonals can often be created in a controlled manner in a pictorial composition – for example, by changing your own viewing angle – curves must be present in the motif from the outset. This makes image composition with curves much more difficult. However, curves do not always have to be real lines. A series of points can also be interpreted as a curve. The Gestalt principles of the "law of proximity" and the "law of good continuation" are effective here. Likewise, a suitable sequence of straight lines can generate an imaginary curve.

The picture on the right, a composition by Caravaggio, is another especially good example of the use of curves. The most important curves are marked by lines. What you immediately notice when you look at the lines is how the viewer's gaze is guided. However, the dynamics and movement in the picture also immediately stand out.

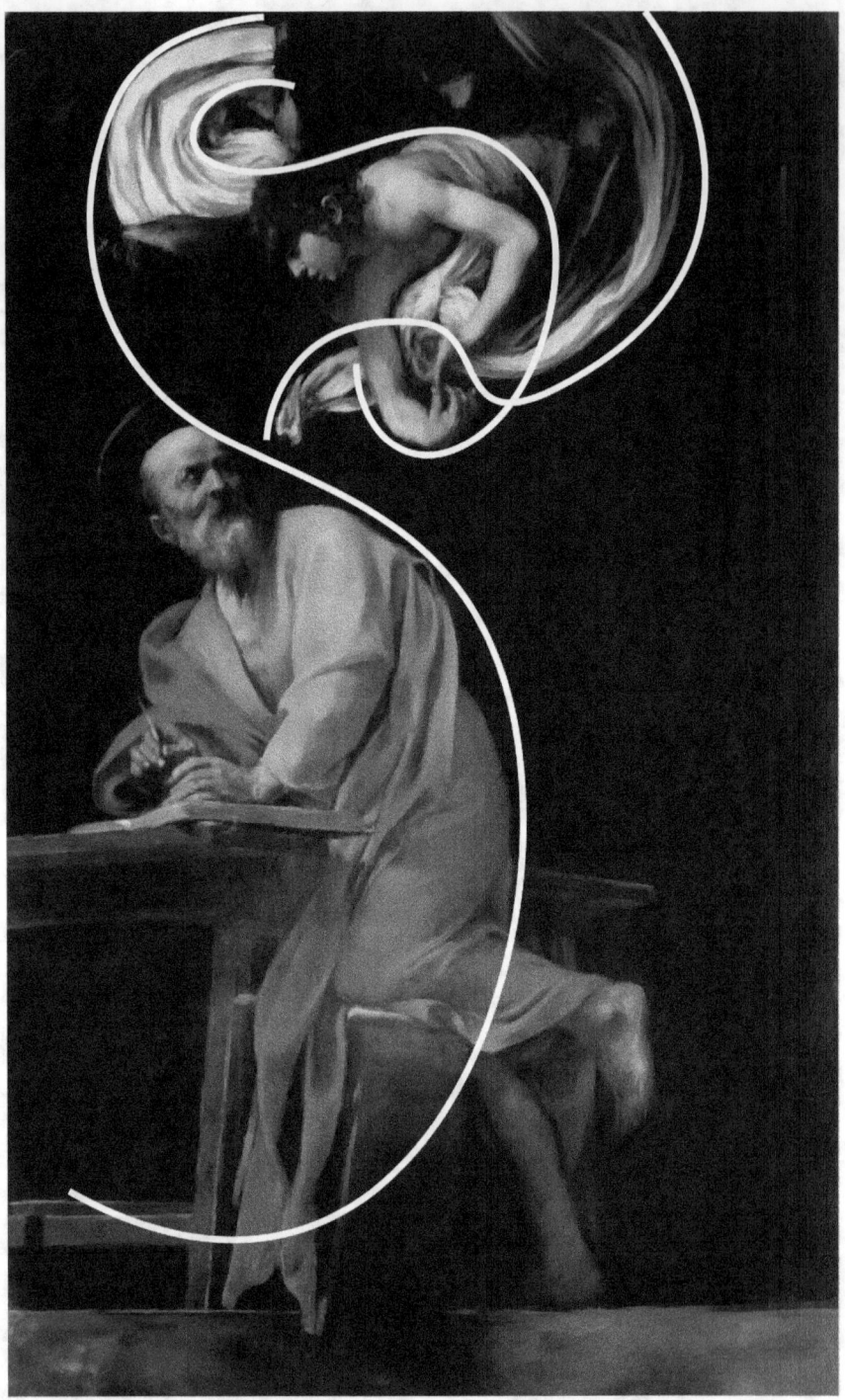

St. Matthew and the Angel – copy – with curved lines drawn in
Original: Michelangelo Merisi da Caravaggio, 1602

Lines of Sight

Lines of sight involve so-called invisible lines. Although no line is actually visible, the viewer perceives an imaginary line that emanates from the eyes of the person portrayed. Lines of sight are perceived by the viewer very quickly because a human face in a painting attracts attention like nothing else. Therefore, these imaginary lines are extremely intense and immediately lead the viewer's gaze in one direction. In many pictures, lines of sight are used very specifically to draw attention to a particular detail.

Similarly expressive are glances that two people reciprocate. We find an example of this in the picture shown in the previous section: "St. Matthew and the Angel" by Caravaggio. Another good example of lines of sight is in "The Calling of St. Matthew," also by Caravaggio. A more detailed description of the painting is given below.

Example Image: The Calling of St. Matthew

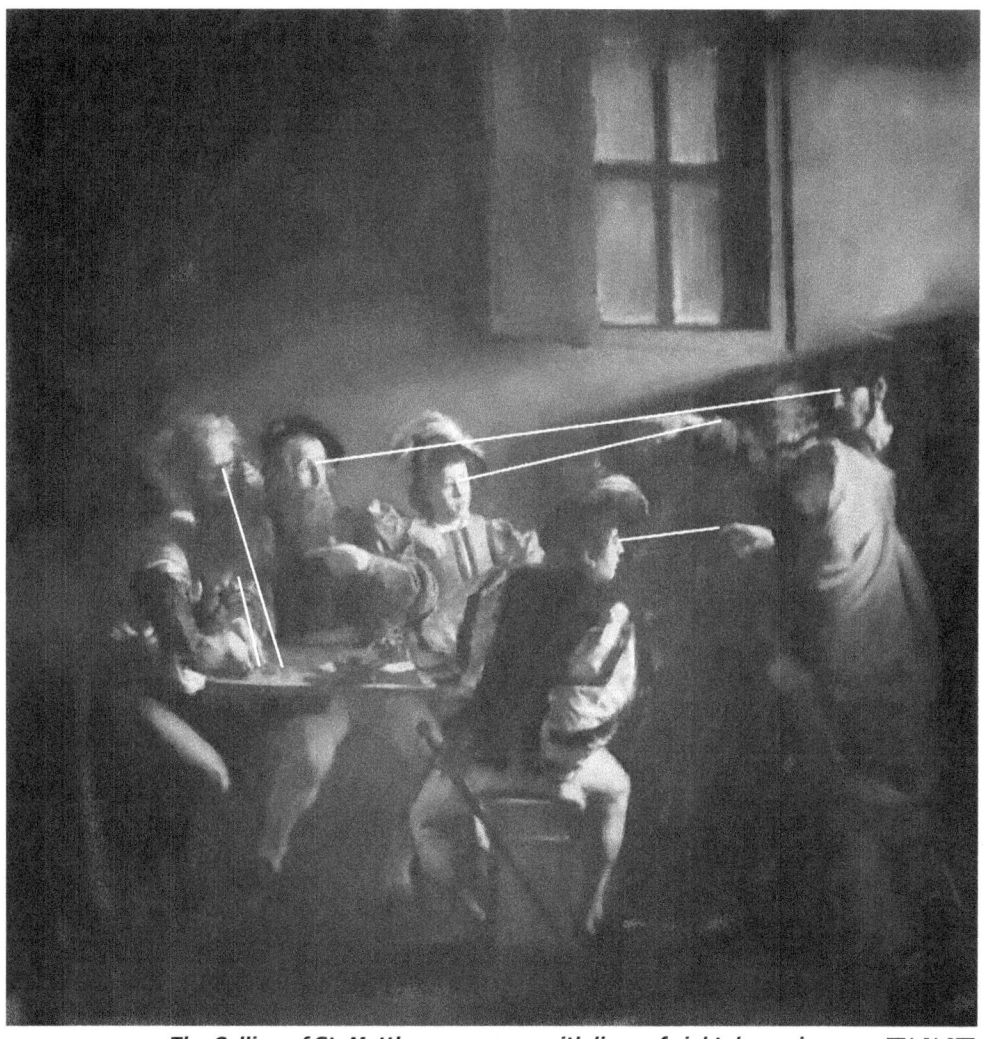

The Calling of St. Matthew – copy – with lines of sight drawn in
Original: Michelangelo Merisi da Caravaggio, 1599/1600

A particularly good example of the use of lines of sight can be found in the painting "The Calling of St. Matthew," which Michelangelo Merisi da Caravaggio painted around 1600. It shows a biblical scene in which Jesus Christ enters a customs house, sees the customs officer Matthew there, and asks him to follow him.

There is direct eye contact between the man with the beard (probably Matthew) and Jesus. The man in the middle of the picture is also looking at Jesus. The two customs officers on the far left of the picture seem to be unmoved by the event and continue to be occupied only with counting their income. The viewer can thus imagine what is going on at this moment by looking at the lines of sight.

In addition to the lines of sight, there are further invisible lines in the picture emanating from the pointing fingers. Jesus Christ and his companion Peter point in the direction of the men on the left and thus automatically lead the viewer's gaze into this area of the painting. Whether the man with the full beard in the left half of the painting is pointing to himself or to one of the men to his left is a matter of controversy in the art world.

Contours

A contour is the outline (or silhouette) of a figurative element. Contours are an important design element in painting and drawing. In painting, contours are created by clear color transitions in a very small area; for example, a transition from blue to yellow produces a visible contour. Even strong differences in tonal value in a small area can make a contour visible.

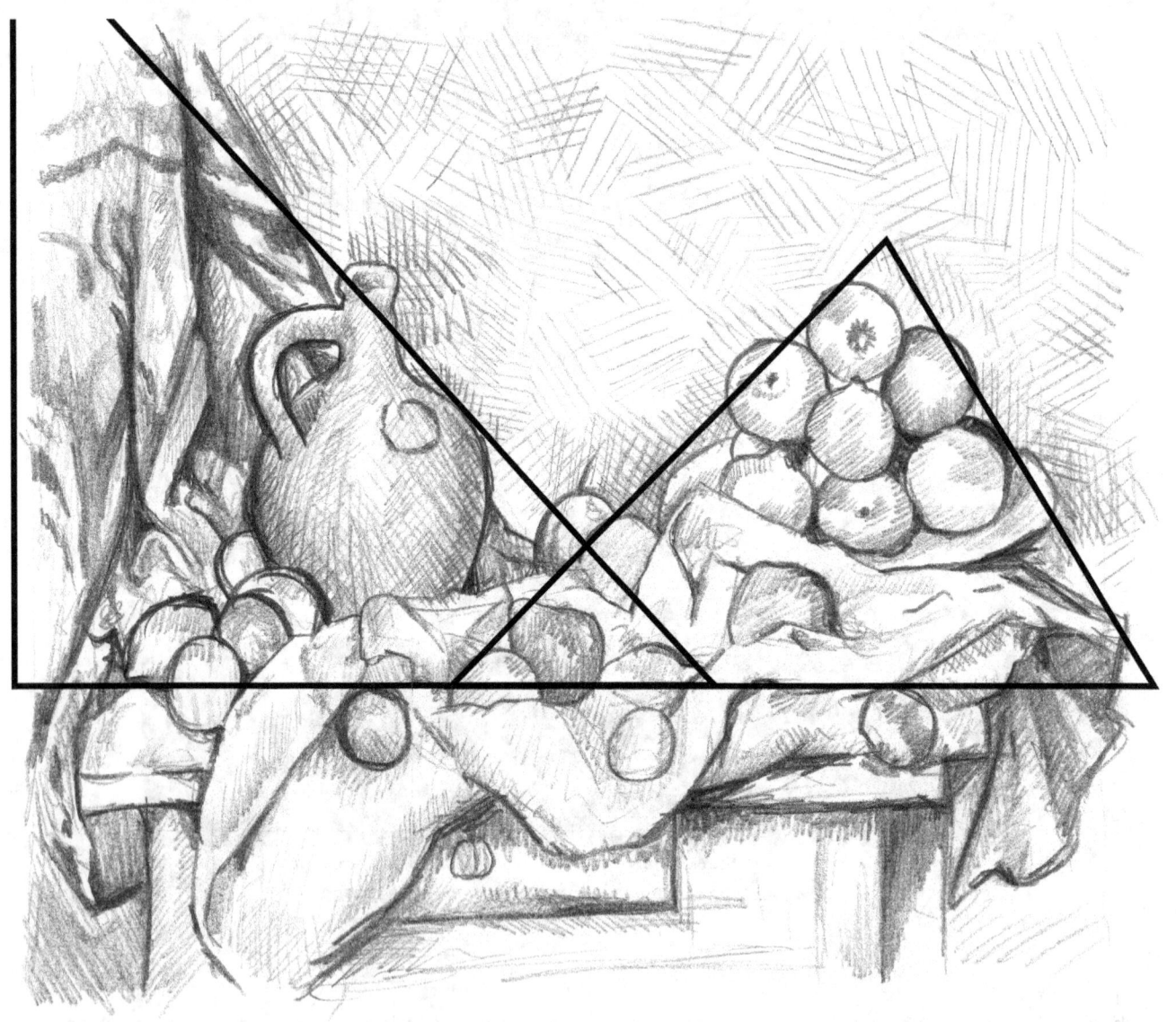

Drawing with clearly defined contours
Sketch of a still life by Paul Cézanne: "Still Life with Curtain, Jug, and Bowl of Fruit"

Contours are graphic design elements. They can only be used to reproduce two-dimensional shapes. In drawing, but also in painting, contours are often reinforced by tracing the outline of an element with a black line. These contour lines also give paintings a graphic aspect. However, these explicitly drawn outlines do not exist in reality.

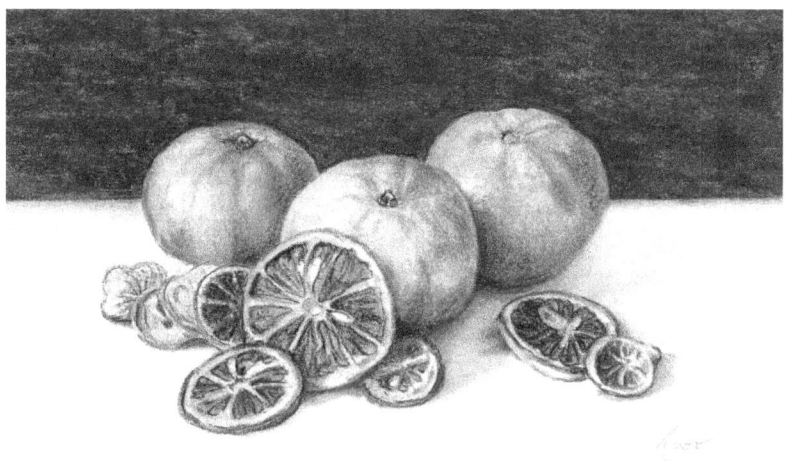

Depiction without explicitly represented contours

Design Using Contours

Depending on how pronounced the contours are, you can develop them into a very dominant characteristic in your picture and significantly shape the overall impression of the picture. As mentioned previously, you can also use them to give a painting an aesthetic and graphic impression. A pictorial composition based on contours can also work using the rhythm of the contours. They can be rounded and curving but also angular and dramatic.

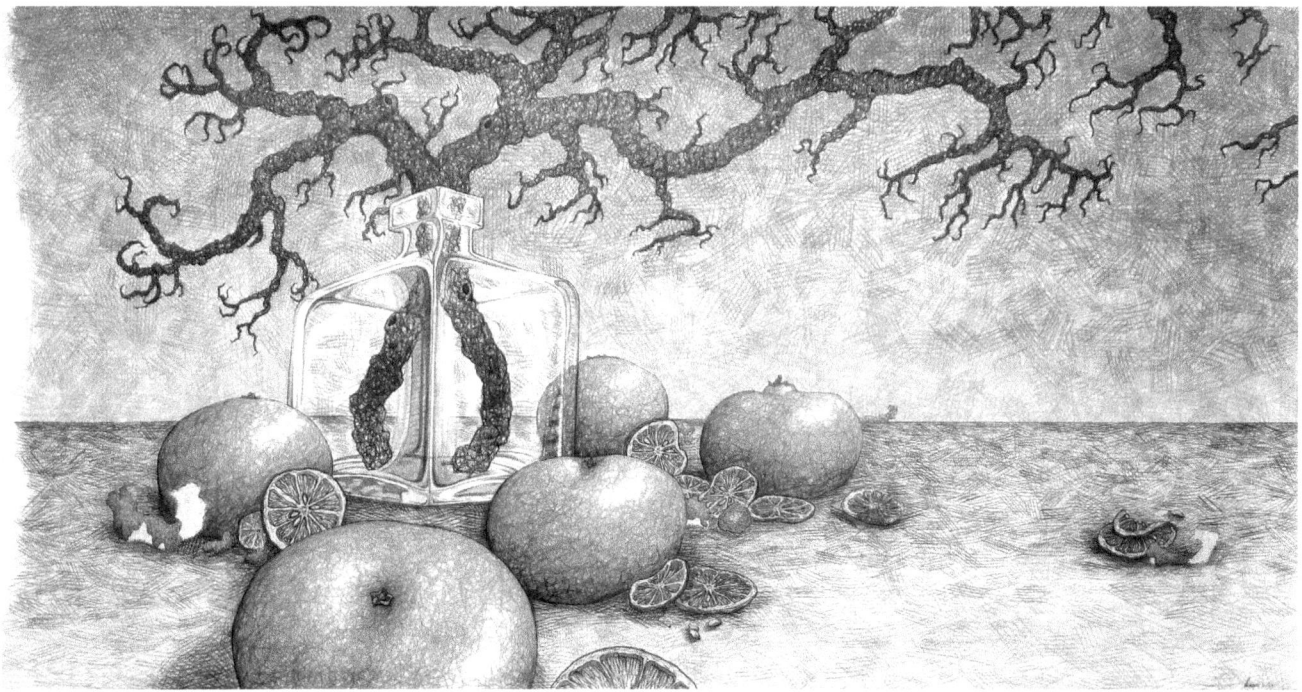

Contrast between rounded lines (mandarin oranges) and angular lines (branches) in a still life

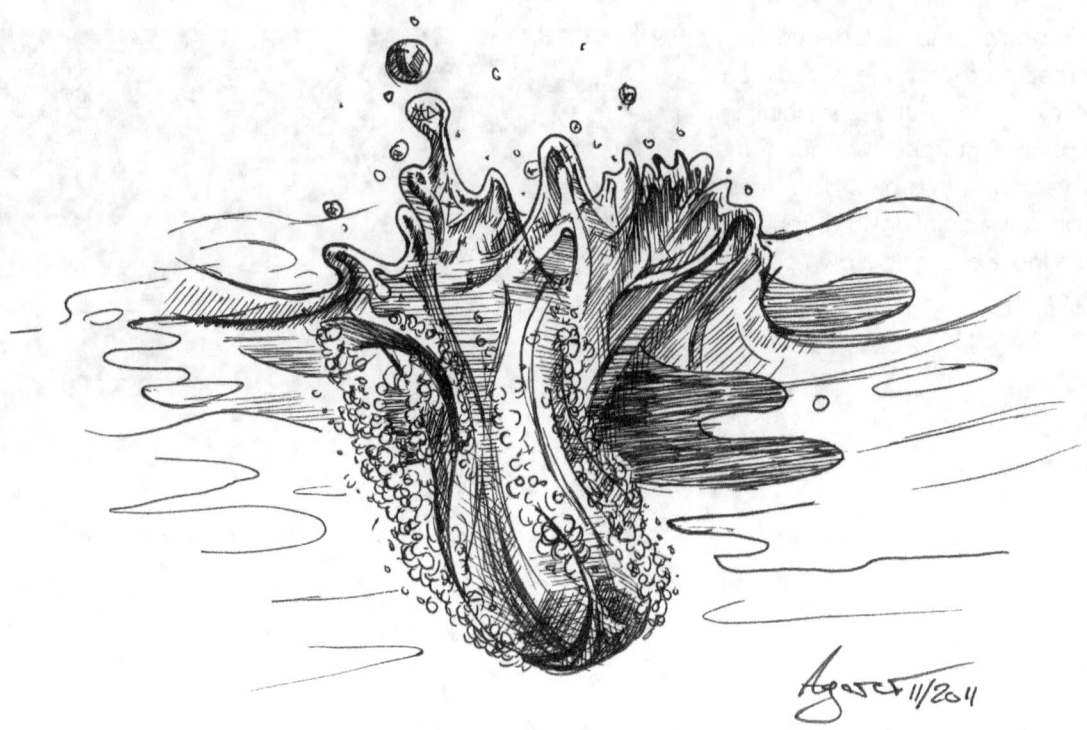

Drawing with mostly rounded contours

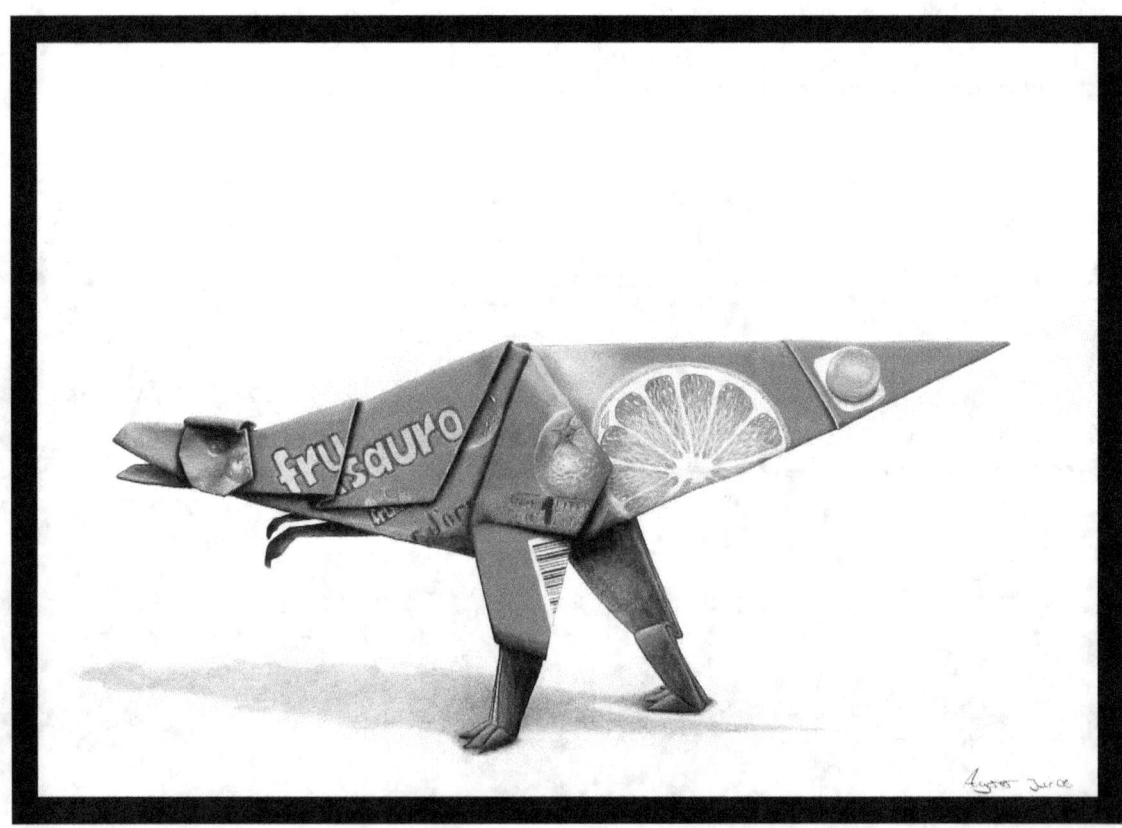

The illustration "Paper Warrior #4 – T-Rex" primarily depicts angular contours

Since contours are for the most part self-contained and enclose forms, they serve as a good transition to the next topic: surface and form.

Surface and Form

As mentioned in the previous section, after the point, line, and contour, we now come to the surface. In looking at surfaces, we open up another dimension in the picture plane and encounter our first two-dimensional graphic design element.

Surface

With the surface, as with the line, we have a pictorial element that is potentially infinite. In this case, of course, there is always the limitation that an image, no matter how large, always has an edge where it ends. However, this does not mean that line and surface are not intended to be infinite, and they can thus be imagined by the viewer as being so.

Here the actual limitations of a work of art enter into a productive tension with the creative imagination of the artist and the viewer. In this respect, the surface as an element of the pictorial composition is simultaneously concrete, in terms of its actual limitation, and at the same time transcends this limitation as an abstract concept. In the composition of the picture, however, the surface is usually only perceived as a carrier of structure/texture or color.

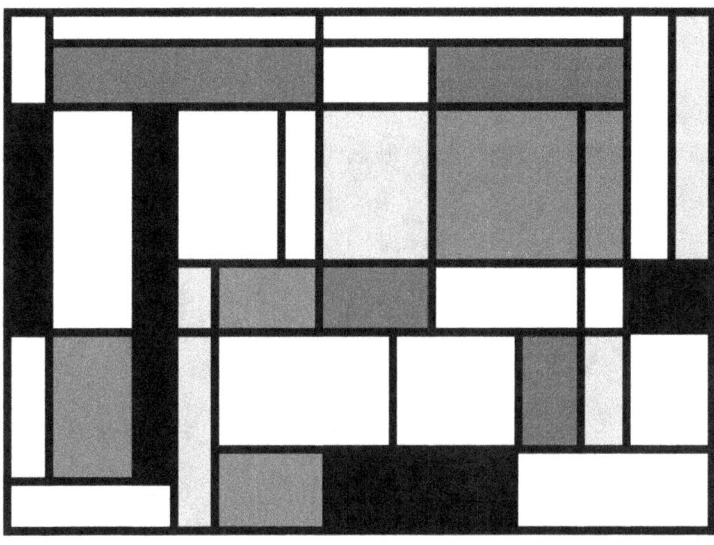

An image based on surfaces
Reproduction of a painting by Piet Mondrian

Form

Every bordered surface in a work of art (even if that border is the edge of the picture) indicates a form. Fundamental to the perception of forms are the simplest basic forms. These basic forms are the triangle, the circle, the oval, the square, and the rectangle. Geometric shapes stand for certain characteristics. They can be formed by the outline of the motif but can also be created by several objects that together form a certain shape. Thus geometric forms are also very suitable as design elements on which the arrangement of objects in a picture can be based.

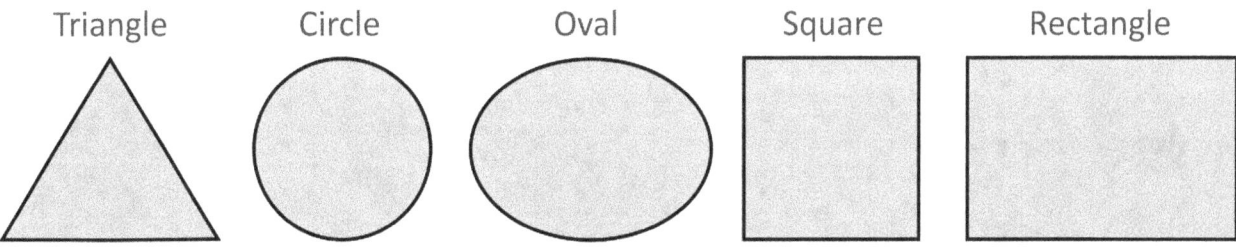

Basic geometric forms for pictorial composition

The Effect of Forms

In human perception, forms seem to have a weight and thus also a focus (i.e., a center of gravity). This focus can also be understood as the center of the form. However, it cannot be understood as a physical "center of gravity" in a scientific sense. It is possible, for example, for complex shapes to be made up of several basic forms which can be perceived as several such "centers of gravity."

Such a center, or perceived center, of gravity marks a special place within the form. It allows the form to additionally acquire the character of a point, and it is thus perceived as an exact location within the composition. If there is a dominant point outside the form, this creates a duality of two elements that are not equivalent. We will come back to this duality of weighted forms and the resulting balance (equilibrium) later in the course of this book.

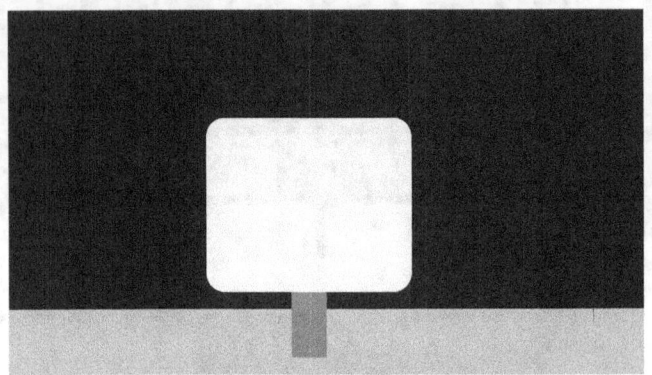 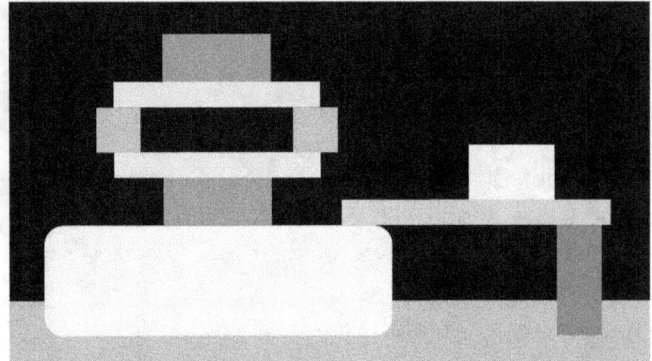

Left: Balanced composition with easily recognized center of gravity
Right: Balanced composition with a complex construction

Like the line, the form also separates two areas. With the line it would be two open areas; with the form we have an open area outside and a closed area inside. Each form thus presents itself from two points of view. Firstly, as a geometric element within a pictorial composition; here the form interacts with the picture surface and other pictorial elements. Secondly, the form has an inner composition that is limited by its contour. In the most rudimentary case, this is the image surface itself. However, every independent form within the image can also represent the frame of a separate image.

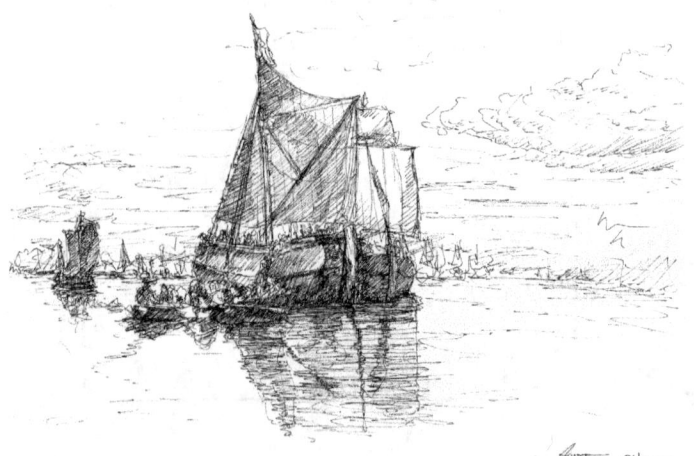 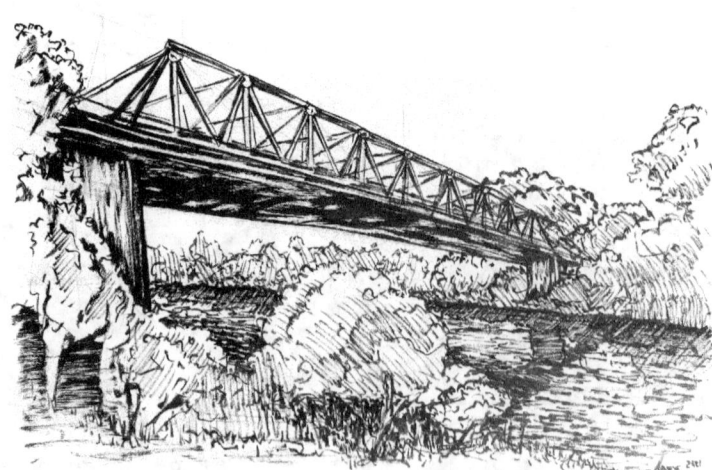

Grouping of objects make it easier to recognize center of gravity
(Ink drawing after a painting by William Turner)

Number of objects make it more difficult to recognized center of gravity

What is key here is the power that draws the eye to the inside of the form. The corners and edges represent the connection with whatever lies outside the form. In addition, the symmetry of the form influences the orientation of the form in the image, which could, for example, be diagonal or straight. In combination with the focal point of the form, this can convey feelings of either instability or stability.

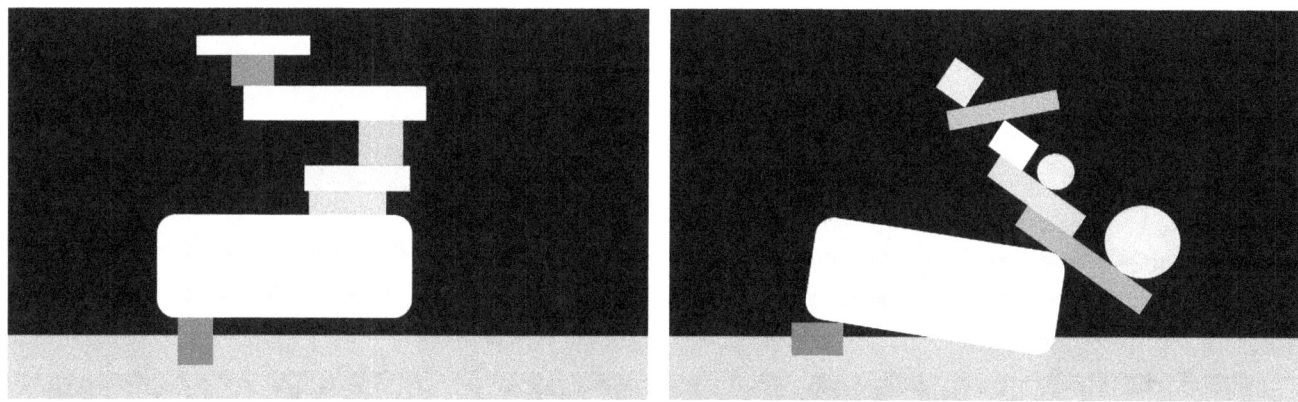

Left: Composition in balance
Right: Tension in the composition due to the unstable balance

In the following chapter, we will discuss the effect of simple basic forms in an image composition. The circle, oval, square, rectangle, and triangle will be analyzed.

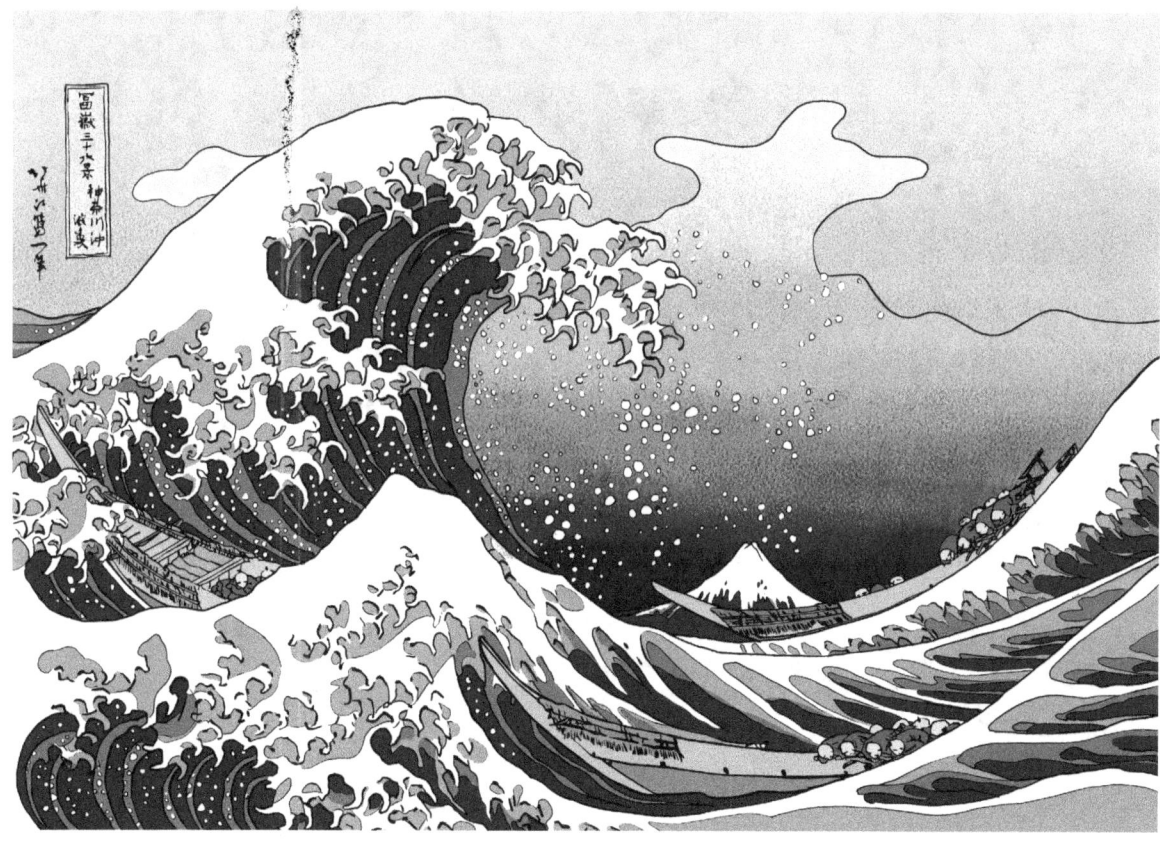

The wave coveys a feeling of instability
(Ink drawing after a picture by Katsushika Hokusai "The Great Wave off Kanagawa"

Geometric Forms

Geometric forms are design elements that have a significant influence on the composition of an image. They represent certain feelings and characteristics, which they convey to the viewer.

Geometric forms can simply emerge through the outline of the motif, but they can also be created by several different objects that together produce a certain form. Thus, geometric shapes are also very well suited as a design element on which to base the arrangement of objects in a picture.

Triangle Composition

One of the most frequently used stylistic devices, which we can find again and again in art, is the triangle composition. The triangle as a principle of the arrangement of pictorial objects embodies clarity, calm, and harmony. The form appears solid like a mountain and thus automatically gives the viewer a feeling of stability.

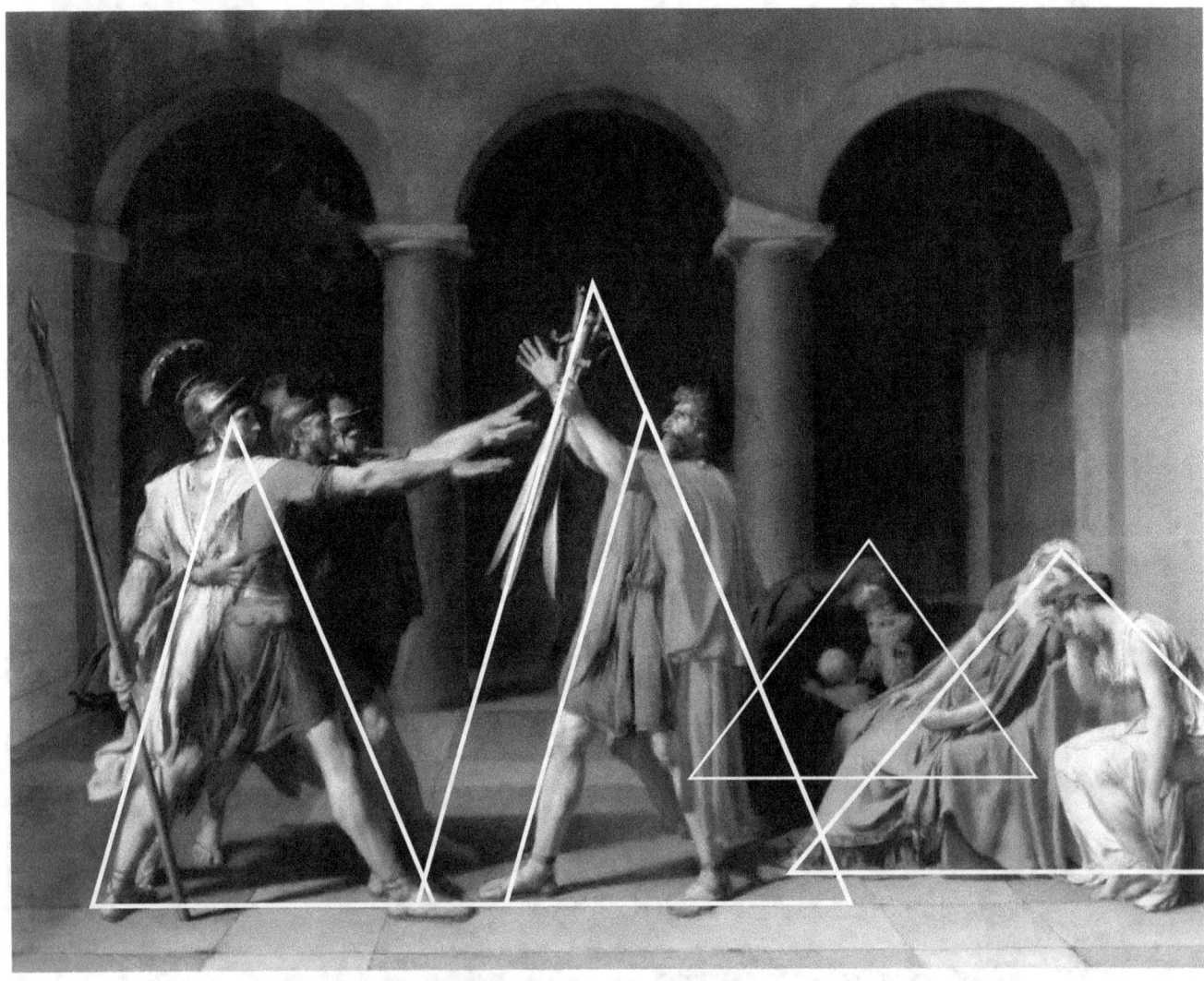

Several triangle compositions in the painting "Oath of the Horatii" (copy)
Original: Jacques-Louis David, 1784

Triangle Composition in Still Lifes

In many still lifes, one can differentiate between two types of triangle composition: the right-angled triangle and the pyramid form.

Right-angled triangle composition

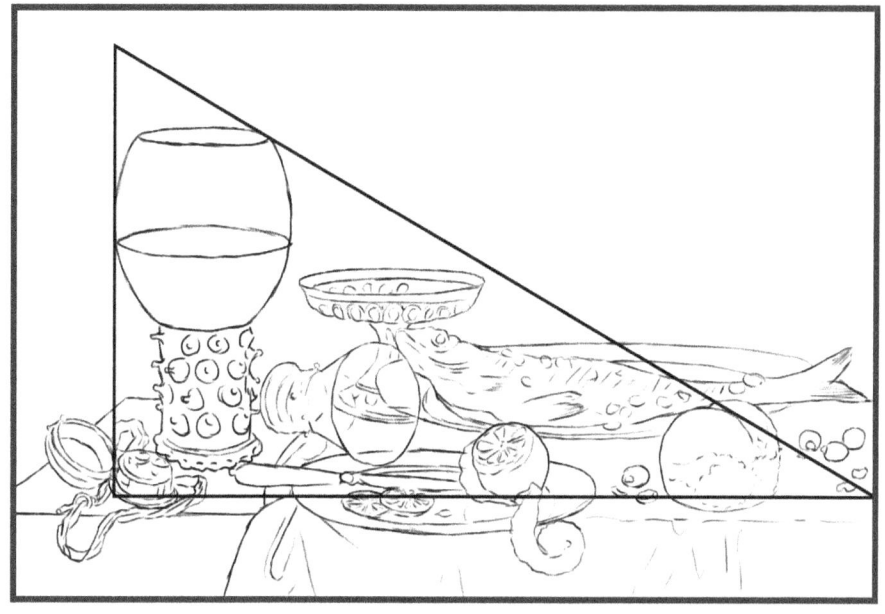

Sketch of a still life by Willem Claesz Heda
"Still Life with Roemer and Watch," 1629

This right-angled triangle composition is an arrangement on a table that starts from one of the two vertical sides of the picture. The vertical side of the triangle can be located far to the right or left of the image and forms a right angle with the horizontal lower side of the triangle.

With this example of arrangement, there is only one compositional support. The mid-section of the picture usually leads the eye automatically out of the center of the picture.

Pyramids

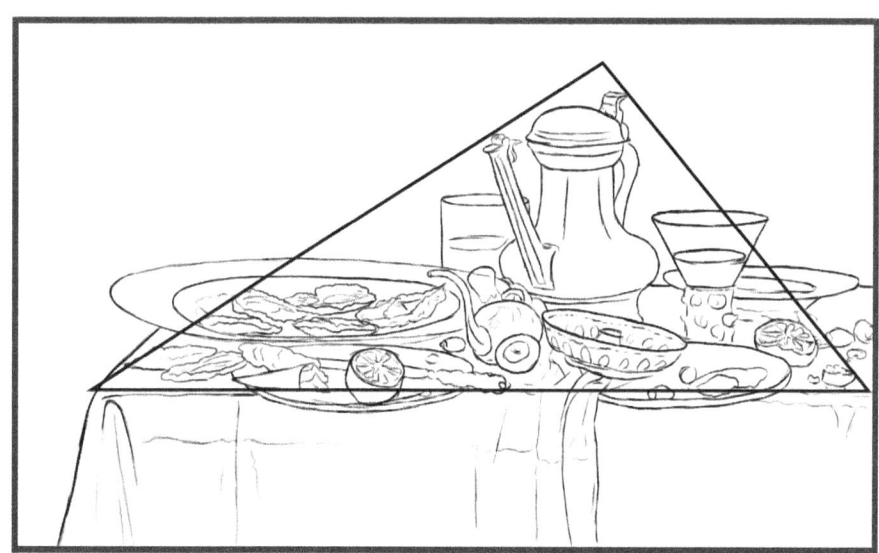

Sketch of a still life by Willem Claesz Heda
"Still Life with Pewterware"

The pyramid shape can correspond to an isosceles triangle – but it does not have to. The diagonal pyramid is more popular as here the center of gravity of the composition comes out of the middle of the image. This makes pictures look less static – as with the compositional techniques of the golden section and the rule of thirds. This composition is well arranged with only one compositional support.

Double triangle

A variation of this is the double triangle, in which two triangles are arranged into an overall composition.

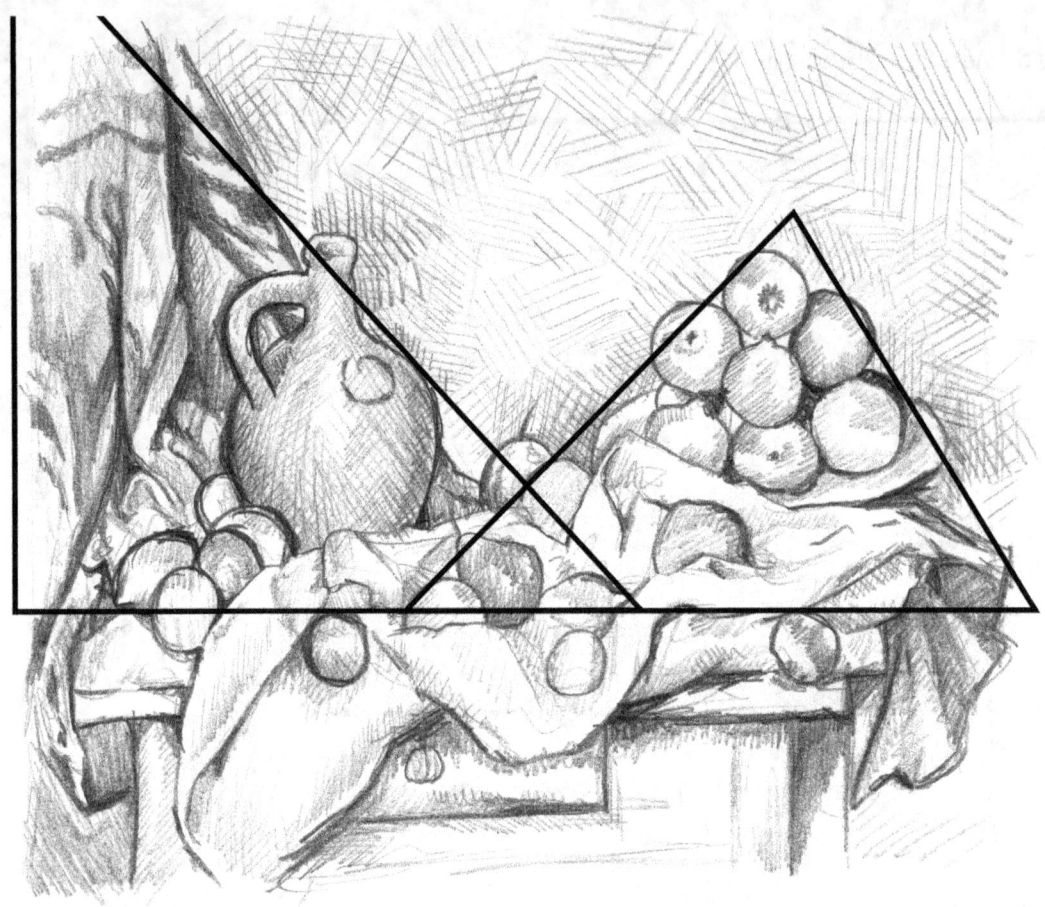

Sketch of a still life by Paul Cézanne:
"Still Life with Curtain, Jug, and Bowl of Fruit," ca. 1894

Circles and Ovals

Circles and oval shapes in a pictorial composition create the effect of unity. Everything that is within this geometric form is bound within it. In addition, round forms create a certain feeling of movement – i.e., rotation.

In order for the shape of a circle or oval in a picture to be recognized as such, it must be very clearly outlined and easily recognizable. The difficulty in achieving this is due to the fact that circles and ovals are often difficult to find or create. A popular example can be found in still lifes. Here, fruit, vegetables, or other compositional objects can be placed in a round bowl, which is then viewed from an angle, typically from above.

However, when using this compositional aid, the draftsperson should always bear in mind that circles and ovals capture the attention of the viewer very strongly. For this reason, these forms should be deployed with care and very specifically.

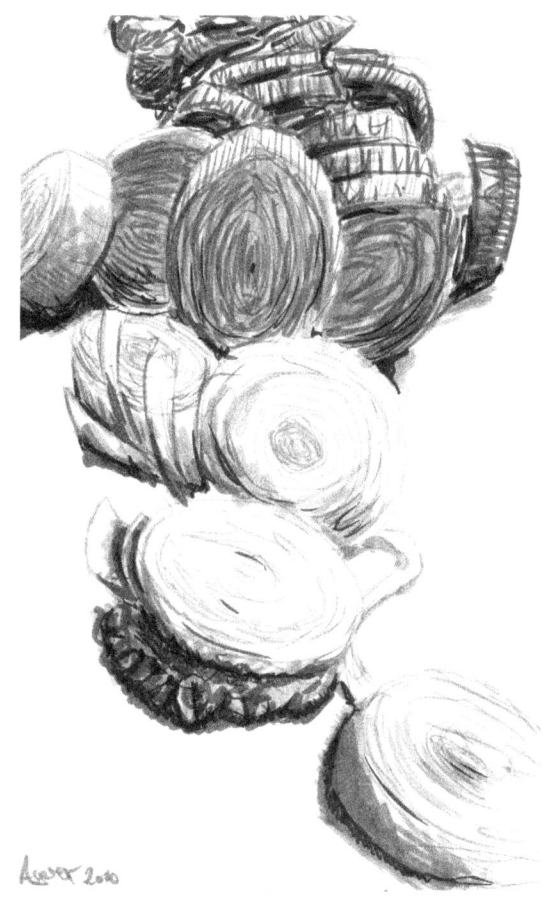

Still life with sliced leeks

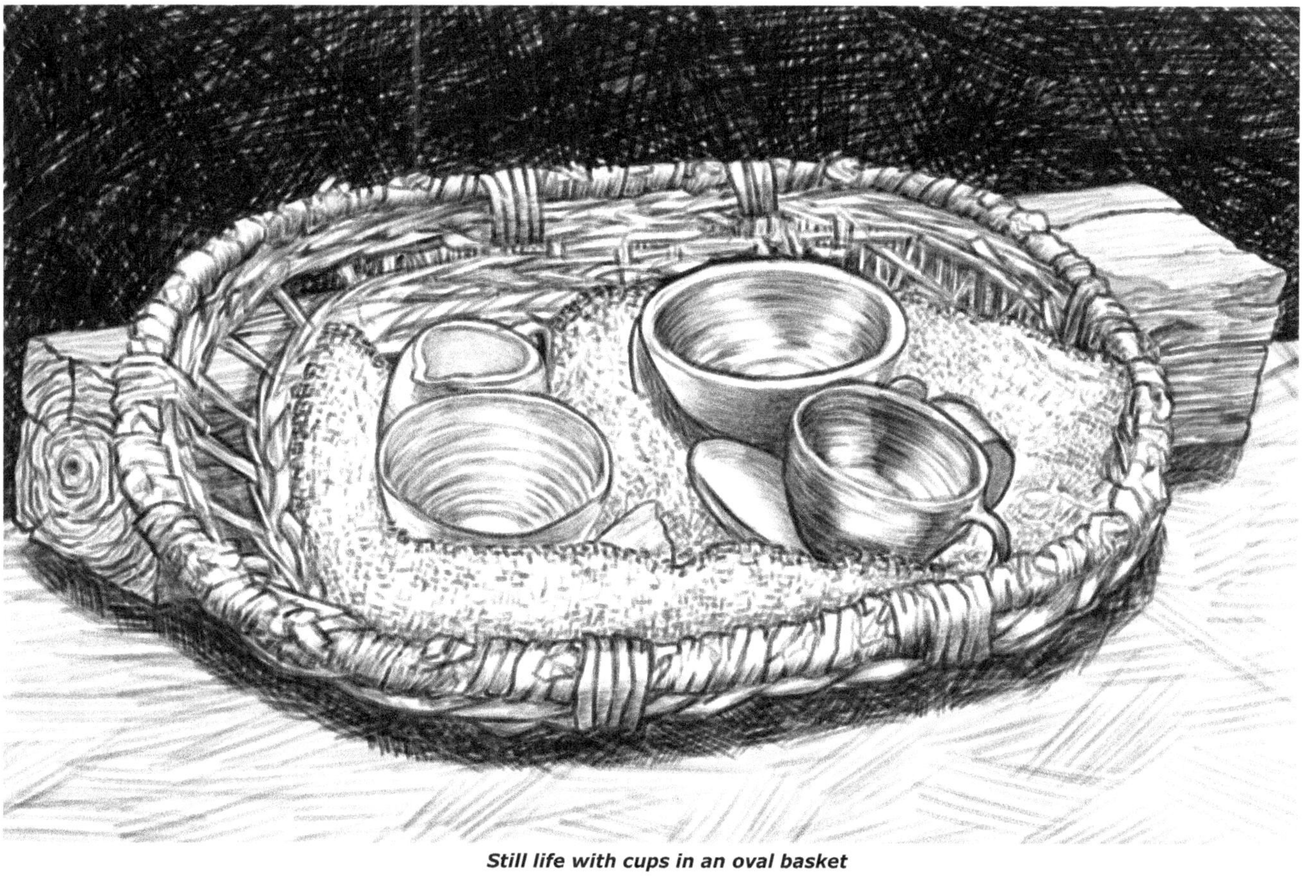

Still life with cups in an oval basket

Squares and Rectangles

The rectangle is rarely used as a geometric compositional aid. The shape does not correspond to typical natural forms and occurs primarily in man-made objects. In still lifes, rectangular objects are often arranged in combination with round objects to create a contrast. In addition, the rectangle frequently appears in the form of a frame within a picture.

Still life with pictures and frames

However, when using rectangles in a composition, it should not be forgotten that these strictly geometric forms appear static and motionless. As a rule, they do not create any dynamics or movement within the picture. Rather, one associates rectangles – above all the square – with gravity, solidity, precision, and a sharp demarcation from their environment. These are various aspects that should be taken into account when creating a picture, but they can also be used in a targeted manner.

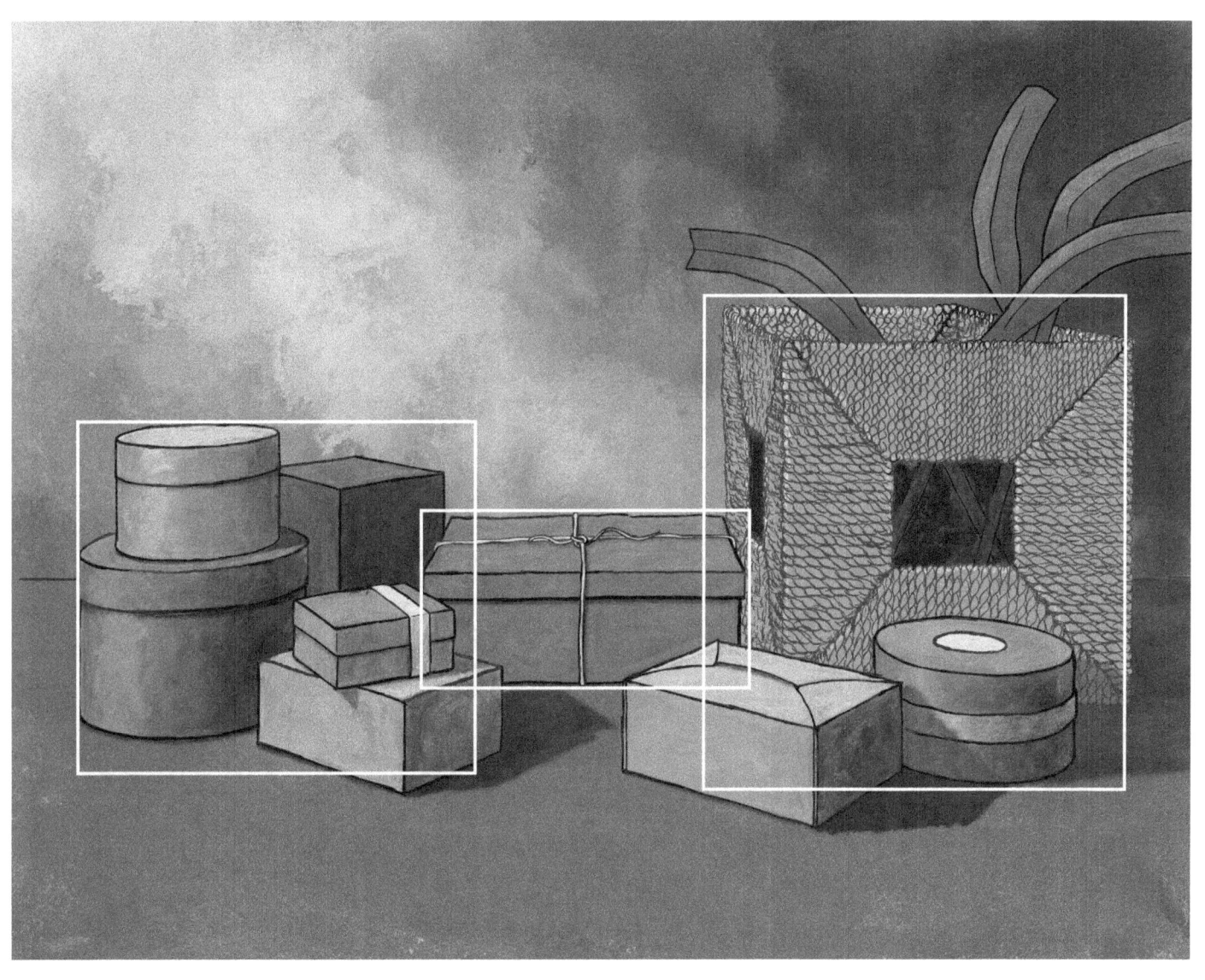

Still life with a rectangle composition

Structure

Lines are used to delimit shapes, creating surfaces. As we have already learned in the previous section, surfaces often serve as carriers of structure. The structure is what you could call the substance of the surface. Compositionally, we thus have the sequence: line – form – surface. The structure is much smaller in relation to the form. It is therefore not perceived by the viewer as a single entity. Nevertheless, structures can dominate not only the form or background of a composition but also entire areas of the image. For this reason, the structure is therefore "surface-forming."

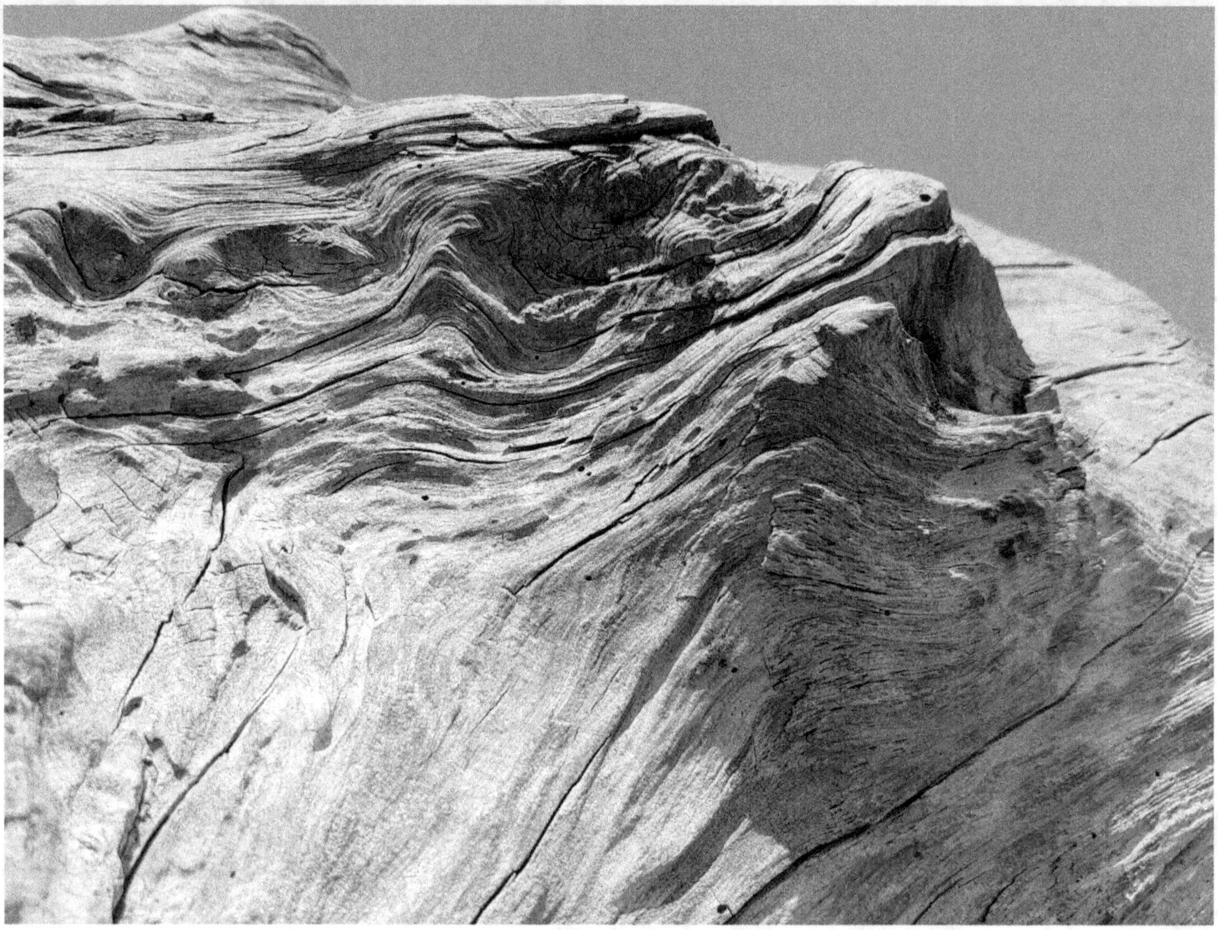

Structures in an old tree stump

Structures reveal certain "organizing principles." Seen from a certain distance or from above, even larger, diverse elements can form a structure. However, their effect on the viewer will be preserved as long as they can still be recognized as single entities. The arrangement of such elements, be it free, rhythmic, or strictly organized, allows different "organizing principles," ranging from the chaotic to very exact patterns.

Such "organizing principles" can be perceived very precisely, especially with structures. In this context, it is also important to distinguish between pattern and structure – although the boundaries cannot always be clearly drawn and sometimes they are "in the eye of the beholder." A pattern is perceived, for example, when many very uniform elements are used.

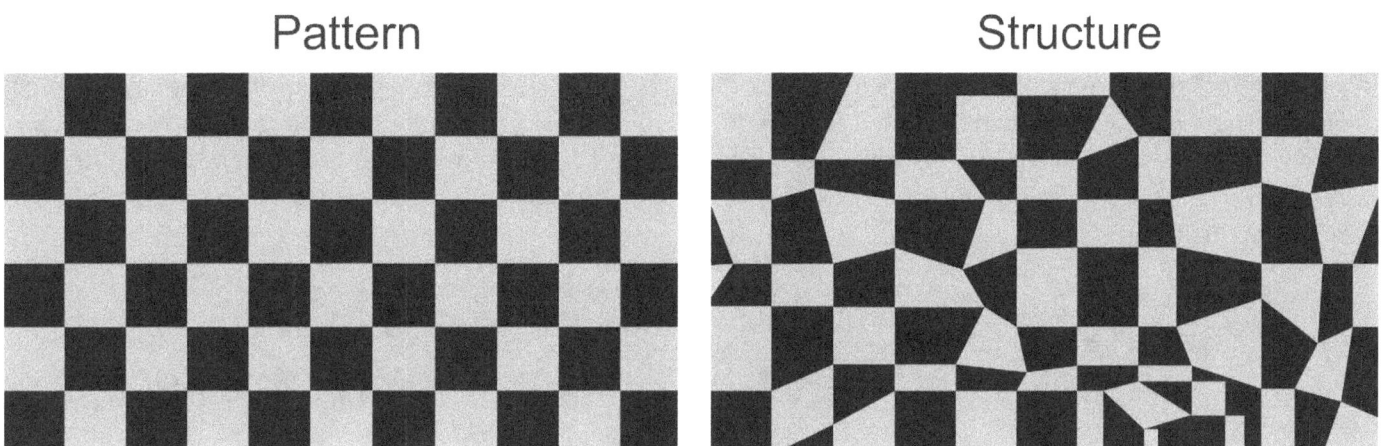
Comparison of pattern and structure

Individual objects can be distorted through the use of structures; for example, by "covering" them with transparent materials such as glass or certain fabrics. Grids and fences fulfill a similar function. The structure of the superimposed object is thus reduced to a certain degree. Distortion through structure can also be caused by the medium itself. Examples include pencil hatchings and brush strokes, or the texture of drawing paper (e.g., roughness) or film material (e.g., film grain). And printing screens also enable the formation of structures.

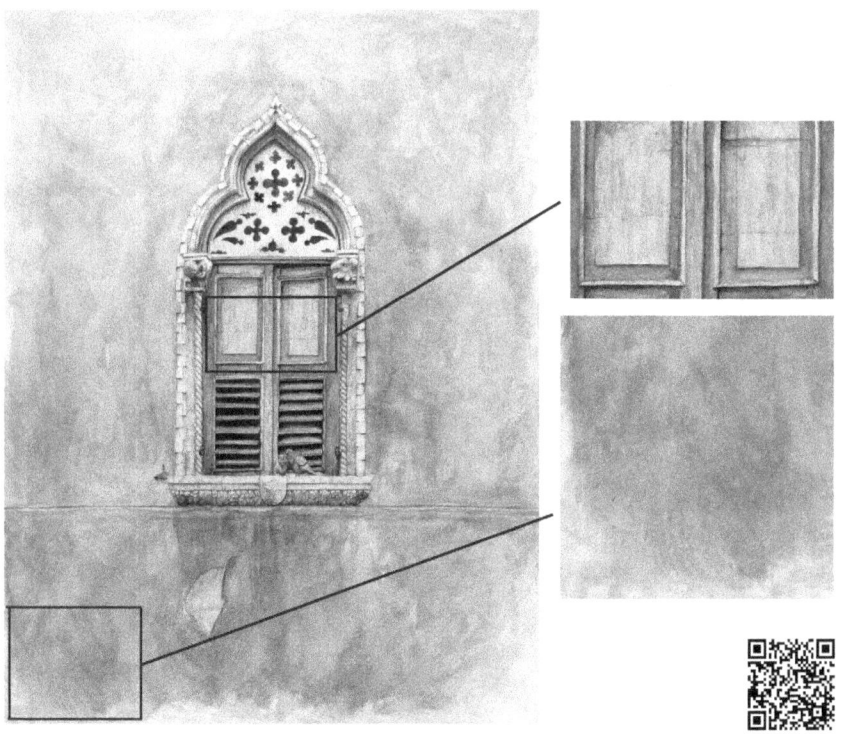
Structures in the wood and structures obtained through strokes of the brush

Composition and Structural Size

Image compositions usually consist of objects of different sizes. Of course, the largest objects can be seen by the viewer from furthest away. The viewer perceives these larger objects in relation to each other. The first level of observation is thus created by the relationship between the main motif and the size of the other components making up the motif.

Viewing the image thus takes place on different levels. It begins with the whole picture and is then "refined" step by step. More and more details are then perceived from an increasingly closer distance. Such an approach is supported by the findings of Gestalt psychology, which assumes that objects are always first recognized as a whole.

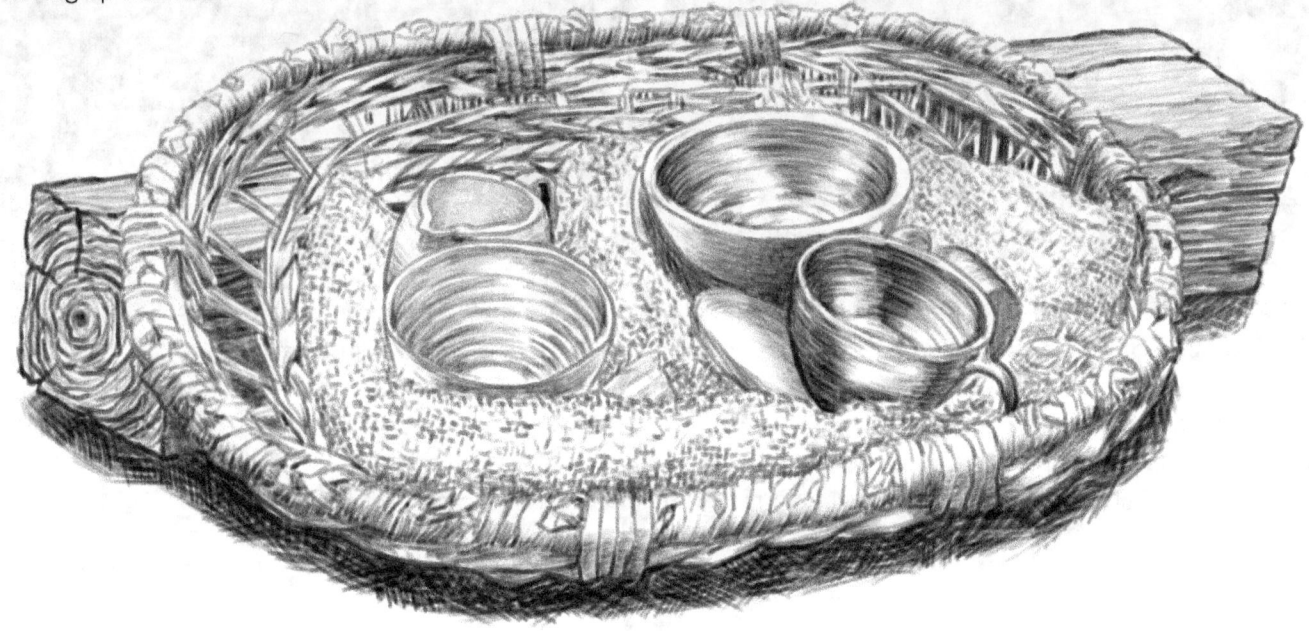

*Several structures in a drawing:
wooden structure, coarsely woven basket, and delicately woven fabric*

The structures are best compared from the same distance. For each size of structure, there is a suitable distance for the viewer. Structures that are very coarse or very delicate are almost never perceived at the same time. In the event that the structure itself is the main motif of the image, a structural contrast is necessary for a satisfactory pictorial composition. This contrast must be effective at the greatest viewing distance.

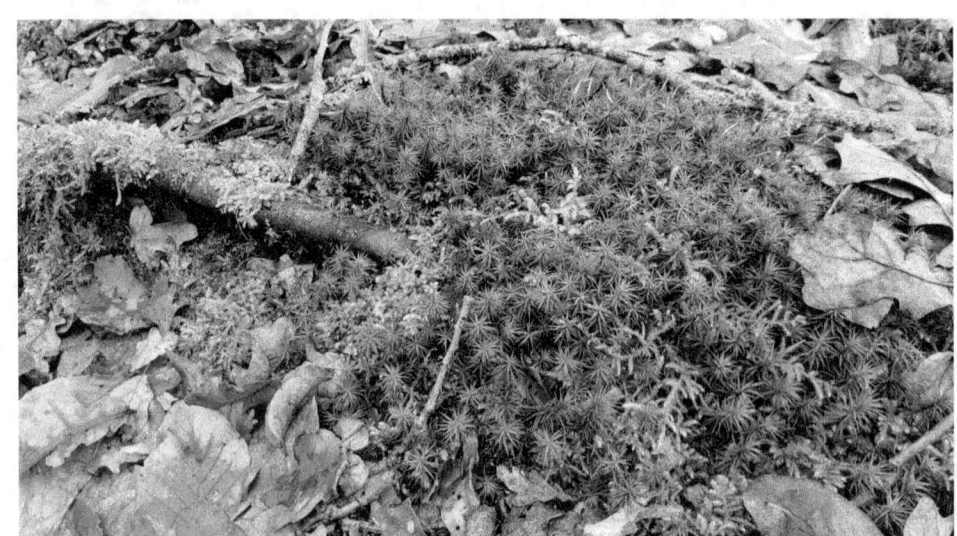

Structural contrast

Example - Composition with Diagonals and Structures

For a better understanding of the previous chapters, we will now take a look at an example. The motif of this still life is a couch which is stacked with books.

The composition of this still life is more multifaceted than you might initially think. At first glance, one recognizes the couch with the books lying on it as a rectangle. The motif seems heavy, block-like, and solid. The depth effect is very slight. Moreover, the image is relatively symmetrical, and you can see horizontal as well as vertical lines. Due to these characteristics, there is little dynamism in the drawing at first glance.

If you take a closer look at the still life, you will notice that there are also many diagonal lines. These are caused by the books, which are not all lying on top of each other in an orderly fashion. Even the cloth that lies on the seat of the couch hangs down at an angle and thus contributes considerably to the lively effect of the picture.

The books also create a kind of structure, which becomes a main element of the composition of this still life. The structure of the books has a certain degree of contrast to the structure of the blanket on the seat, the blanket hanging over the backrest, and the hatching in the background.

The interplay between these design elements creates an appealing pictorial composition that is not necessarily recognizable at first glance.

Example - Composition in Landscape Art

A very successful and extremely well-known example of composition in the visual arts is the painting "The Windmill at Wijk bij Duurstede" by Jacob van Ruisdael. Van Ruisdael was a Dutch baroque landscape painter who was born in Haarlem, Holland, in 1628/29. The windmill is one of his most important works.

The main focus of the painting is on the sky, with its dramatic arrangement of clouds. However, the composition as a whole is also remarkable. Use your knowledge from the previous chapters on pictorial design and composition to decipher van Ruisdael's methods.

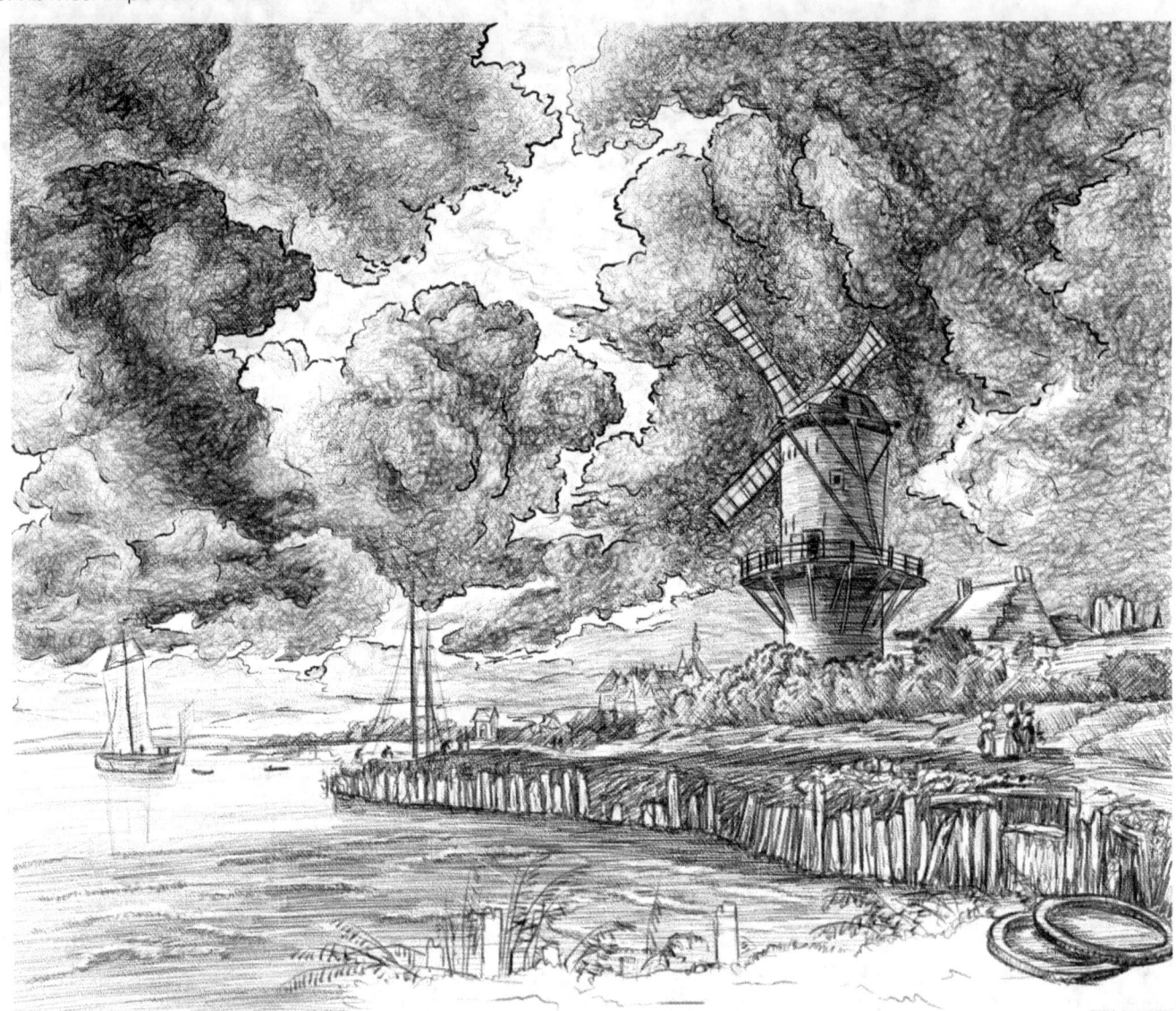

Landscape sketch of a painting by Ruisdael: "The Windmill at Wijk bij Duurstede"

When you look at a picture by an artist, always pause for a while and examine the composition of the work. The composition of "The Windmill at Wijk bij Duurstede," for example, is very well thought out. The spatial layout corresponds approximately to the rule of thirds, with about two thirds being occupied by the sky.

The windmill protrudes into the sky area and extends into the second third. Several diagonals appear in the form of the bank, the windmill wheels, and the clouds. They open up the space and direct our gaze around the picture. People at different distances away also lead us through the picture at the level of the horizon. The impressive cloud formations are also very dynamic.

80   Graphic Design Elements

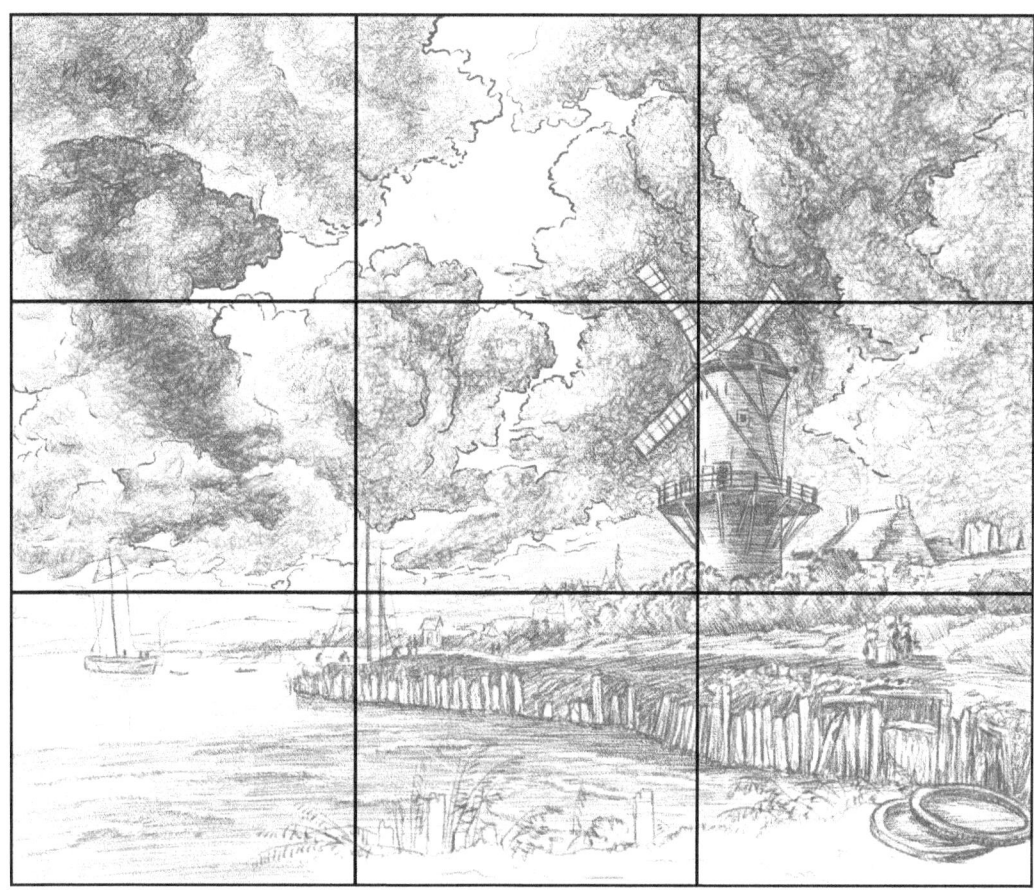

The rule of thirds in the picture

A Few Art-Historical Facts

While earlier landscape paintings tended to divide the picture surface into two thirds land and one third sky, in the seventeenth century Dutch painters reversed this weighting. More and more often, landscape pictures now showed the sky taking up two thirds of the picture surface.

This development is evidence of the fact that even artists hundreds of years ago were well aware of compositional methods like the rule of thirds.

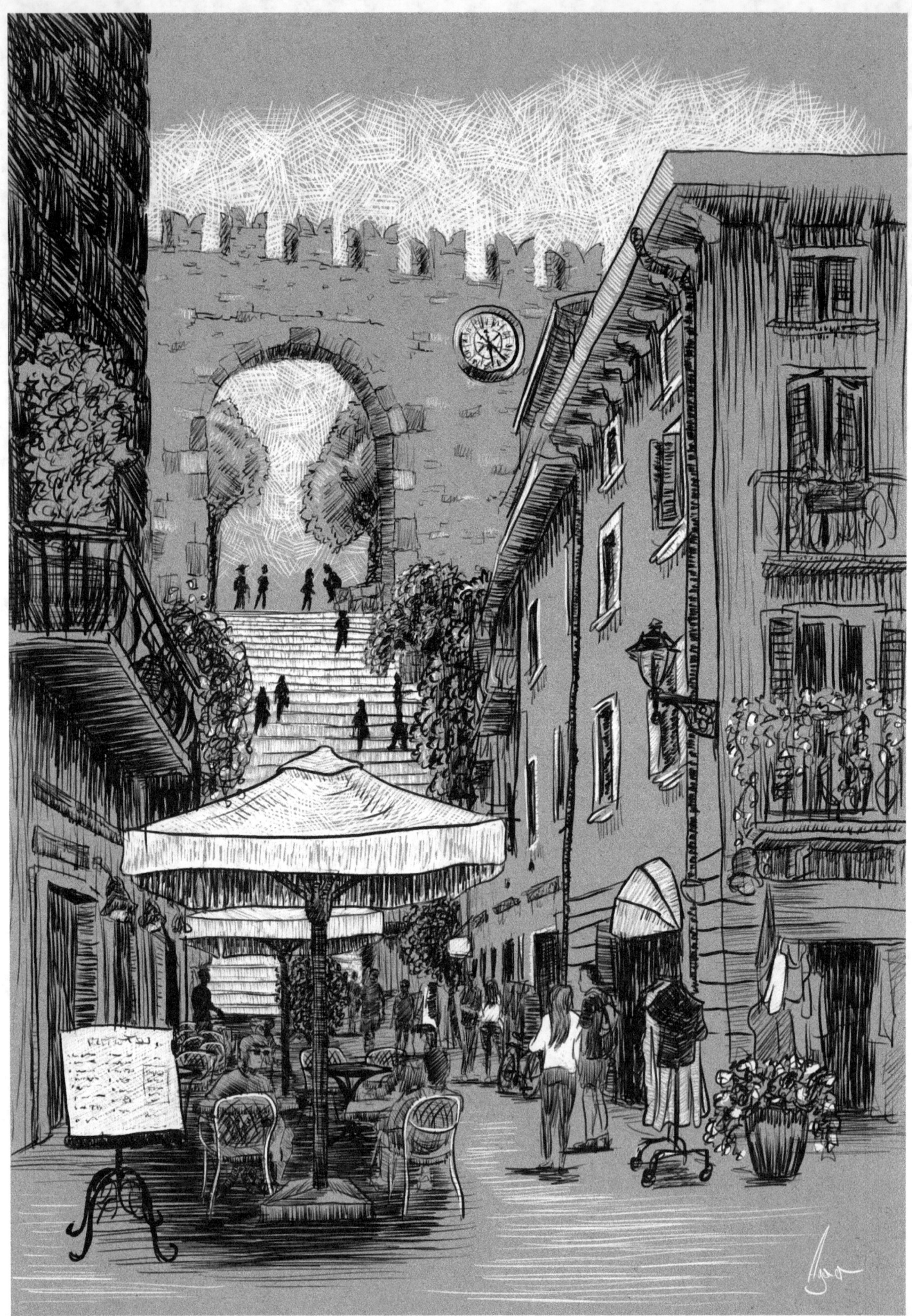

Further Design Elements

» Drawing is a form of contemplation on paper. «
- Saul Steinberg -

Further Design Elements

In addition to methods of subdividing the picture background and the graphic design elements, there are also other design techniques that are just as important for the composition of the image but function in a different way.

The Format

A fundamental decision in pictorial composition is the choice of format. First of all, a distinction can be made between portrait and landscape format. The same motif can have a completely different effect on the viewer depending on the choice of format. The two most important formats are the landscape and the portrait format. In general, it can be said that landscape format emphasizes width, while portrait format mainly emphasizes the height of an image. Accordingly, certain formats are generally suitable for certain motifs.

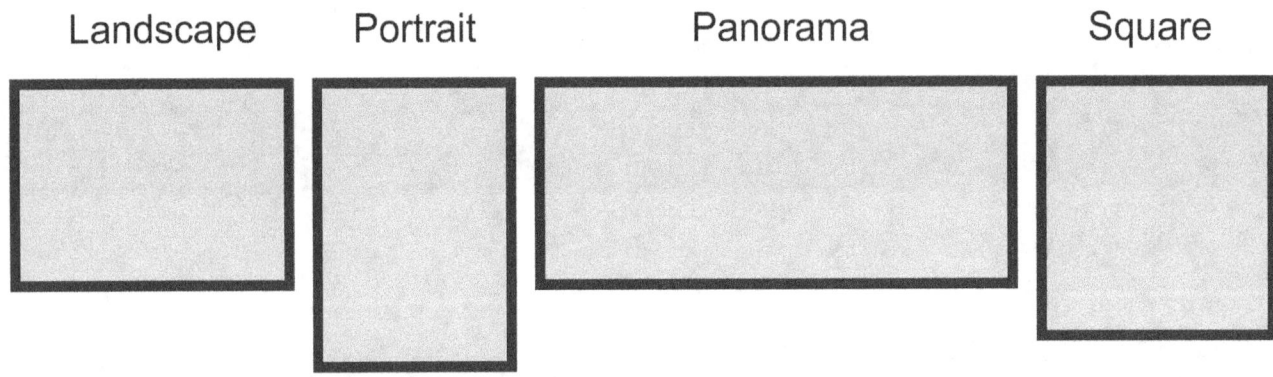

Various canvas formats

Landscape (Horizontal) Format

Landscape pictures typically use a horizontal format, as this format mainly emphasizes width. This fits in with the way landscapes are usually presented. Furthermore, the landscape format corresponds to our own field of vision since our eyes are arranged next to each other. Still lifes and scenes in which several people can be seen are also very often depicted in landscape format. In the composition, the main motif is often positioned off-center to the left or right, as recommended by rules such as the golden ratio.

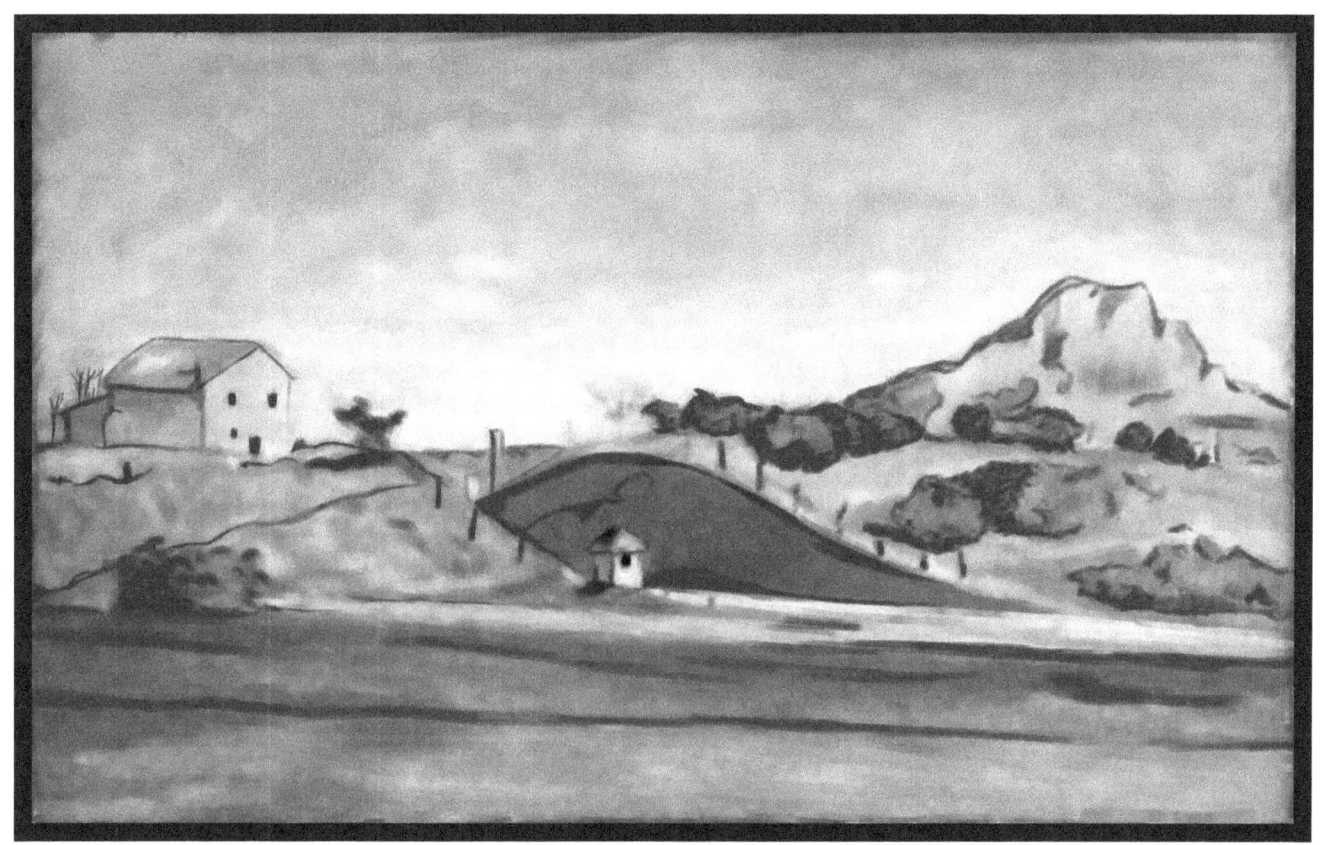

Landscape in horizontal format: "The Railway Cutting" – copy
Original: Paul Cézanne, ca. 1870

Portrait Format

Portraits are a typical application of the portrait format, as the vertical alignment of the image matches the shape of the human body and face. Also, when tall buildings are depicted, portrait format is commonly used. For landscape pictures, portrait format is suitable when the sky needs to be emphasized – even if you normally use landscape format for landscapes.

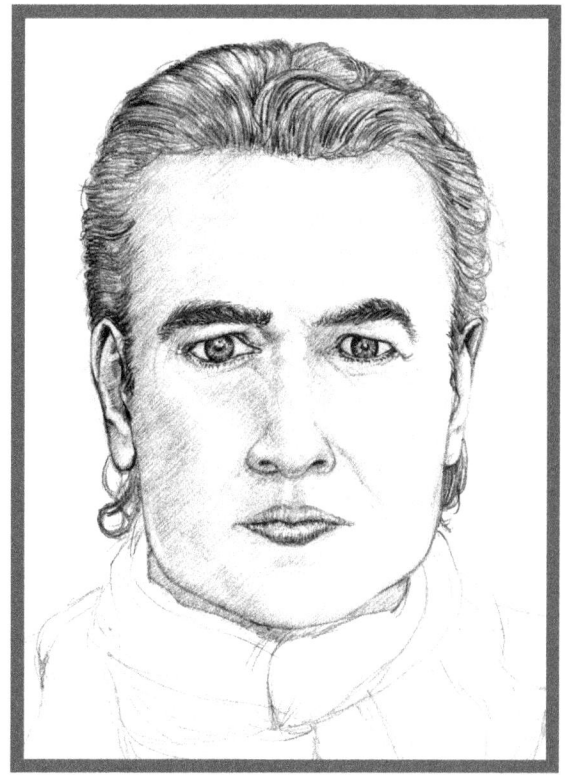

Portrait drawing in typical vertical format

Panorama Format

The panorama format is an extension of the landscape format. It is a format that is even wider than the usual landscape formats. The fascination of the panorama format lies in the fact that our view goes beyond what we can see with our human field of vision.

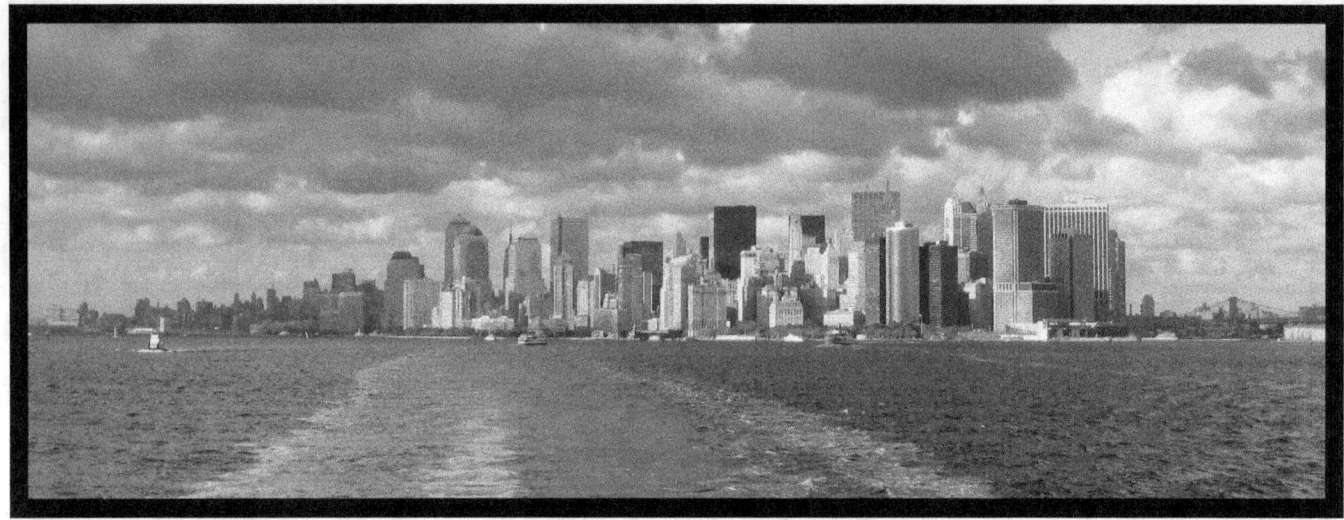

Panorama photograph of a New York cityscape

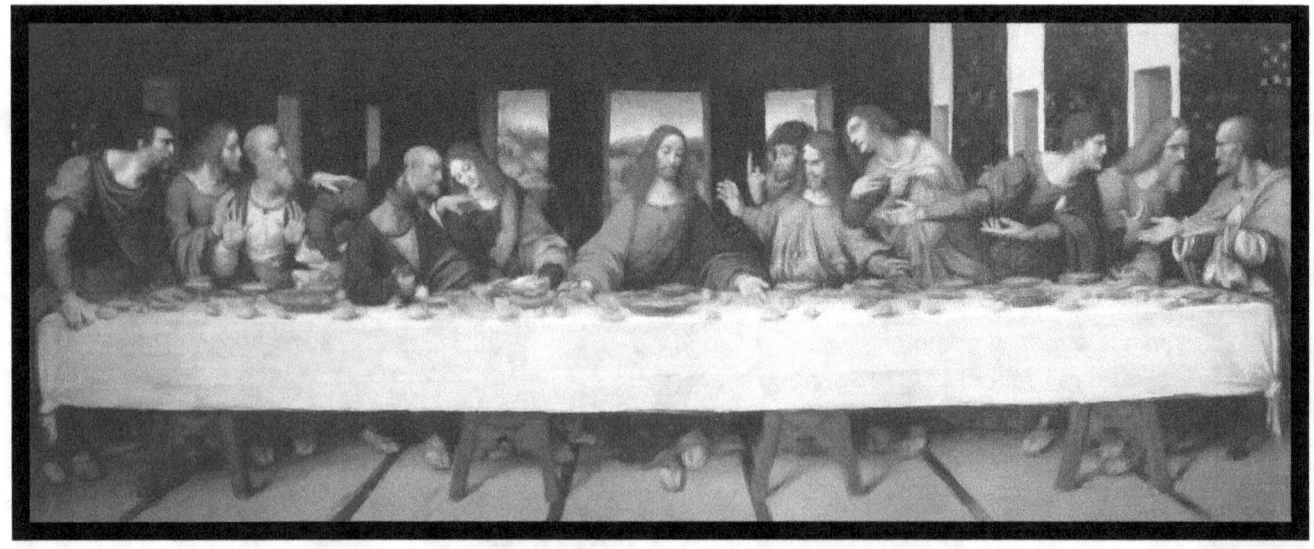

Panorama format in a group portrait: "The Last Supper" – copy
Original: Leonardo da Vinci, 1494 to 1497

Square Format

For the square format, it is not so easy to find a suitable pictorial composition. Very few motifs are square. Therefore, the square format is chosen less often. With a square image format, some kind of square geometry is usually expected in the motif, but it can also be suitable in certain other cases.

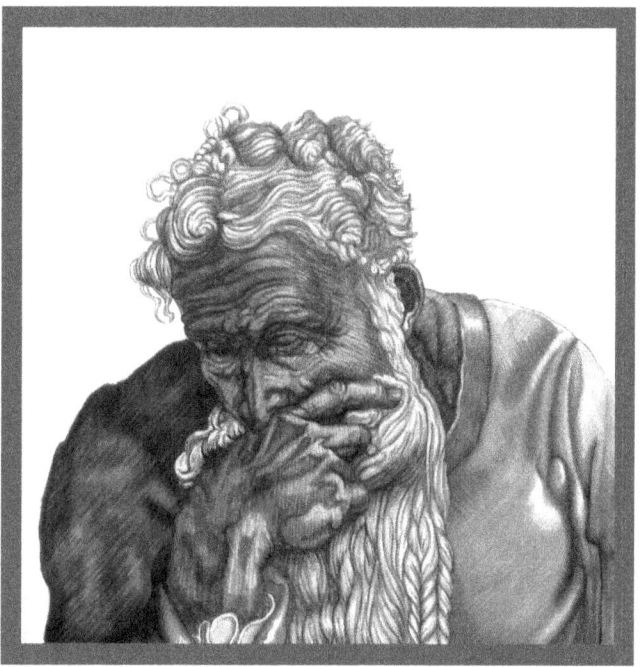

Portrait in square format
"Jeremiah" after a painting by Michelangelo Buonarroti

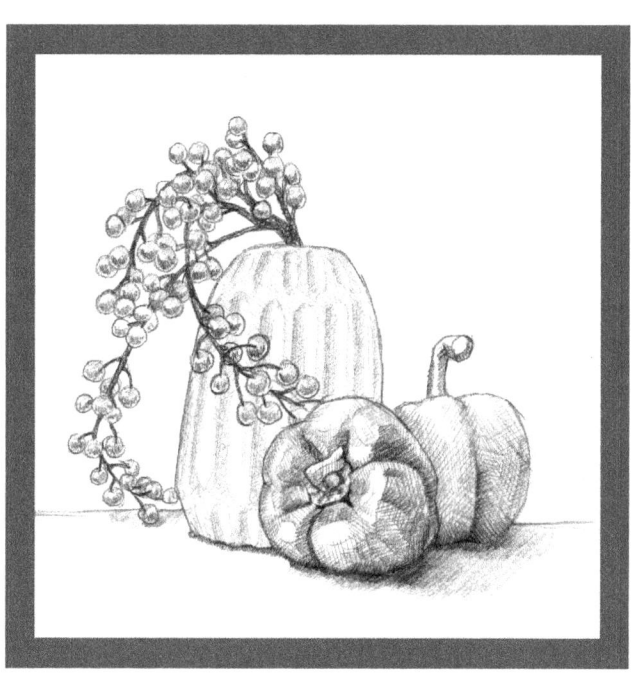

Still life in square format

Using Contrasts

With the skillful application of contrasts, images can be made more exciting and specific objects can be highlighted. There are several different types of contrast that work in different ways.

So, which contrasts do we have at our disposal? Often the word contrast automatically implies the light-dark contrast. But there are many more types of contrast. In principle, contrasts are simply opposites that differentiate from one another considerably. In the following sections, the most important types of contrast will be described in more detail.

The Light-Dark Contrast

The light-dark contrast results from the different brightness of elements in a picture. This tonal value contrast can occur with the achromatic colors black, white, and gray, but is also found with the primary and secondary colors to the same extent. In the case of chromatic colors, one speaks of the color brightness.

Light-dark contrast is used very frequently and very specifically in image composition. It can be used to add depth to an image or to draw attention to certain elements. For example, surfaces with the same level of brightness appear to be on the same plane. Strong tonal contrast, on the other hand, creates plasticity. Bright elements appear as if they are further in the foreground, while dark elements recede into the background. Painters and draftspersons consciously use the light-dark contrast to clearly separate light and shadow. In the motif depicted below, the contours become more recognizable, which leads to an impression of corporeality and three-dimensionality.

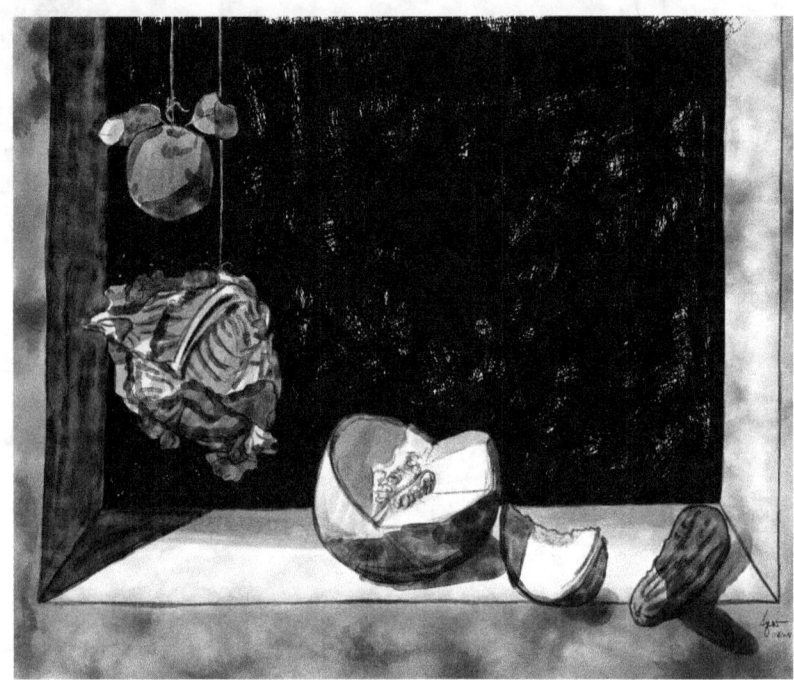

Still life with strong light-dark contrast
Drawing after a painting by J. S. Cotán

Strong contrasts are also a tool for directing the viewer's gaze to the most important areas of the picture. Use the strongest contrast for the elements of your drawing that you want to focus on. Drawing the less important areas with low contrast will make them less prominent.

The other effect of light-dark contrast is the weighting of pictorial elements or picture areas. Because bright elements attract the viewer's attention, they appear more important than things that lie in the dark. This method can be found in countless pictures by different artists from different epochs of art history. Again and again, we see significant elements being depicted in a bright light, while things that the viewer is not supposed to focus on are obscured in darkness and disappear.

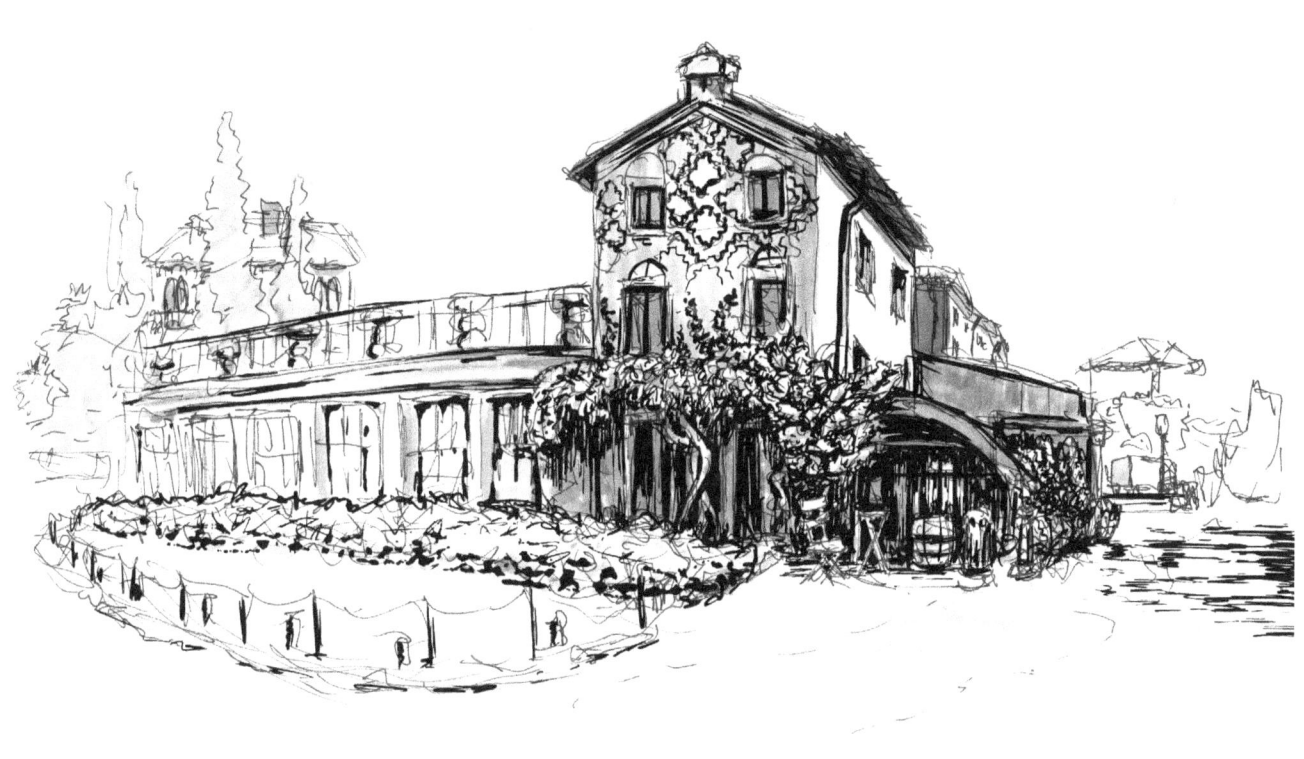

Stronger light-dark contrasts in a drawing lead one's attention directly to the most important element of the picture

Example Image 1: The Calling of St. Matthew

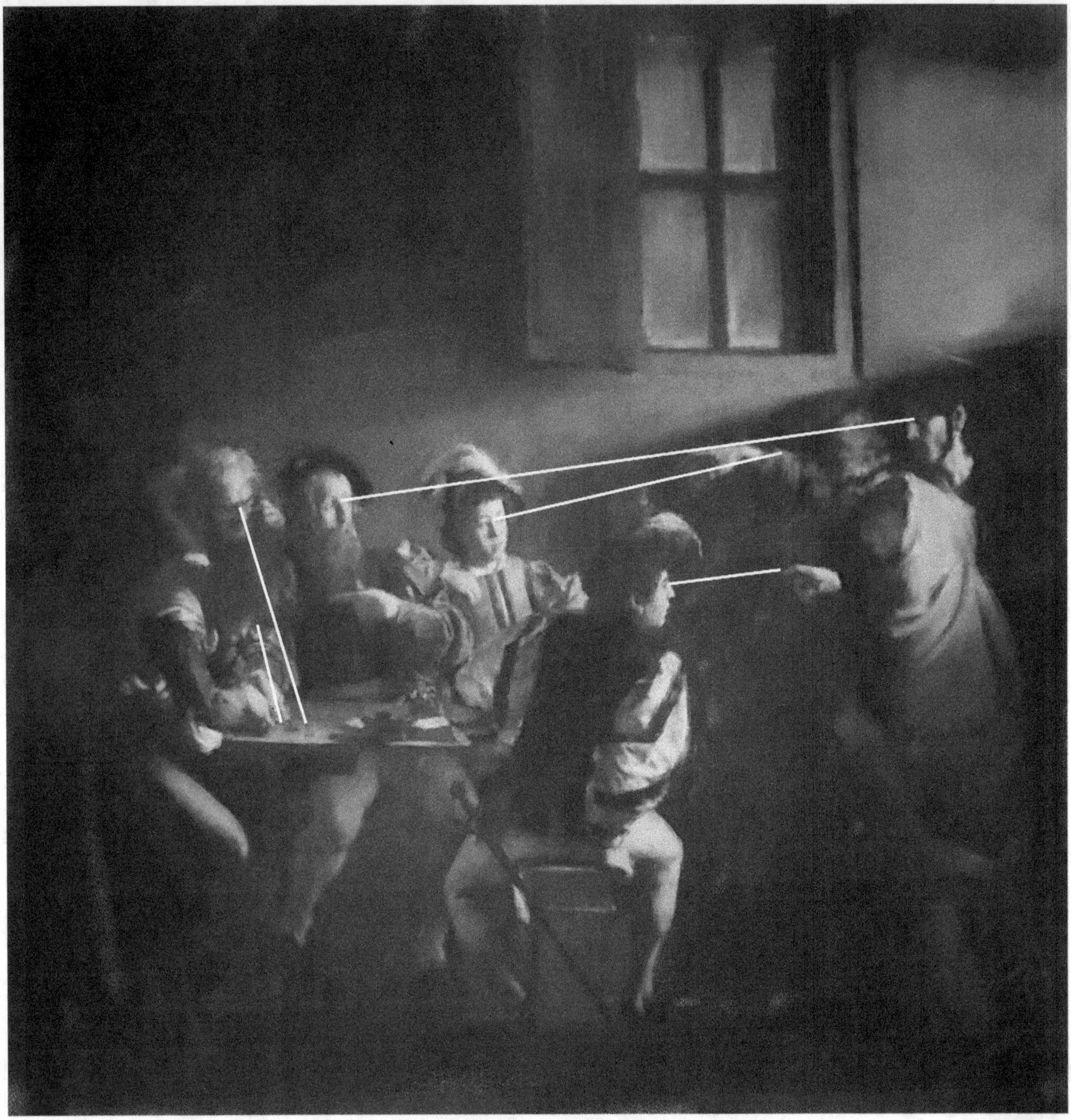

The Calling of St. Matthew – copy
Original: Michelangelo Merisi da Caravaggio, 1599/1600

A particularly fitting example of the use of light-dark contrast is "The Calling of St. Matthew" by the painter Caravaggio. In the painting, you can see very distinctly that a clearly defined light falls into the room from the right. The light falls on the individuals in the room and seems to cut them out of the darkness. However, areas of the picture outside the beam of light sink into the shadows.

Example Image 2: The Night Watch

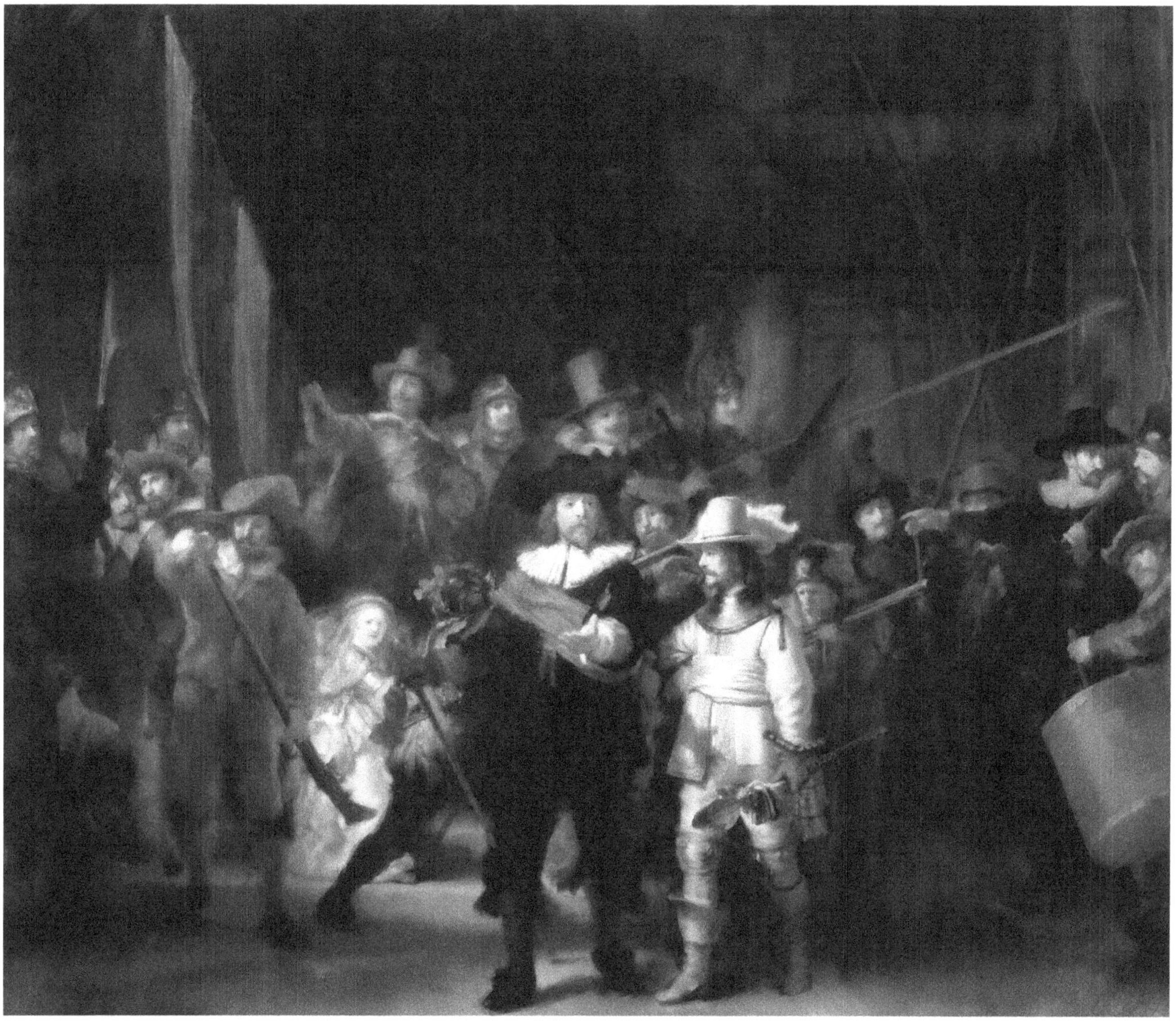

The Night Watch – copy
Original: Rembrandt van Rijn, 1642

In the example image "The Night Watch," you can clearly see how different elements within the image are weighted by means of lighting. The painting is a group portrait of a marksmen's guild in which 34 people are portrayed. Two figures are clearly emphasized through the targeted use of lighting and their bright clothing. They are the lieutenant in the foreground and a girl in the middle ground.

The second figure in the foreground is the captain. He is quite clearly emphasized by a strong light falling on his face and collar. The rest of the scene is presented in much darker tones. It should be noted, however, that the particularly strong light-dark contrast may also have been caused by the natural darkening of the numerous layers of varnish. In the original state, the contrast may not have been developed so dramatically.

Further Color Contrasts

According to Itten's theory, seven color contrasts can be distinguished. This includes the light-dark contrast described in the previous section, since this can also be found in color brightness. Due to its outstanding significance in the field of drawing, however, the light-dark contrast has been described in more detail in the previous section.

- Light-dark contrast/tonal value contrast
- Color-in-itself contrast
- Cold-warm contrast
- Quality contrast
- Quantity contrast
- Complementary contrast
- Simultaneous contrast
- Successive contrast

Since this book is dedicated to monochrome drawing, the individual color contrasts will not be discussed further. However, for the sake of completeness, they are listed above.

Content Contrast

A completely different kind of contrast is content contrast. It arises from contradictory or antithetical content in a picture. This includes contrasts such as hard-soft, big-small, poor-rich, or ugly-beautiful. For example, people going swimming in snow and ice in winter create this contrast in content. Another good example is a delicate flower breaking through asphalt.

Through high-contrast image content, one can evoke certain feelings in the viewer. If the contrasts in content are intensified at the same time as the color contrasts, these impressions can be intensified further.

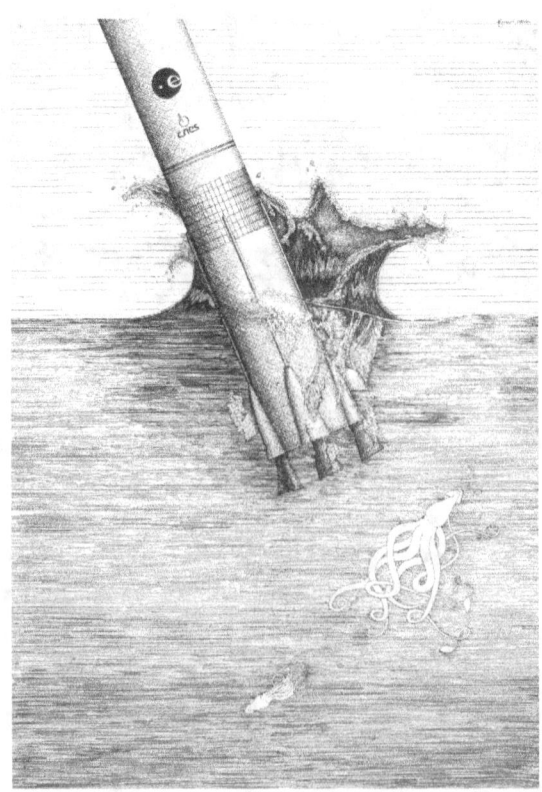

The content contrast here comes from the fact that the rocket is not flying in space; rather, it is sinking into the water

Contrast in Shape

Contrasts in shape arise when different shapes meet, as is the case when round and angular shapes are combined. Frequently, shapes also form surfaces, which in turn create a surface contrast, for example a contrast between symmetrical and asymmetrical surfaces. Contrasts in line can also give rise to contrasts in shape. These arise when lines of different thickness, direction, color, continuity, etc. are present.

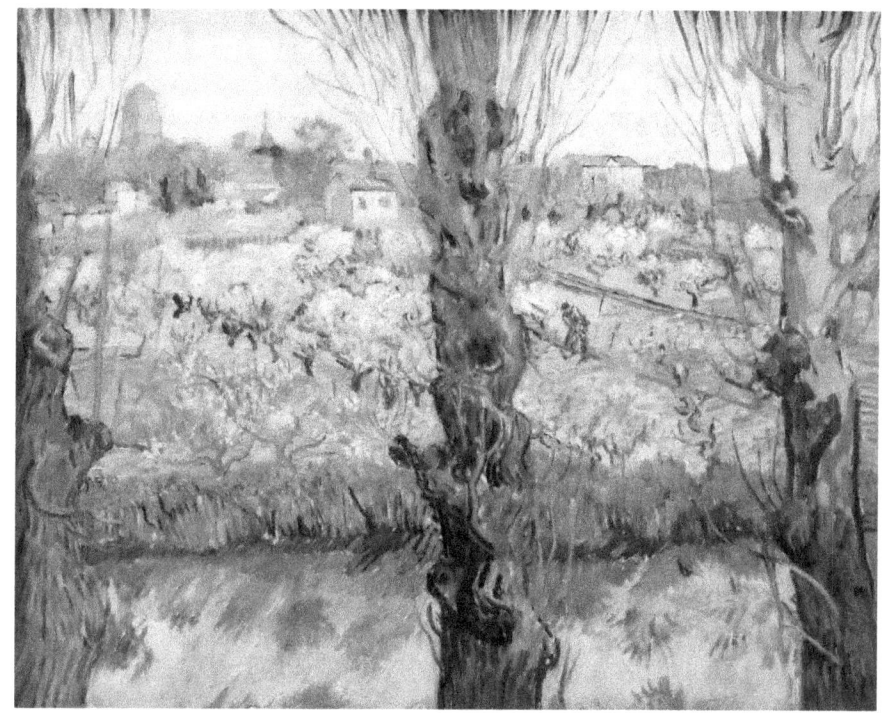

A contrast emerges between the vertical trees and the horizontal riverbank

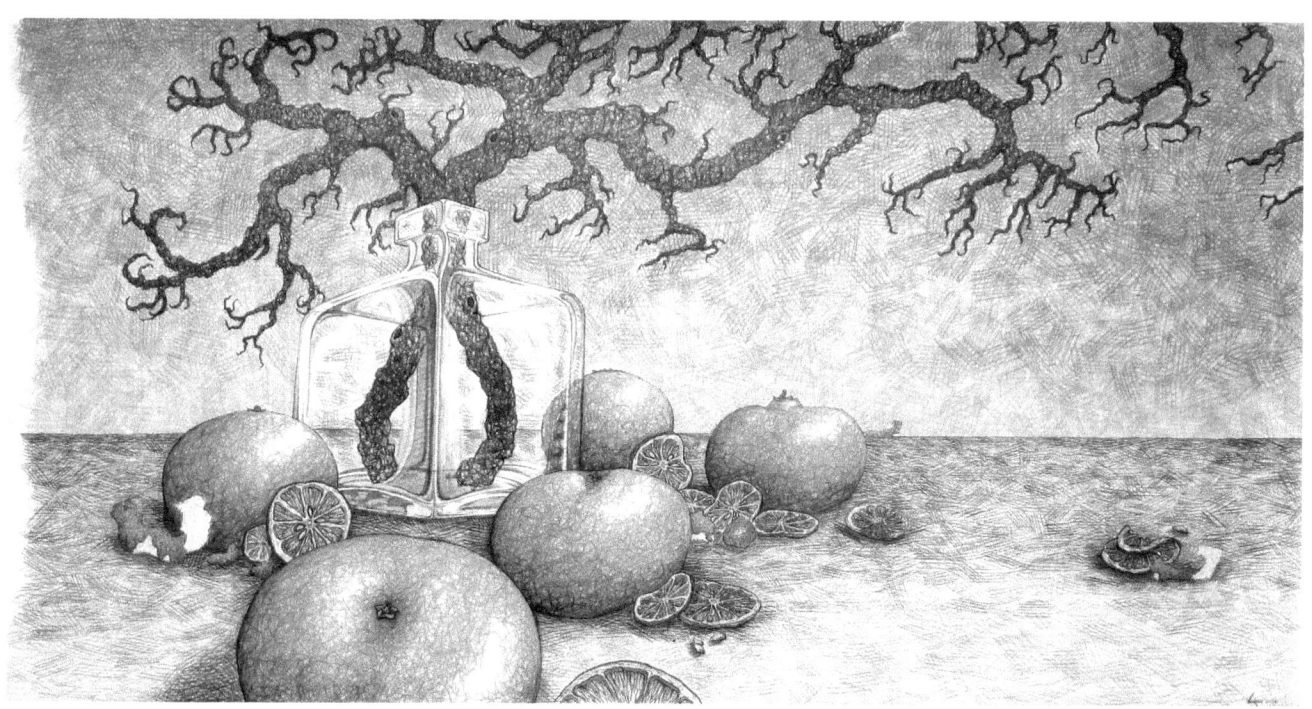

Contrast between rounded lines (Mandarin oranges) and crooked lines (branches) in a still life

Perspective and Space

The term perspective refers to the angle from which the artist depicts a motif. Conversely, it is also the point of view from which the viewer sees the scene. The perspective changes automatically when the artist moves – be it up, down, left, right, forwards, or backwards. Every inclination or new orientation of the vista also changes the perspective.

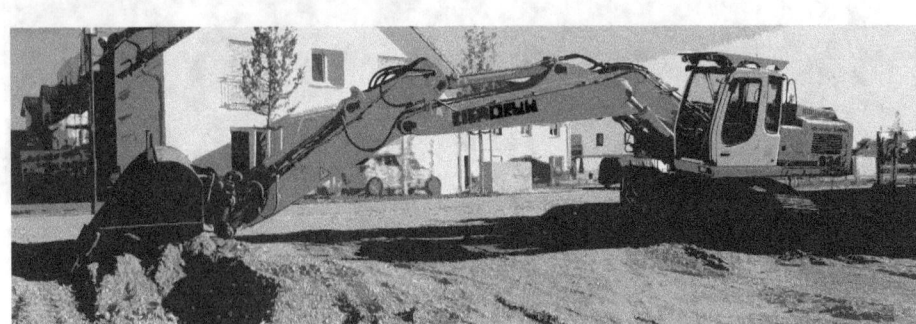
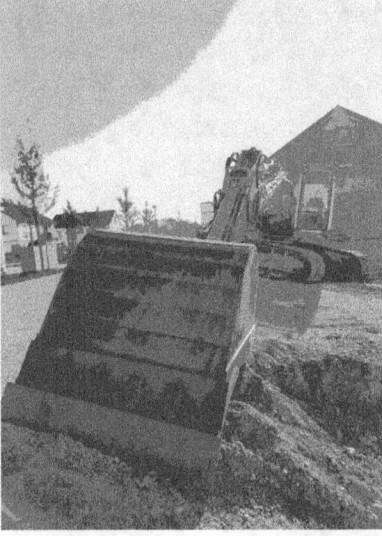
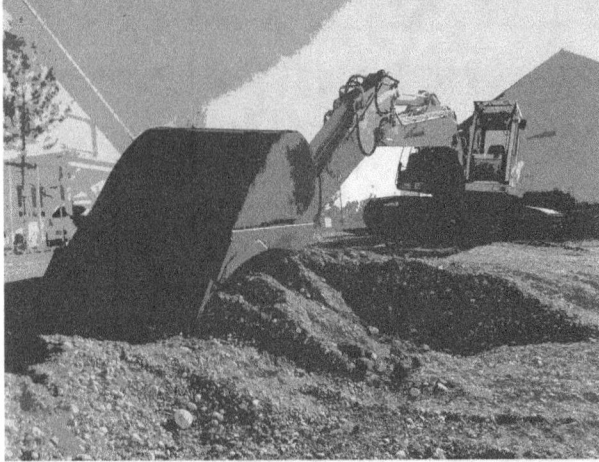
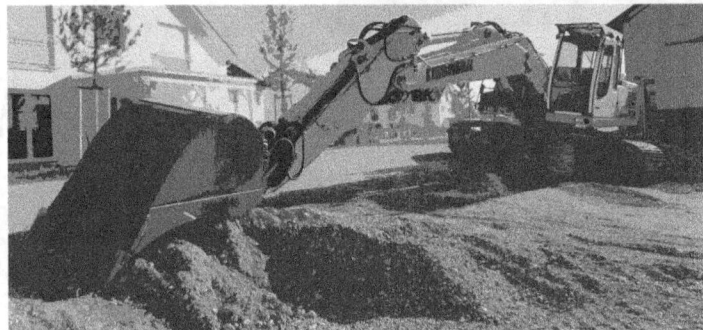

The same excavator from different viewpoints

Perspective is a particularly powerful instrument of image composition as it can be used to directly influence the effect of the image and to create targeted effects. A view from above (bird's eye view), for example, creates a completely different impression than a view from a low point of view – even if nothing else changes in the motif.

Spatial Depth

The representation of spatial depth is an important and challenging element in composition. If you are capable of achieving the effect of three dimensions in a painting, this will play an important role in your ability to create a realistic depiction of your subject matter. In order to allow this sense of space to emerge on a two-dimensional drawing surface, diverse graphic aids are frequently deployed. The following methods can be used to create spatial depth:

- Suitable image composition
- Overlapping
- Levels
- Repetition of objects at varying distances
- Reducing the level of detail
- Aerial perspective
- Perspective foreshortening
- Vanishing point perspective

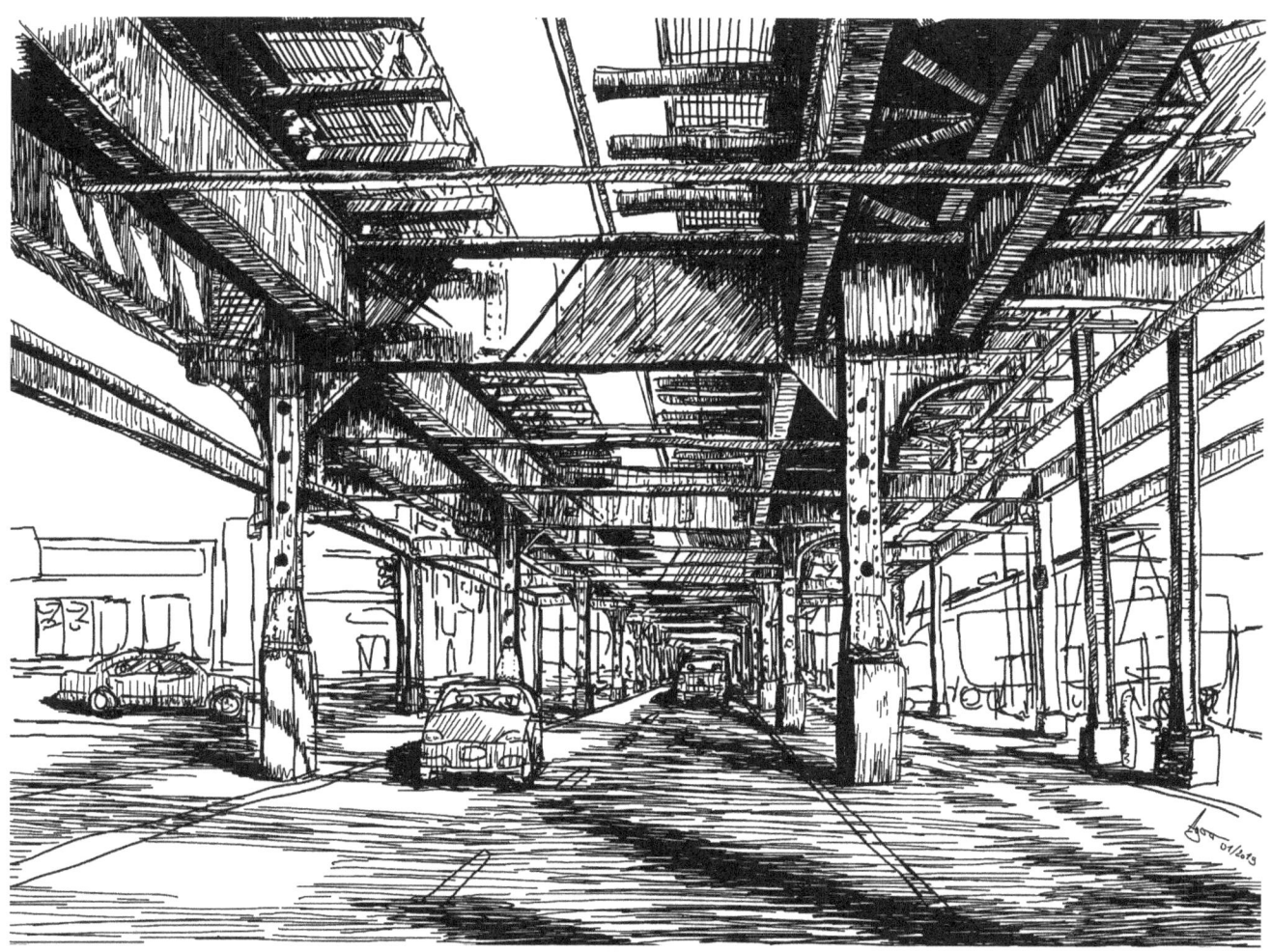

Central perspective in this city scene draws the viewer's gaze into the depth of the picture

Suitable Image Composition

A basic precept of achieving the effect of space and depth is to fulfill the expectations of the viewer. This means that we represent the space in a manner that they are accustomed to and anticipate based on their experience. Specifically: those objects that lie on the ground, i.e., in the lower area of the drawing, are located in the foreground, and those objects that are in the upper section are more likely to be located in the background. In this way, we can make it easier for the viewer to get their bearings within an image, and the impression of a three-dimensional landscape is more readily conveyed in this manner.

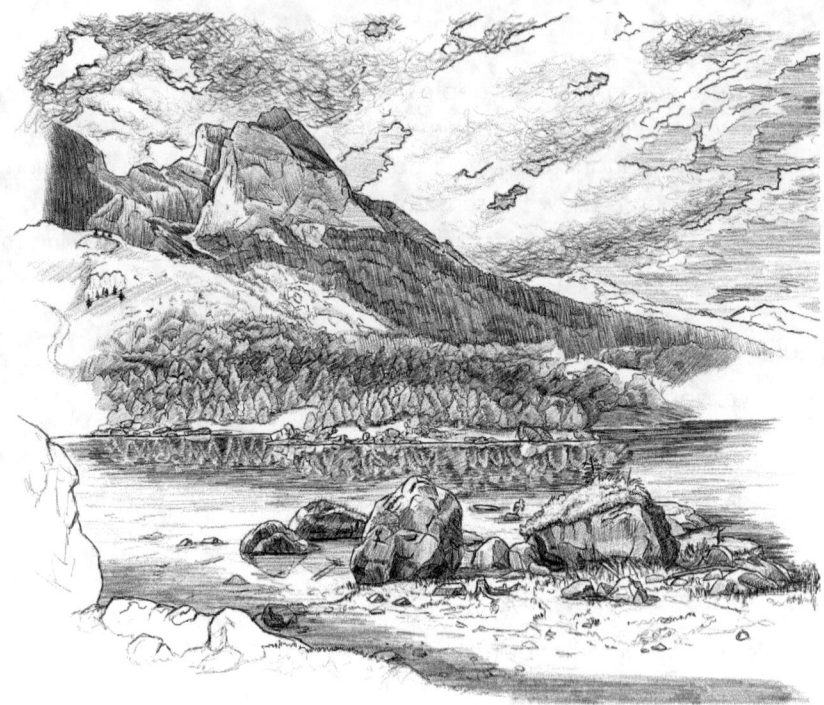

Landscape with a classic composition
(Drawing based on a painting by Carl Rottmann)

Overlapping

The effect of spatial representation is optically reinforced when the image is constructed from several upright planes. These planes could contain trees, a house, a car, etc. The planes should be laid out at varying distances and overlap one another. Due to the fact that the planes overlay one another, it is immediately obvious to the viewer that the various objects in the image are located at different distances.

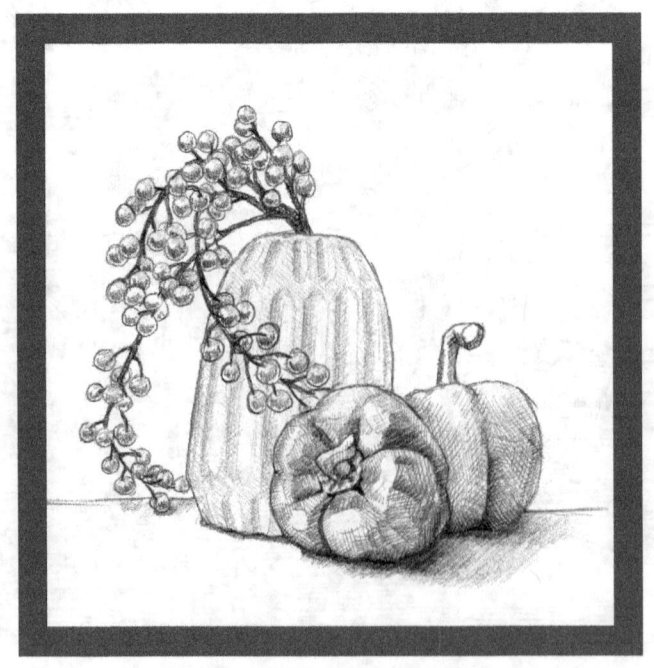

Spatial effect via overlapping objects

Levels

The effect of spatial representation can be visually enhanced by building up the image in several levels. These levels could include trees, a house, a car, etc.

In many cases, the overlap method is combined with the level method; the levels are at different distances and overlap each other. As the levels overlap, it is immediately obvious to the viewer that the different image objects are at different distances.

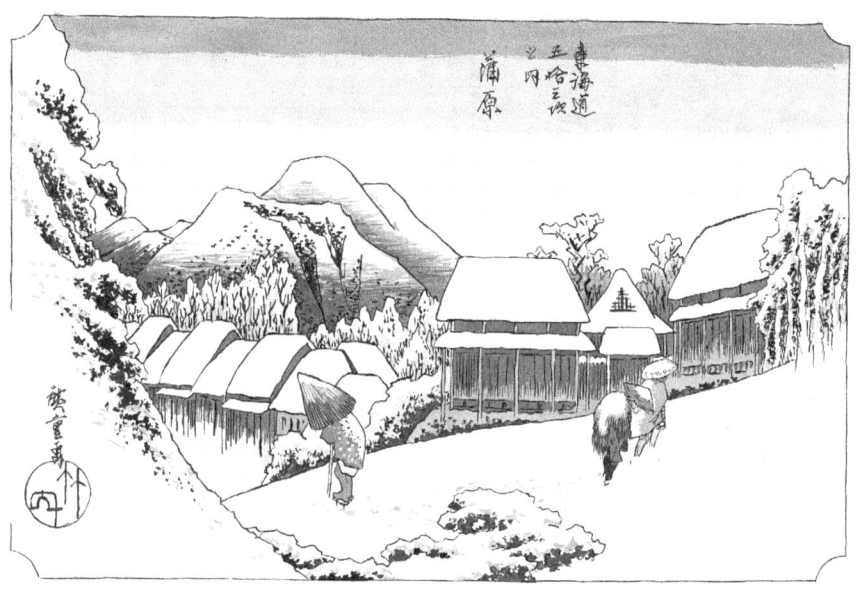

Copy of a Japanese woodblock print: "A Snowy Evening at Kambara Station" from the series "The 53 Stations of the Tōkaidō"; original: Utagawa Hiroshige

Repetition of Objects at Varying Distances

The spatial effect in a drawing can be further increased by varying the viewer's perspective of an object. Specifically, this can be achieved by repeating similar objects.

The effect of depth emerges as a result of representing the objects – depending on how far away they are – in varying sizes. Thus one person, for example, can be drawn somewhat taller and a second person noticeably smaller. It is evident to the brain of the viewer that these two individuals must be of approximately the same height, and they will automatically assume that one person is standing in the foreground and the other in the background. The impression of depth thus emerges.

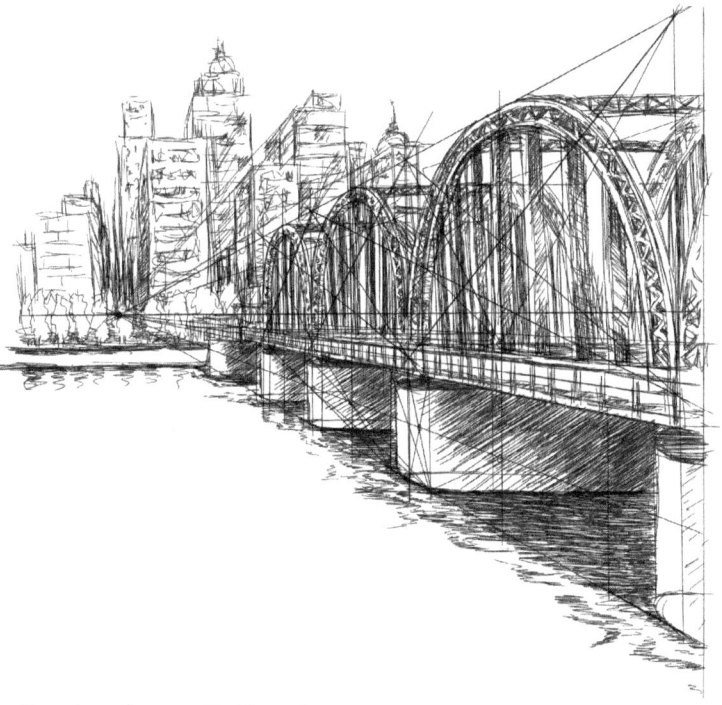

Drawing of a steel bridge with arcs that get smaller in the distance

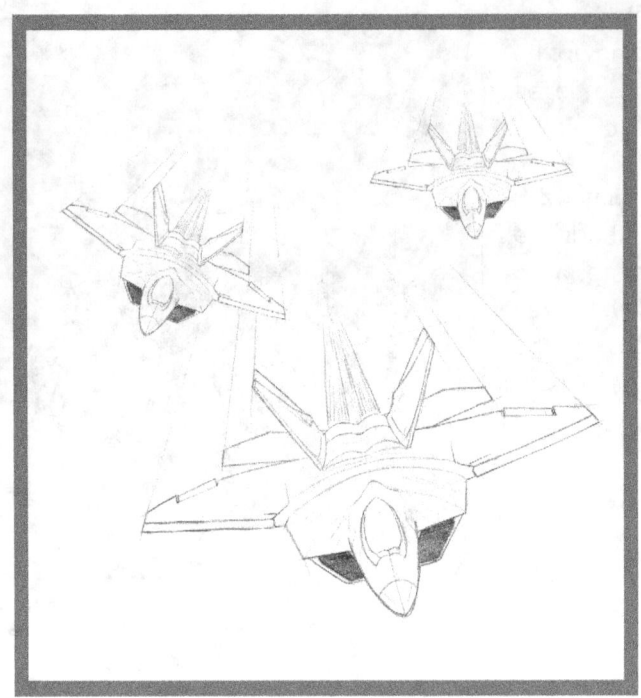

In this drawing, the viewer recognizes immediately that the jets must be different distances away

Reducing the Level of Detail

The methods described above can be perfected further by making the level of detail in the objects correspond to their distance away from the viewer. It is possible to recognize many details in an object that is close by. Conversely, if something is located further away, you can no longer discern these details. In drawing, the further away an object is located, the fewer details we include.

This method can be seen in the landscape sketch on the right.

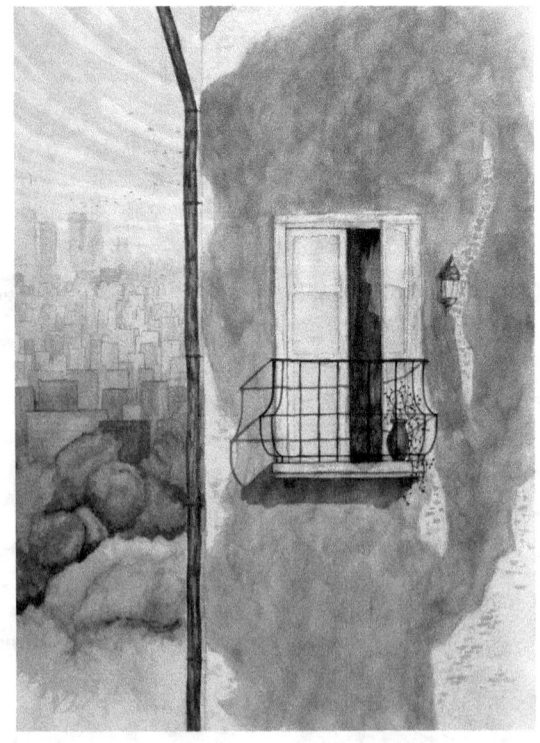

Cityscape with reduced detail in the background

Further Design Elements

Aerial Perspective

Aerial perspective is used in drawings and paintings in order to produce an impression of depth. In reality, this is based on an atmospheric effect. Light is deflected by air molecules, haze, and dust. This causes distant objects to acquire a light blue tinge, while also appearing lighter in color and lower in contrast. Due to this blue tinge, one oftentimes refers to a "blueing" effect and/or color perspective.

Since we do not use color in a pencil drawing, this effect can only be produced by making the distant objects paler and reducing the contrast.

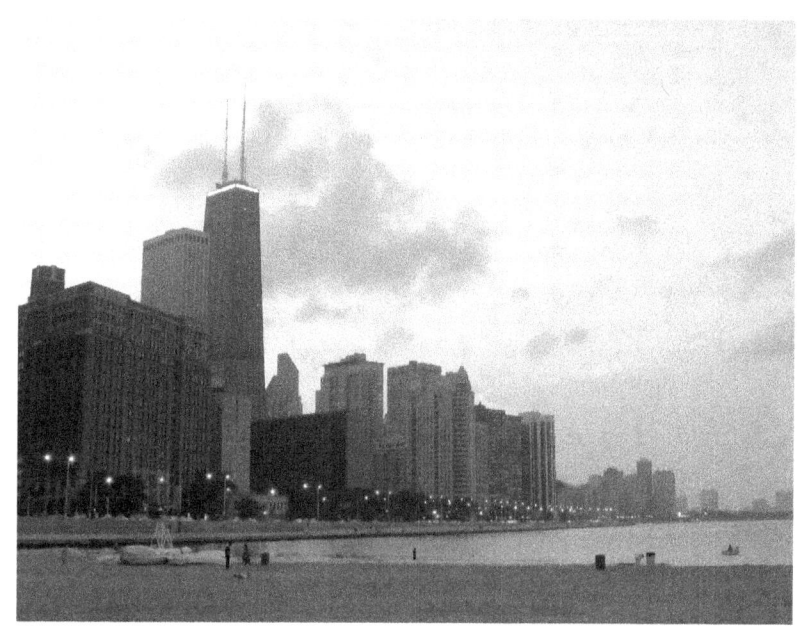

Example of aerial perspective

Perspective Foreshortening

Perspective foreshortening is an effect that becomes particularly distinct when we view, from straight on, an object that stretches out into the distance. For example, when we look at an outstretched arm or a branch head-on.

This creates a problem in terms of drawing as a lot of "information" is compressed into very little space due to the foreshortening. Such views are not only difficult but also unusual to draw. They often contradict what we know from experience.

Unbiased seeing and observing are important approaches here. Vanishing point perspective is also a particularly effective method for representing such views.

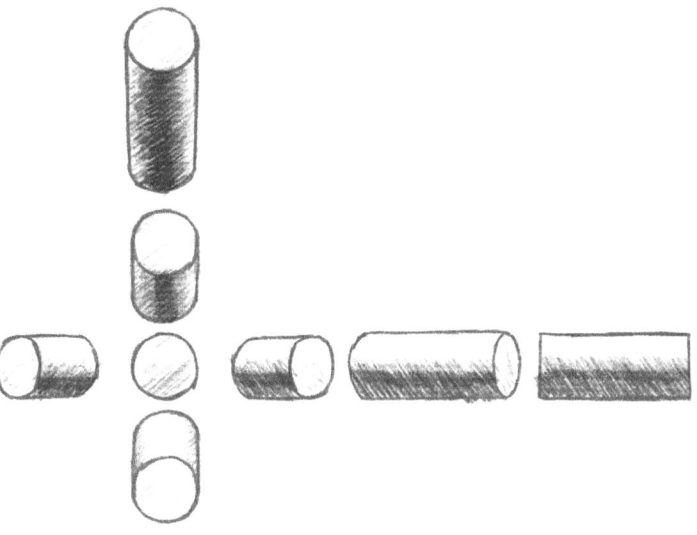

Perspective foreshortening of a cylinder

Vanishing Point Perspective

The last method of spatial representation we will look at here is vanishing point perspective. This procedure is much less characterized by feeling and intuition than the previous methods. Vanishing point perspective is first and foremost a technical method.

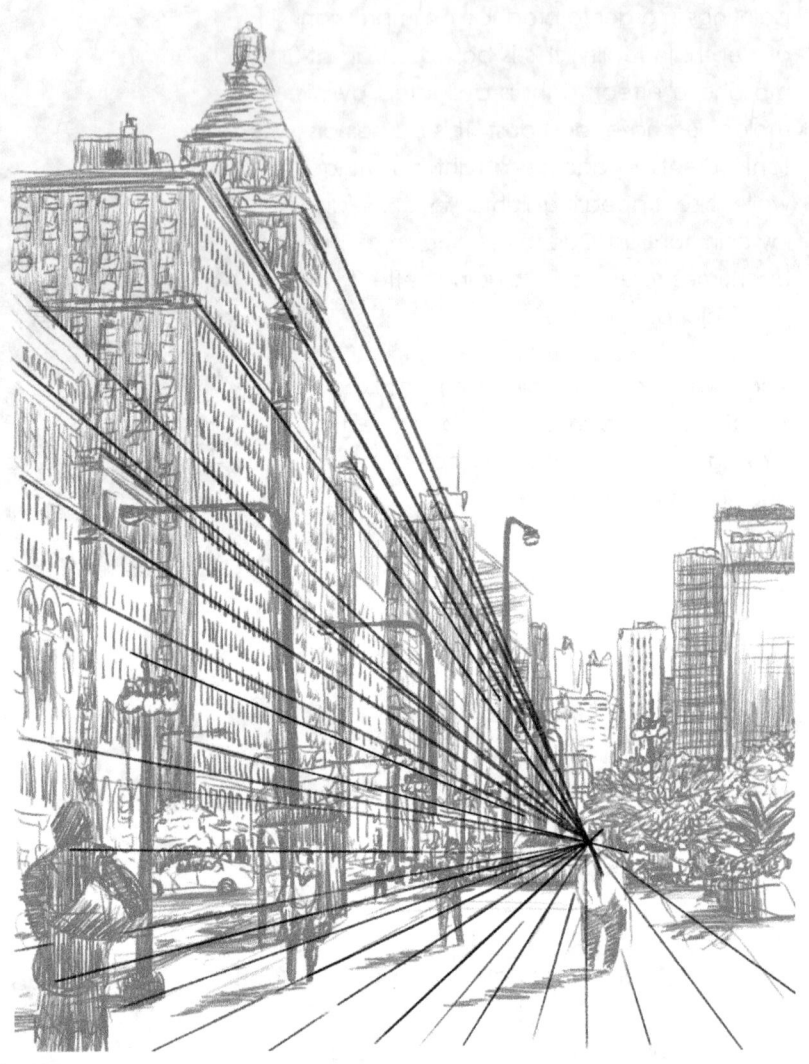

Sketch of a street scene using vanishing point perspective

Example Image: Art and Science

The picture in this example is a copy of Carl Spitzweg's "Art and Science." In this painting from the Biedermeier period, several spatial representation techniques are used. The scene is set in the open space in front of a building with a view of its front. Objects in the foreground, such as the fountain and the doves, convey an awareness of the three-dimensionality of this area.

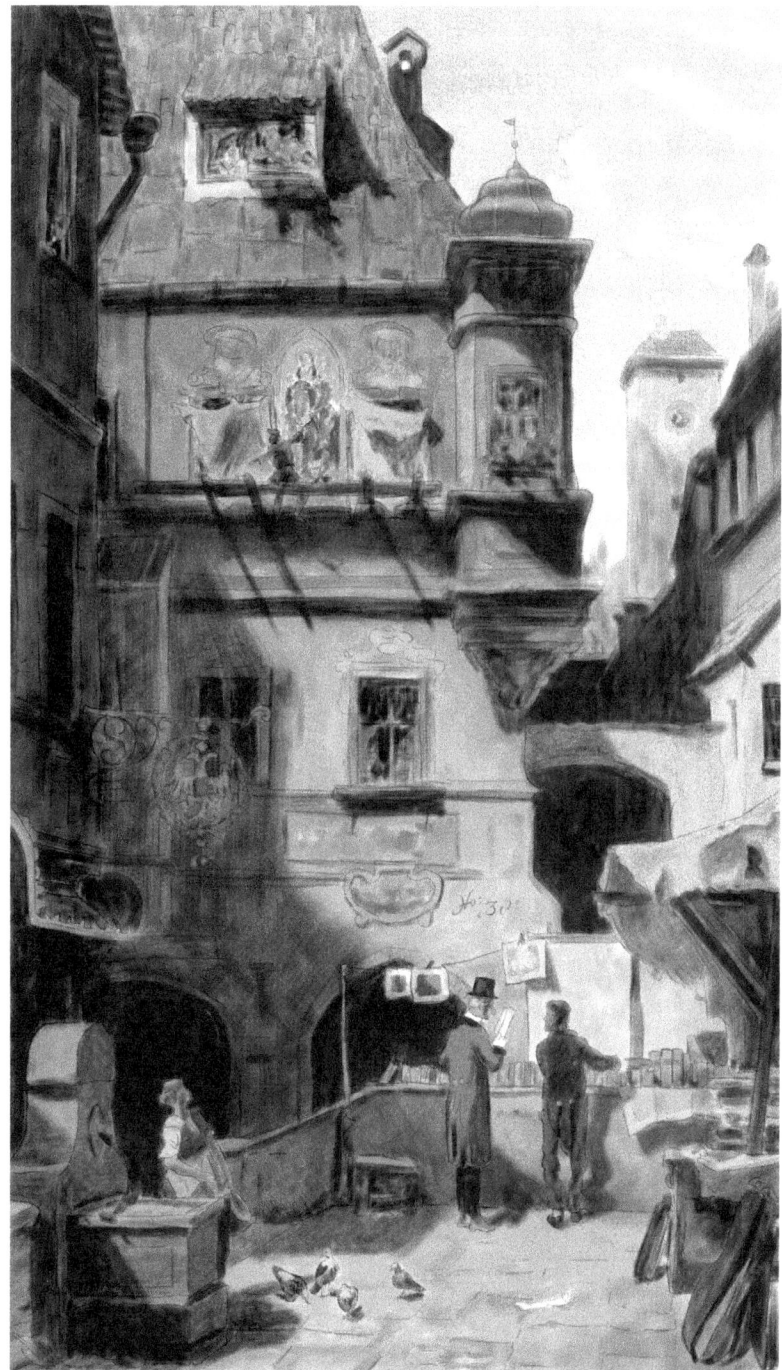

People stand on the ground in the lower part of the picture while the houses tower above them. A sign hanging on the left of the building creates an additional spatial effect, as do the shadows cast by the buildings. The painter also offers the viewer a look into the distance – in the upper right corner. This view is effective because of the tower in the distance that the painter has depicted using air perspective. The gate on the right, which is partially concealed, also contributes to a sense of depth.

And to return once again to the theme of contrast from the previous chapter: Note the pictures and linen sheets near the two people. They form particularly bright image areas and thus attract the viewer's attention. The same applies to the collar, the cuffs, and the book of the main actor.

The man on the right, with his dark coat in front of the light linen cloth, stands out particularly well. In contrast, the man to his left wears a lighter coat, which creates a strong contrast to the dark gate in the background.

This painting contains many more interesting features, but the examples already mentioned show how the painter Carl Spitzweg purposefully used the most diverse design techniques to create appealing pictorial compositions.

Example of spatial effects in a city scene: "Art and Science" (copy)
Original: Carl Spitzweg, 1880

Conveying Three-Dimensionality through Light and Shadow

Through the targeted use of light and shadow, the three-dimensional effect of objects can be increased. Light and shadow describe the shape of both small and large bodies, even at greater distances. Vanishing point perspective is another suitable technique for perfecting your representation as it can be used to construct shadows correctly.

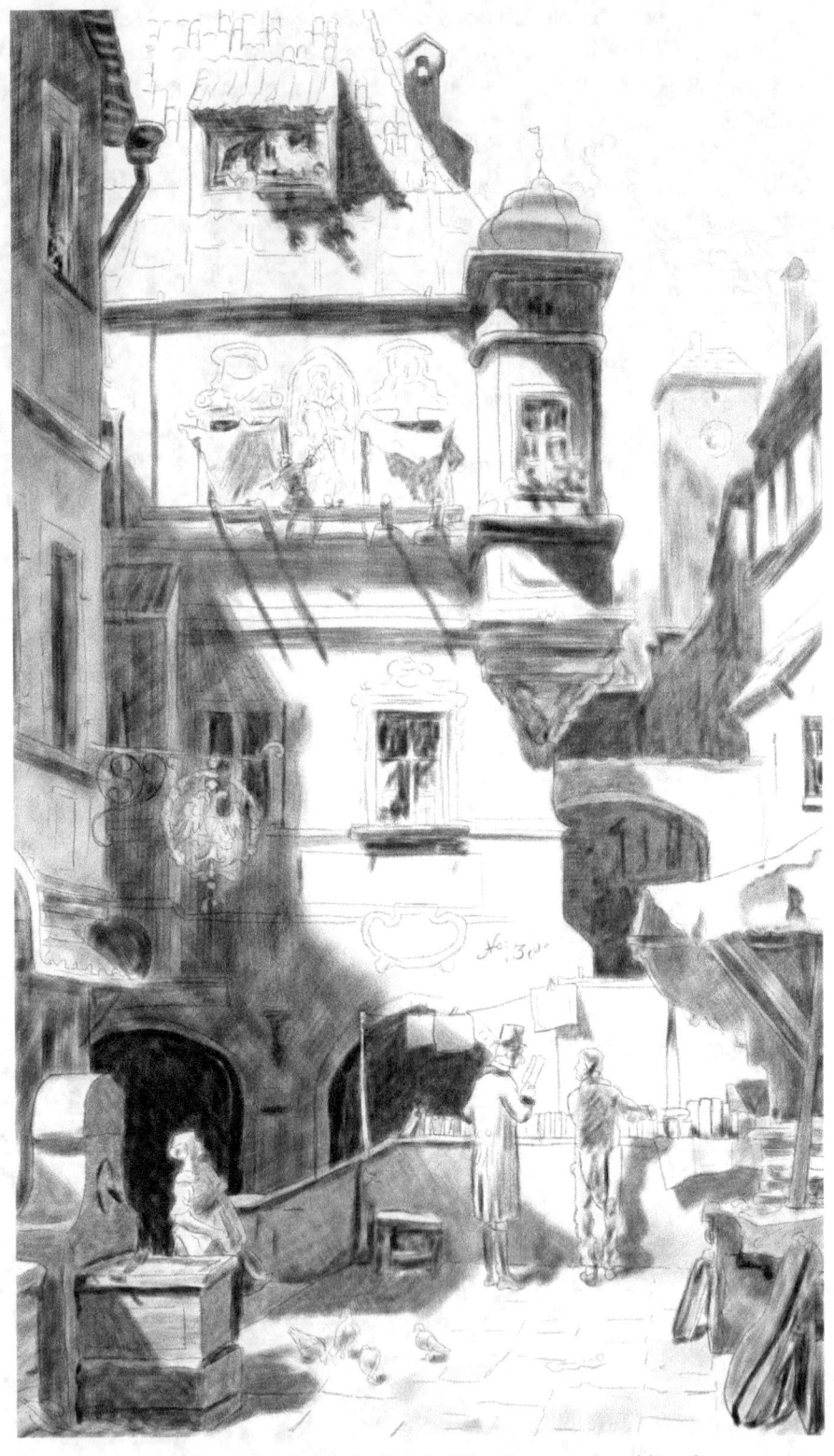

The three-dimensional effect in this city scene is achieved by means of light and shadow
Picture: "Art and Science" (copy) reduced to shadows
Original: Carl Spitzweg, 1880

Tricks for Mastering Space

For a composition that makes good use of light and shadow, landscape painters often choose the time of day based on the position of the sun and the shadows it will cast. In some landscape paintings, you will notice that the arrangement of the clouds creates a play of light and shadow that additionally supports the illusion of a deep space.

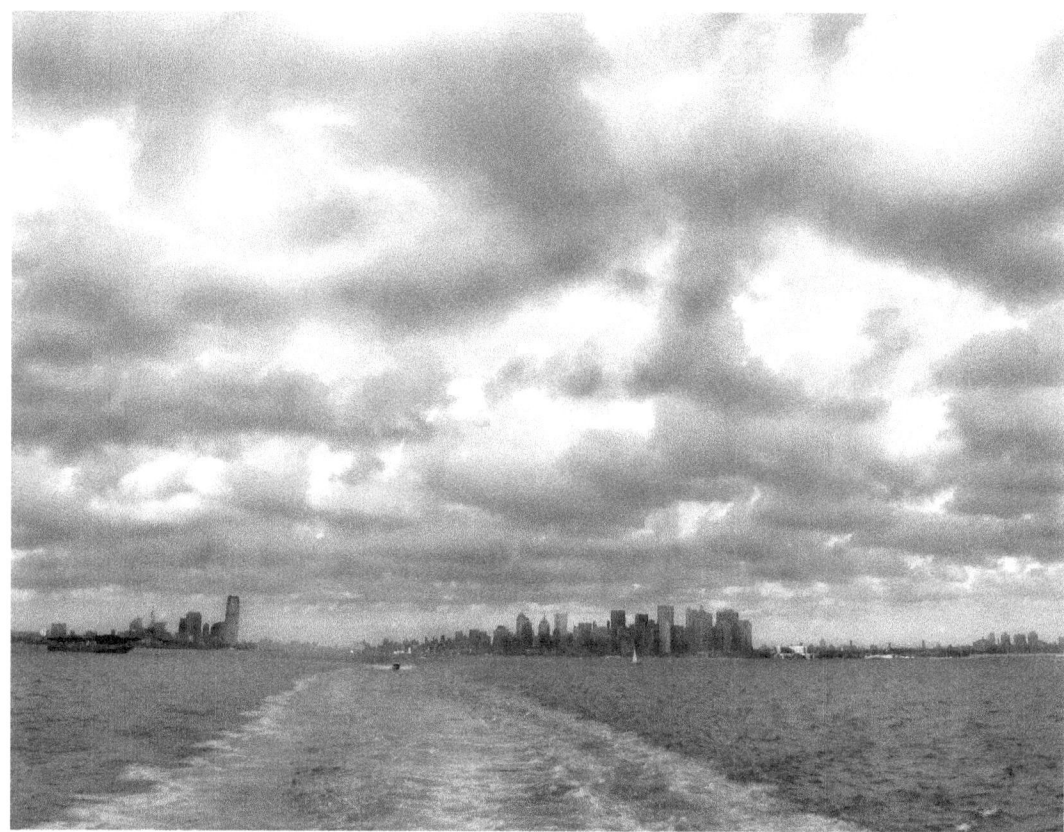

The arrangement of the clouds in this picture conveys a better impression of depth

Another little trick involves the use of shadows: If you show the shadows of objects that cannot be seen in the picture, you expand the space in the mind of the viewer; the artist conveys the feeling that the true space goes beyond the visible part of the picture.

Plasticity

As previously mentioned, plasticity in this context means that objects appear three-dimensional. This optical effect is especially noticeable in objects in our immediate surroundings. To draw plastically means to depict bodies and objects spatially. Their three-dimensional form becomes recognizable on paper due to special drawing techniques; they appear three-dimensional, tangible, and lifelike.

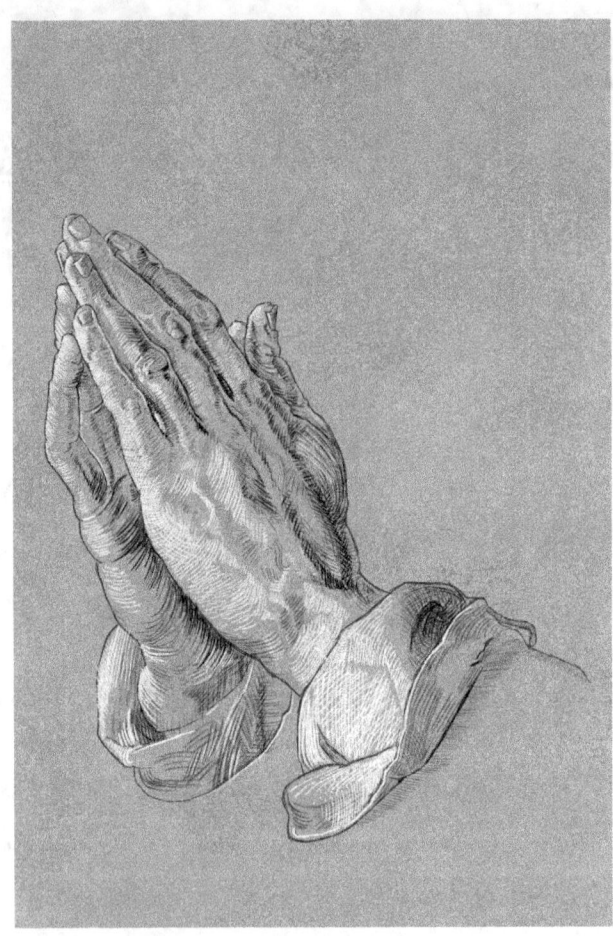

The plasticity has been developed here in the drawing of shadows and white highlighting
Image: Praying Hands (copy)/Original: Albrecht Dürer, around 1508

While a contour alone is sufficient for the two-dimensional representation of shapes, shadows are particularly important for the representation of the third dimension – and, of course, light is a prerequisite for shadows. Light and shadow are wonderful facilitators of form. By intensifying the light-dark contrast, the three-dimensional impression is further enhanced.

In addition, the position of the light source that illuminates the motif is particularly important. The angle of incidence determines the shape of the shadow, which sometimes makes the illuminated body appear more or less three-dimensional. The type of lighting also plays a role: Plasticity manifests itself differently depending on whether the lighting is hard or soft.

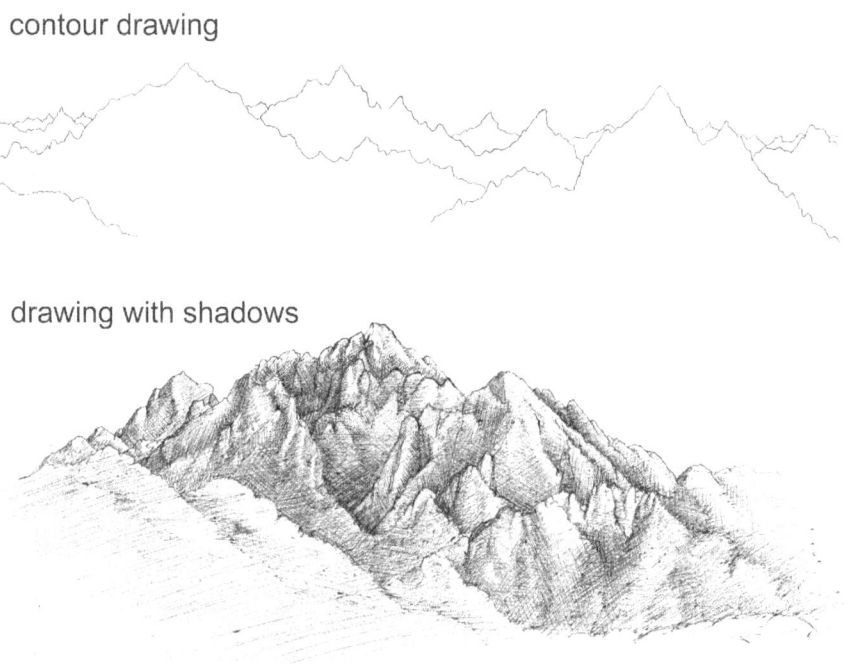

Comparison between contour drawing and drawing with shadows using mountains as an example

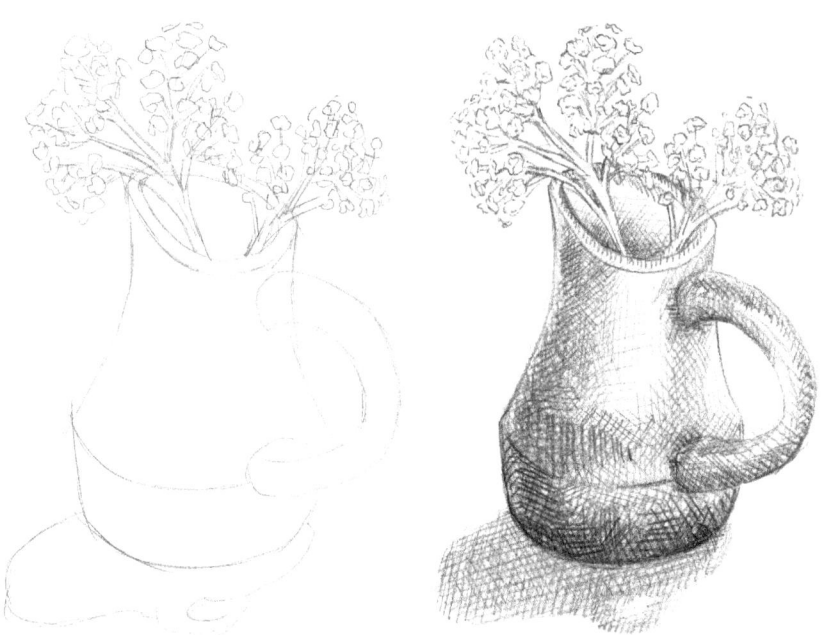

Another comparison between contour drawing and a drawing with shadows using a vase as an example

Another way to draw objects in a particularly plastic manner is to change the angle of view. For example, a hand can be drawn from above or below, but also from an oblique point of view. When looking directly at the back of the hand or the palm of the hand, the hand cannot be drawn very vividly. An oblique point of view or a changed hand posture, such as the spreading of one or more fingers, improves the spatial effect of the drawing. Be sure to pay attention to the perspective foreshortening, which has already been discussed.

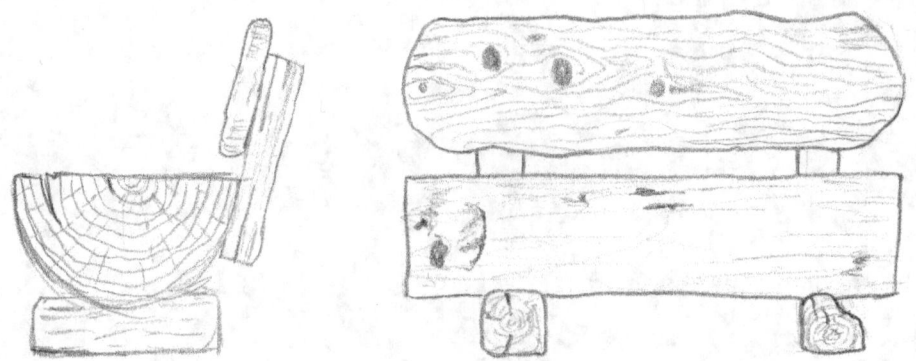

Presentations from directly in front or from the side are not conducive to strong plasticity

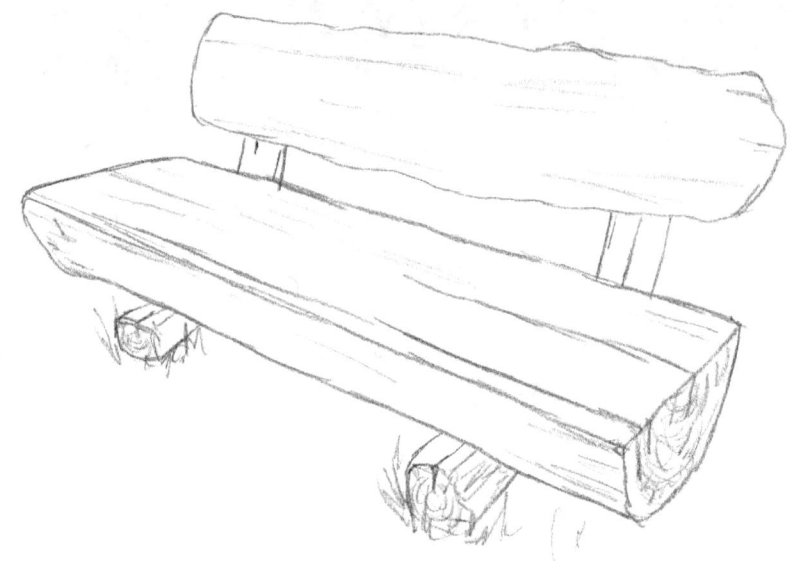

On the other hand, a representation of the same object from an oblique perspective facilitates plasticity

Careful elaboration of details such as contrasts, contours, and the casting of shadows allows an object in a drawing to stand out even more. If the drawing is a still life including several objects, beautiful effects and interesting variations can be achieved by arranging the objects and experimenting with the lighting.

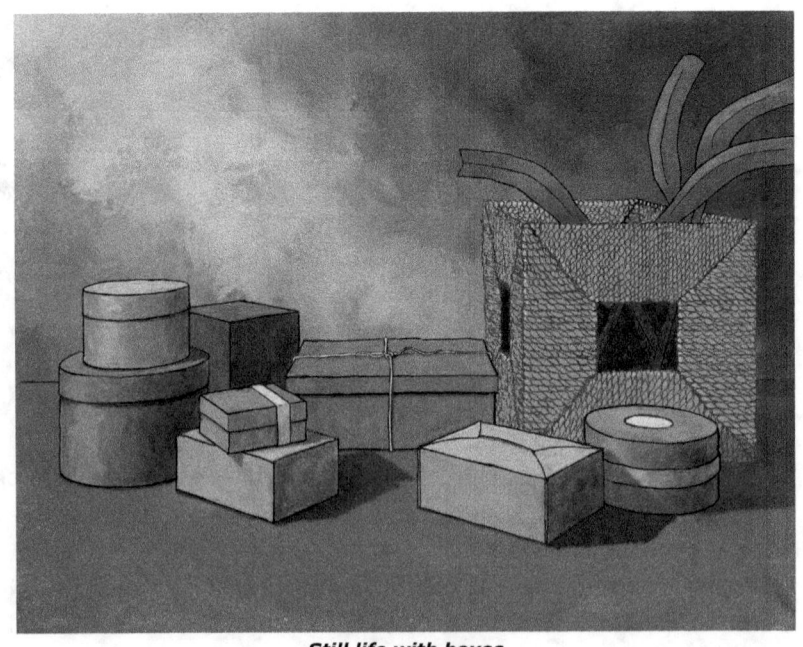

Still life with boxes

Light and Shadow

Light and shadow are among the most important – perhaps even THE most important – means of composing an image. This is because everything we see only becomes visible through light. And it also plays a significant role in how we see things. Light can be hard or soft, the level of light can be high or low, light can come from different directions, and light can also have a certain color.

The factors that you can influence here include important image properties such as plasticity, three-dimensionality, and, last but not least, the atmosphere. By positioning the light source accordingly, you can create dramatic shadows or a contemplative mood with soft lighting.

Direction of Light

As previously explained, it is very important for the overall effect of the image to clearly depict the direction from which the light hits the motif in relation to the position of the viewer. Possible types of lighting include: incident light, frontal light, side light, grazing light, and back light.

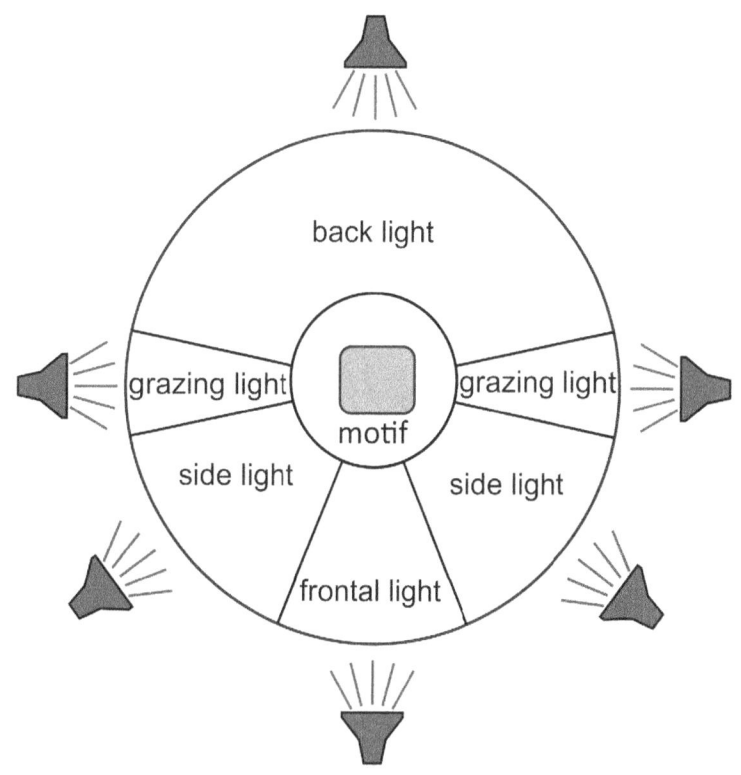

Frontal Light

In the case of frontal light, the light shines onto the motif from the front, which means that the light source must be located behind the artist. The result is that hardly any shadows are visible on the motif as they are located behind the motif. With monochrome drawings in particular, this type of lighting often seems unspectacular. In the case of colored paintings, however, the effect may be desirable since this makes the colored areas the main focus of attention and three-dimensional forms fade into the background.

Incident Light

Incident light involves a light source shining onto the subject mainly from above, as is the case with landscape pictures around midday. Incident light ensures good illumination, with short shadows being cast. Depending on what one wants to achieve, incident light can either be advantageous or best avoided. In particular, if you want to play with light and shadow during the creation of your pictures, you should choose a more suitable type of lighting.

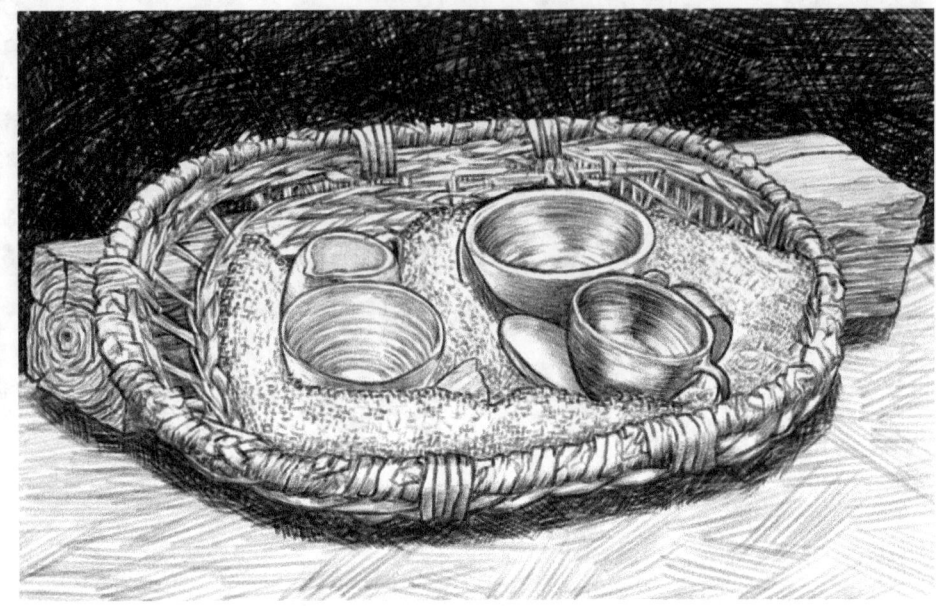

Side Light

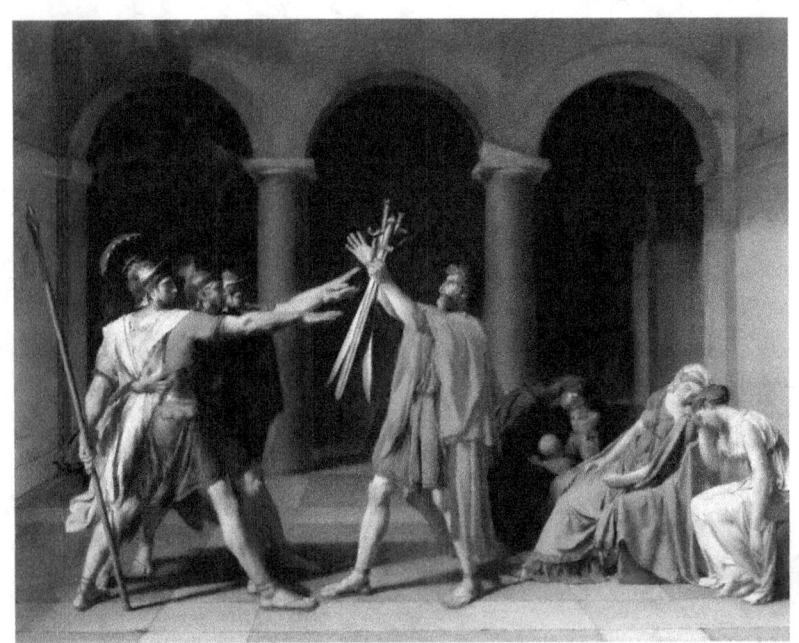

"Oath of the Horatii" (copy)
Original: Jacques-Louis David, 1784

When light falls on the subject at an angle from the side, this is called side light. This category includes lighting at an angle of approximately 30 to 60 degrees to the viewing direction. Side light is ideal for describing the three-dimensional shape of the motif by means of striking shadows. Effective shadows are also created in landscape pictures, which can bring tension and atmosphere into the composition. Side light is therefore the most popular type of lighting for drawings and paintings.

Grazing Light

If the angle between the line of sight and the lighting exceeds 60 degrees and thus hits the motif very much from the side, this is referred to as grazing light: the light grazes the motif from the right or left side. The result is that surface structures are very clearly visible and appear particularly three-dimensional. Grazing light is usually used very specifically for this purpose.

However, this characteristic of grazing light is often undesirable because the way it makes a motif look can quickly become unsuitable. Depending on the result you are trying to obtain, the cast shadows often appear exaggerated and create a drama that is not desired.

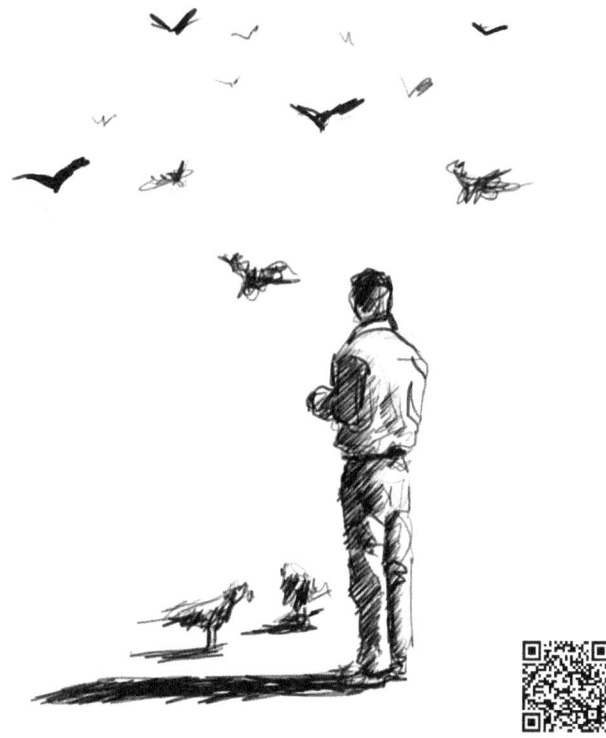

Person with pigeons in grazing light

Back Light

Back light means that the light comes from the direction of the subject and shines toward the artist. Backlit objects usually appear silhouette-like and become very dark. The background is cross-faded by the light source and often no longer visible. These effects offer interesting creative possibilities but also represent a certain challenge for the artist.

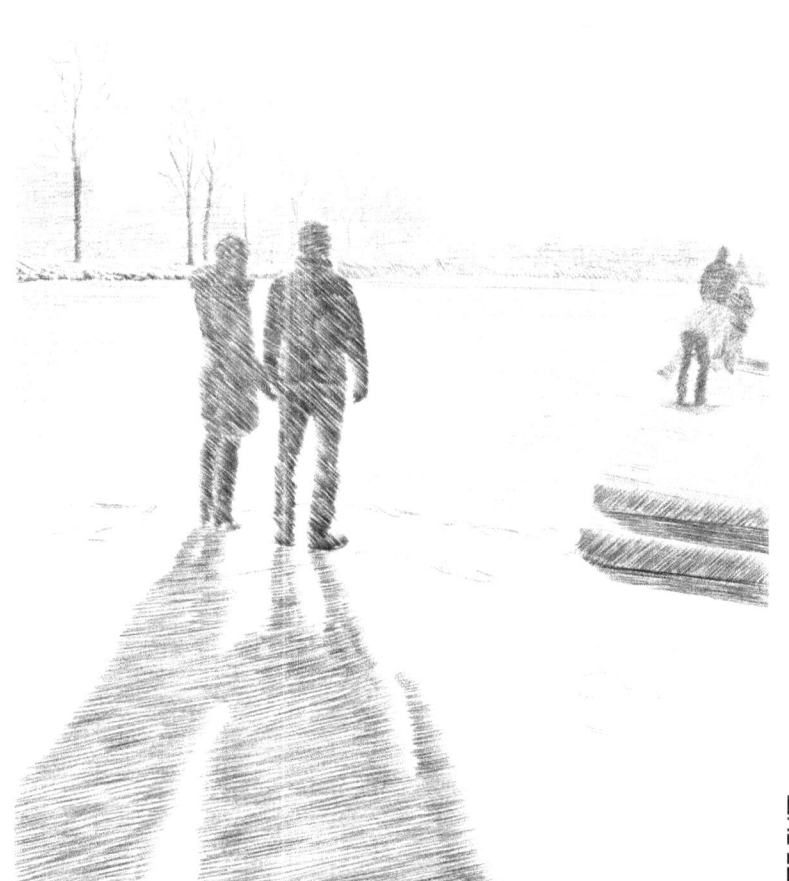

Couple standing on a waterfront, backlit by the sunset

Direct and Diffuse Light

The quality of the light in a picture has a great influence on its visual effect. Light can be direct or diffuse. For example, if strong light hits an object directly, it will be highly illuminated on the side facing the light. The opposite side will almost disappear in the shadow, being only slightly illuminated by the small amount of light scattered through the surrounding area. Through this hard light, extreme tonal contrasts can be created. This kind of lighting quality is called direct light.

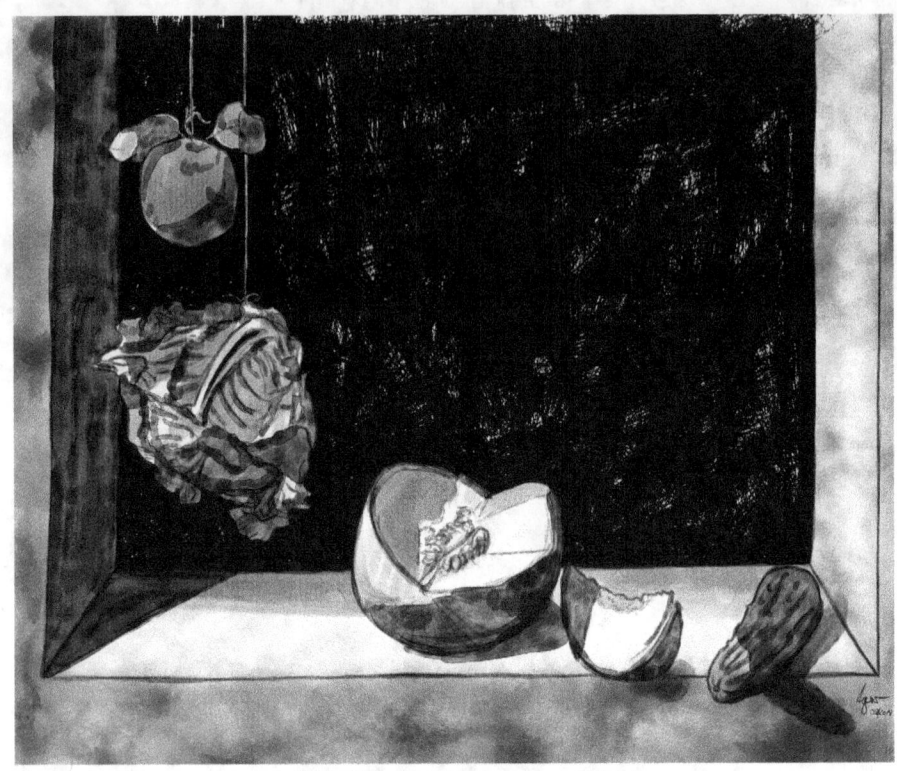

Still life with direct, extreme light
Drawing after a painting by J. S. Cotán

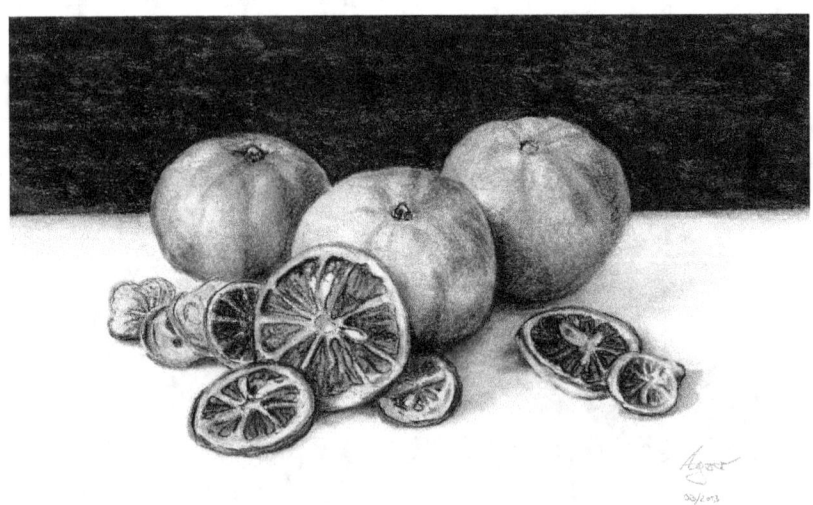

Still life with more diffuse light

Diffuse light occurs when, for example, the light is rather soft and the surroundings scatter or reflect the light strongly. As a result, the sunny side of the object experiences less light intensity, while the shady side is brightened by an increased amount of light. In extreme cases, there will be few or no visible shadows. The tonal value contrast in this type of lighting is thus correspondingly low.

You can observe and analyze the creative use of light yourself in most of the pictures shown in this book.

Using Direct and Diffuse Light to Depict Weather

With the help of light and contrast, you can give the viewer information about the weather in landscape pictures. Depending on the weather conditions, the light can be direct or diffuse and thus cause stronger or weaker contrasts.

If, for example, the sun hits an object directly on a cloudless day, it will be very strongly illuminated on the side facing the light. The opposite side will almost disappear in the shadow, being only slightly illuminated by the small amount of light scattered through the atmosphere. This hard light creates very strong tonal contrasts and is called direct or directional light.

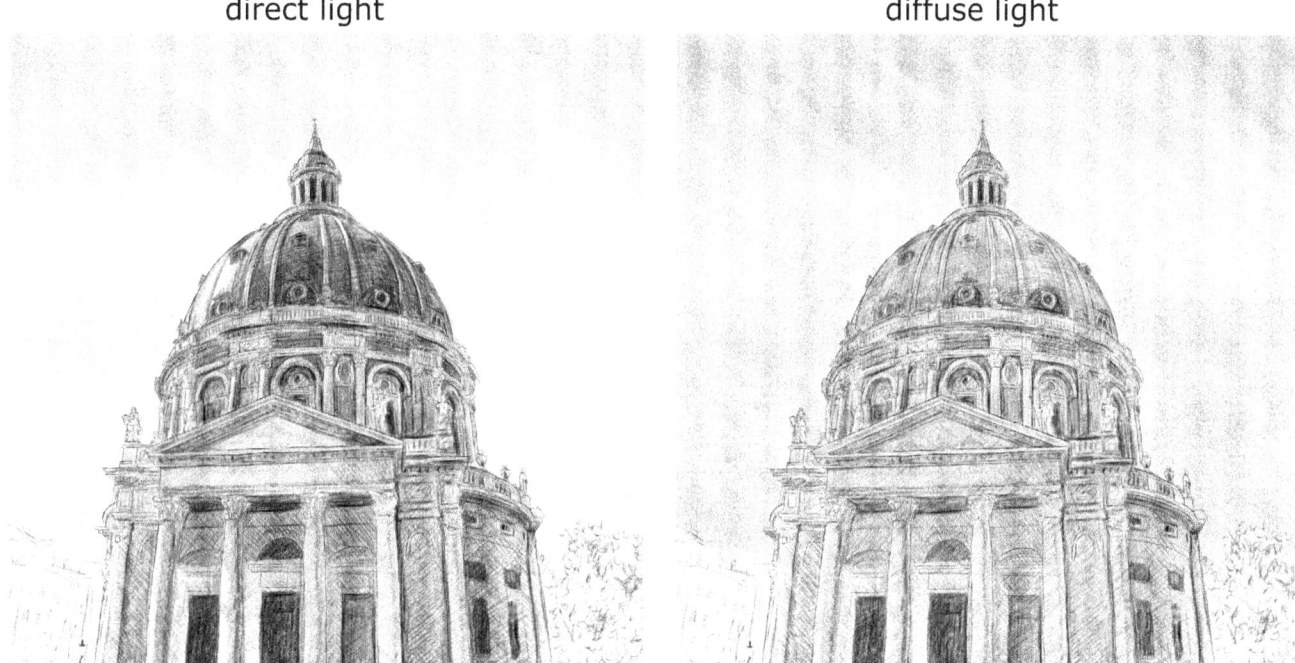

Comparison between direct and diffuse light

Diffuse, soft light is produced when, for example, the weather is cloudy or foggy. The sun's rays are then scattered by the increased amount of molecules in the air, resulting in much more indirect lighting. As a result, the sunny side of the object receives less intense light, while the shady side is brightened by an increased amount of light. In extreme cases, hardly any or even no visible shadows occur. The tonal value contrast in this type of lighting is correspondingly low.

Tricks for the Use of Shadows

The use of shadows has already been discussed in the chapter Perspective and Space, including the trick of illusorily extending the space by including shadows of objects that are not visible in the picture. However, there are a few more ways to use shadows.

Shadows as a connecting bridge

Shadows can form a bridge between two or more objects when a shadow extends from one object to another and thus connect them visually. For example, the shadow of a tree or that of a bridge can be used for this purpose. The objects casting the shadows do not necessarily have to be visible in the image – which in turn introduces the above-mentioned trick for expanding the space in the image.

The use of shadows to accentuate motifs

Another method that uses shadows very deliberately is the highlighting of objects. This highlighting is basically done by creating a strong light-dark contrast. The object that is in the foreground and is supposed to attract attention is rendered relatively brightly. The contrast that makes this object stand out is created by a dark shadow in the background. The contrast can only be created by the background shadow.

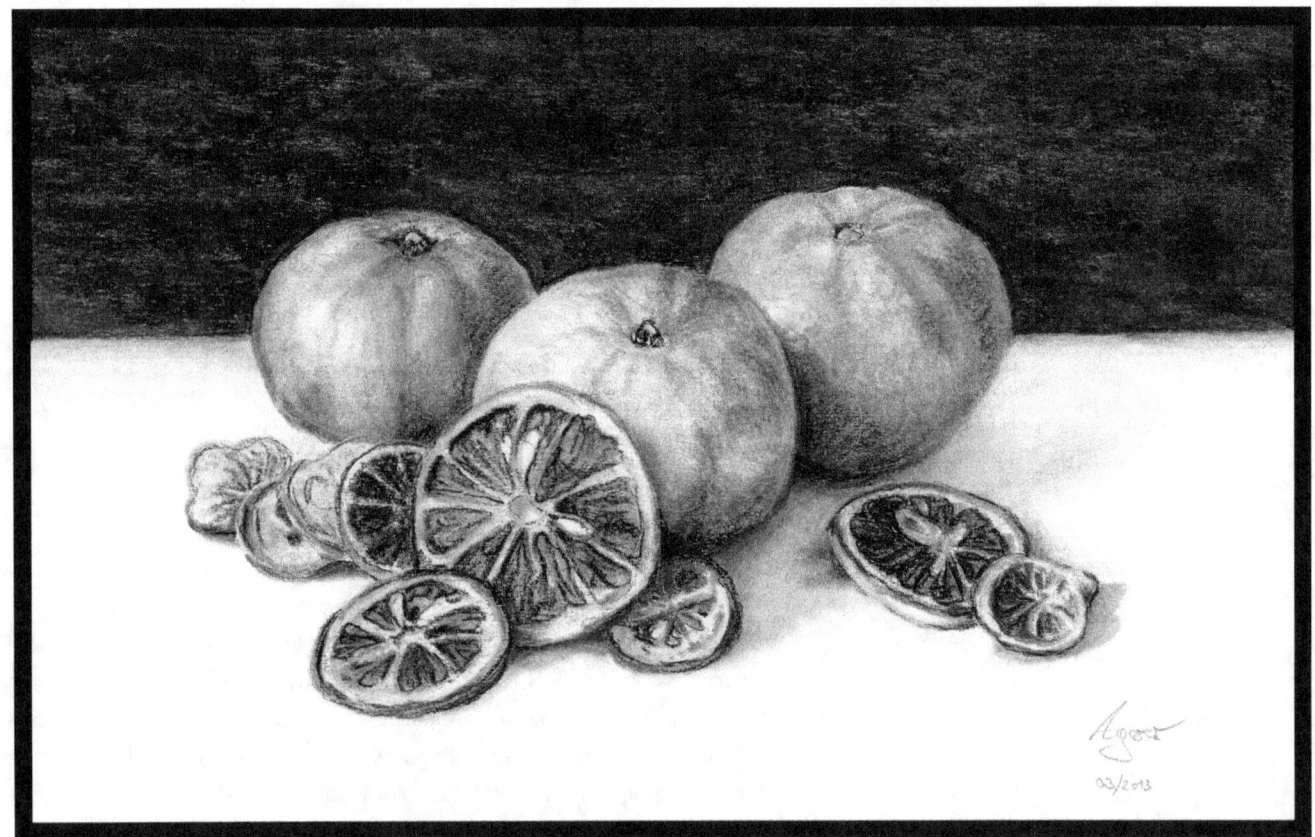

The shadow in the background accentuates the Mandarin oranges

The object from which this shadow emanates is not so relevant here. In still lifes, for example, the background is often kept very dark to achieve this effect. In scenes in which a room with windows is clearly visible, the position of a light-giving window can be chosen so that figures are brightly lit while the background remains dark. A perfect example of this method is the painting "The Calling of St. Matthew" by Michelangelo Merisi da Caravaggio.

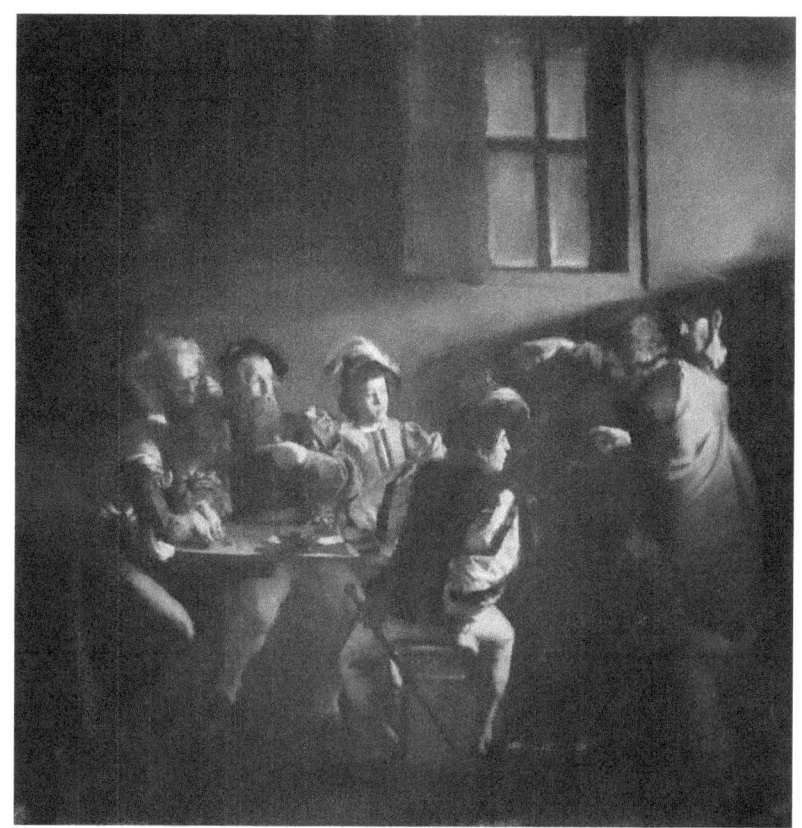

The figures in the painting are considerably accentuated by the dark shadows in the background
Painting: The Calling of St. Matthew (copy)/Original: Michelangelo Merisi da Caravaggio

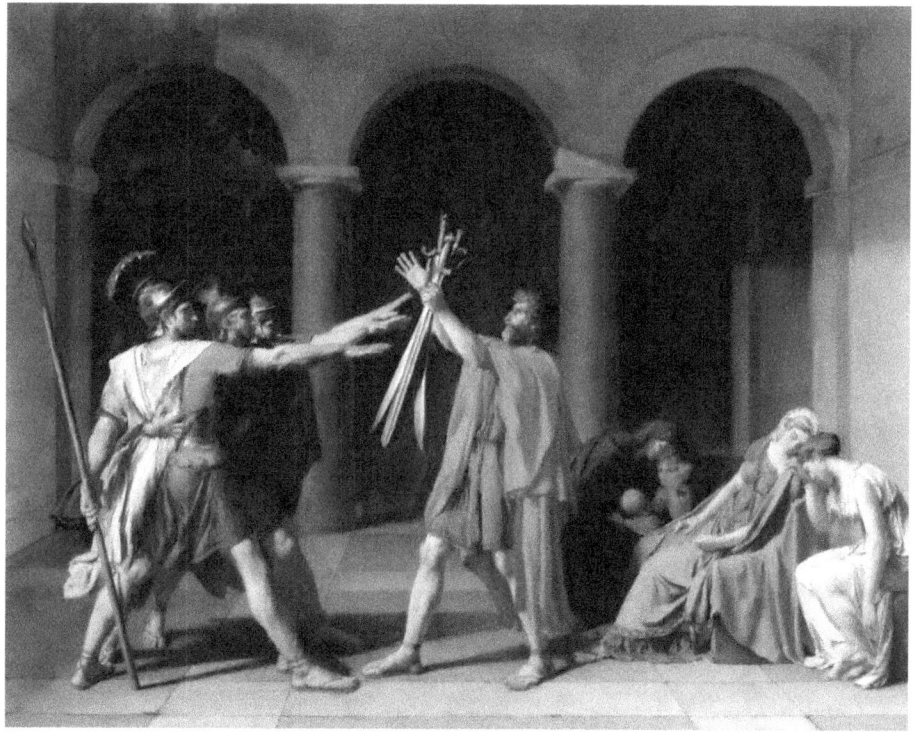

The figures in this painting are depicted in front of dark archways
Painting: "The Oath of the Horatii" (copy)/Original: Jacques-Louis David, 1784

Movement

Bringing movement into an image may not be easy, but it often has a particularly strong effect. Movement makes pictures seem more alive and therefore more interesting because it leads to a change in the present moment. Since movement cannot, of course, be shown directly in a still image, it must be implied by the use of appropriate methods.

One way to convey movement is by introducing an imbalance. This imbalance must, according to the experience of the viewer, be one that will automatically lead to a movement that cancels out the imbalance. An unstable composition will also have a similar effect.

The following two graphic representations depict a supposedly unstable situation in which one is almost waiting for everything to fall out of balance. You can imagine the objects already falling to the ground in your mind's eye. The other graphic shows a dynamic composition in which the movement can be perceived straight away.

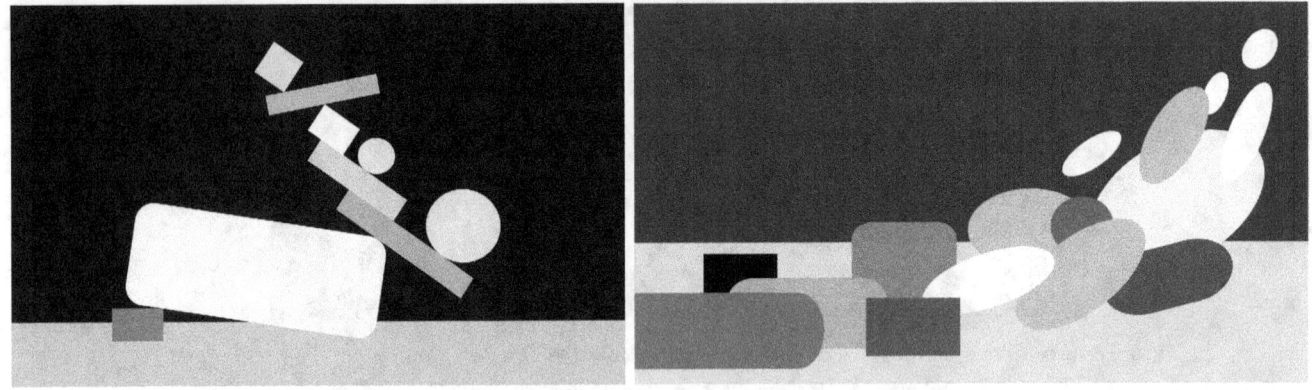

Unstable construction (left) and dynamic forms (right)

In contrast, still lifes usually do not show any movement. As the name suggests, everything here stands still and rests.

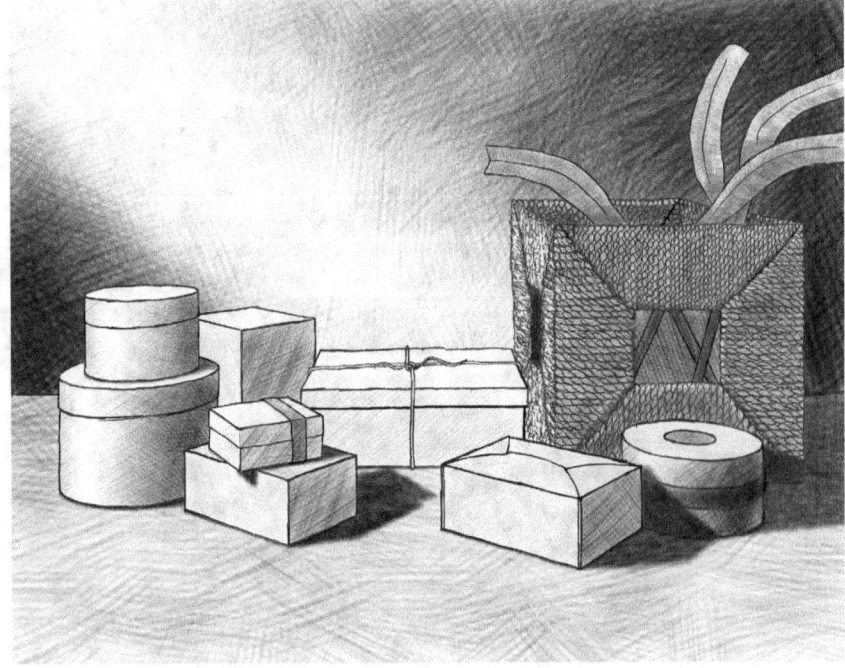

Still life without movement

However, the representation of movement is relatively easy with the help of human figures. The runners in the graphic below clearly illustrate movement. The standing person in the background provides a certain contrast.

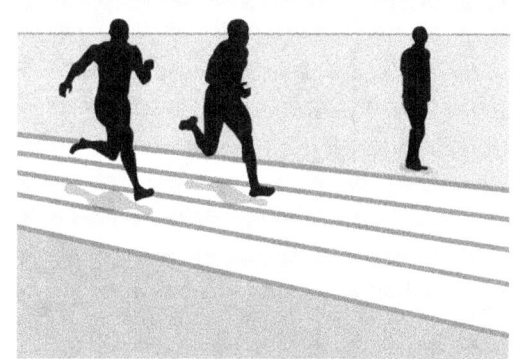
Movement through the representation of people

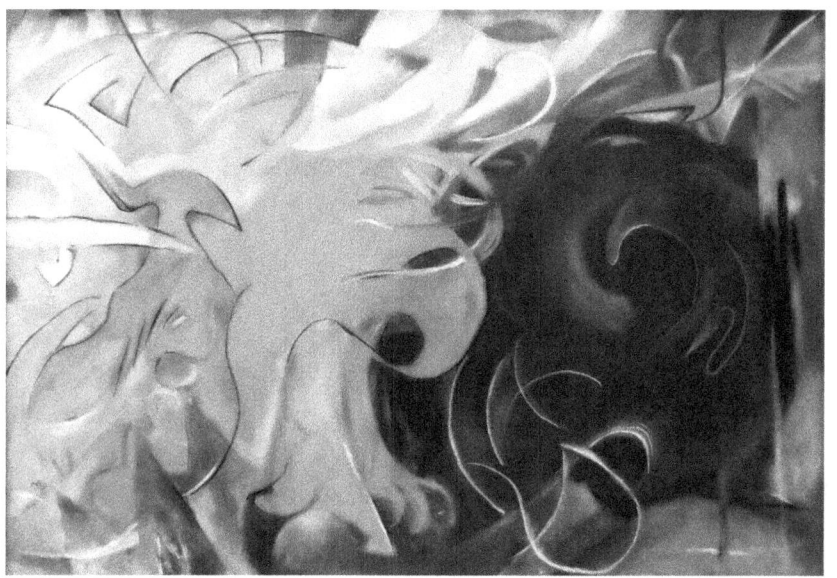
Abstract painting in motion
Painting: "Fighting Forms" (copy)/Original: Franz Marc, 1914

In abstract pictures, movement can be conveyed by means of the design alone. Curved lines best give the feeling of movement. A good example of this is the painting "Fighting Forms" by Franz Marc.

One method that is mainly used in comic drawings involves motion lines, also referred to as speed lines. In the image below, you can see the technique used in the depiction of an aircraft squadron. The movement is already implied by the motif itself, but the motion lines make the action clear. The lines also provide information about the direction in which the motif is moving. Additional dynamics are added to this drawing by the sloping position of the aircraft.

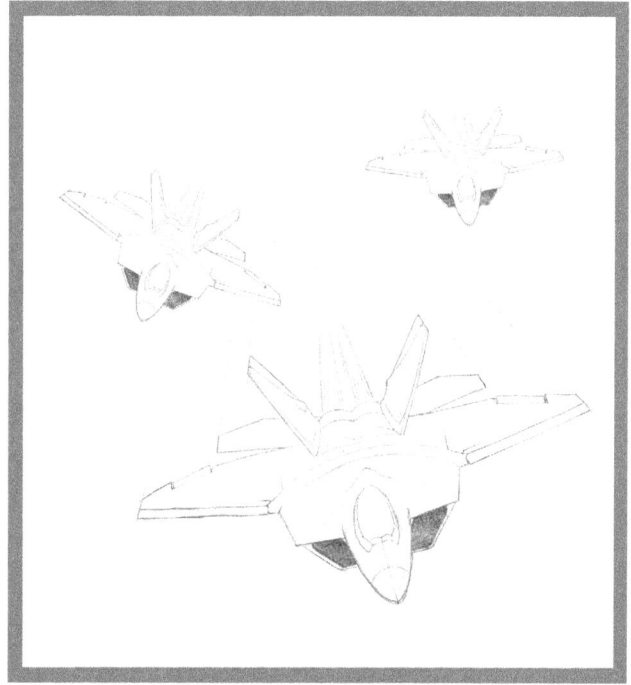
Three jets with motion lines

115

In the following picture, you can see how motion can be represented through the use of curves. The jellyfish is clearly in motion, which you can see from its curved shape. It seems to be meandering through the water.

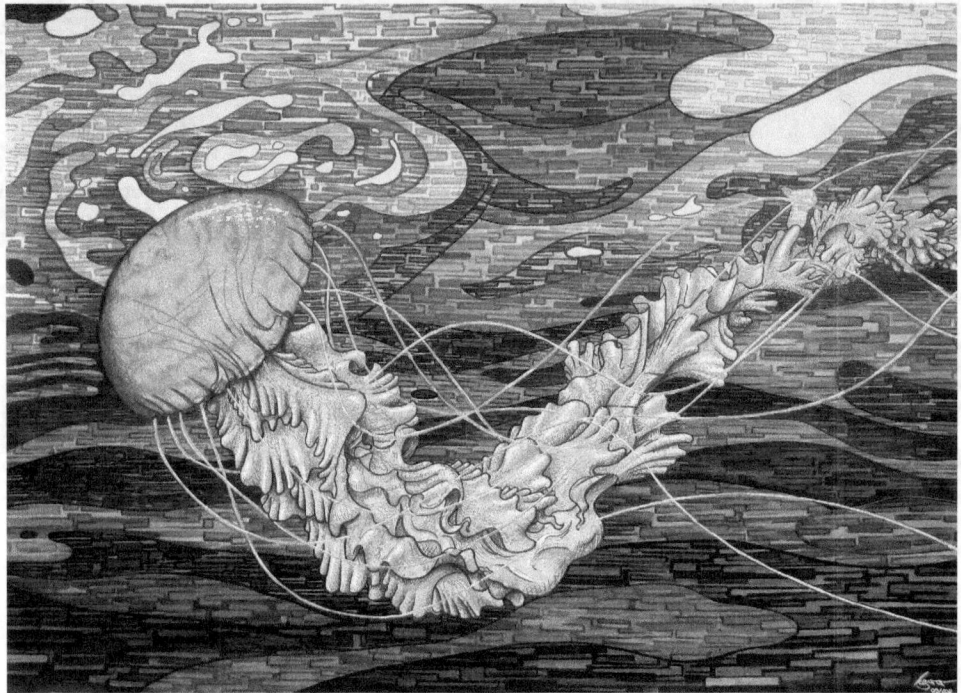

Using shapes to depict movement (the curve)

Similar methods were use for the picture with the turtle.

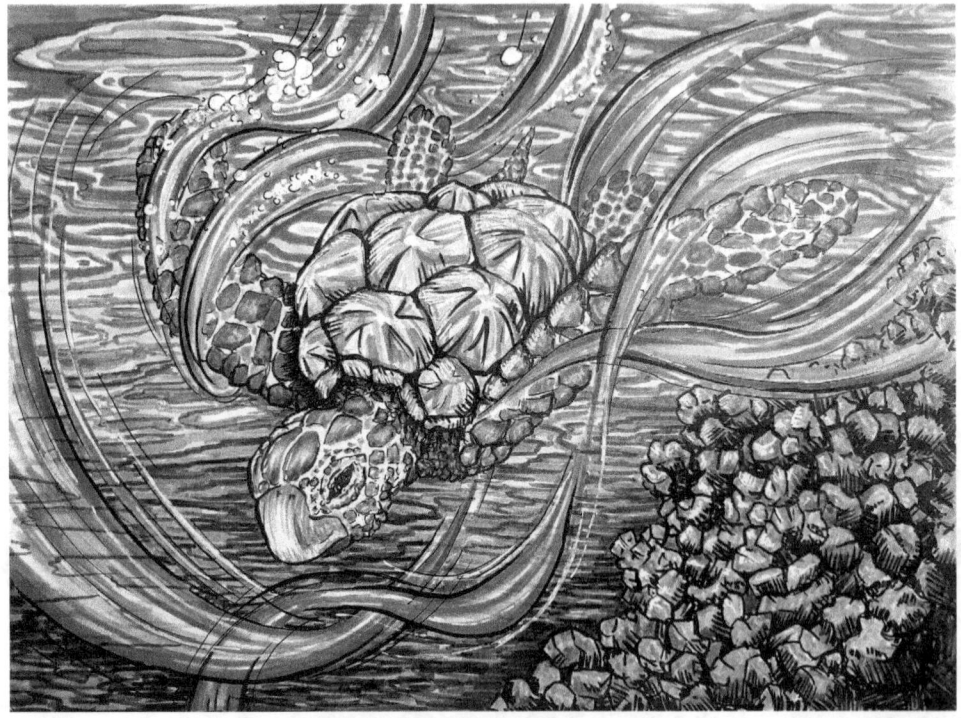

Using shapes and cures to depict movement

Balance in Pictorial Composition

It is natural that the human eye automatically looks for a certain balance when looking at an image. This corresponds to our usual way of understanding things and our striving for harmony. When the eye finds this balance, a picture feels aesthetically pleasing to us.

This kind of balanced pictorial composition can be achieved by the clever arrangement of the objects in the picture, and can also be achieved without having to create a symmetrical composition. The design method that can be used for this is based on the principles of balance. For a better understanding of the method, we can turn to the law of the lever, which we know from physics.

In order to make the principle of the balance of forces in pictorial composition understandable, it is best to imagine a set of scales. If there are equal weights on both sides, the scales are balanced. If the weights are different, the larger weight must move closer to the center of the scales or the lighter weight must move further outwards. In physics, one would speak here of a balance of forces or the law of the lever.

In a painting or drawing, the objects in the picture correspond to the weights, which are ideally in balance with each other. If there is harmonic equilibrium within the picture, the objects in the picture can be in either symmetrical or asymmetrical equilibrium.

Symmetrical equilibrium

We speak of symmetrical equilibrium if, for example, two identical image objects in a photograph lie on the left and right.

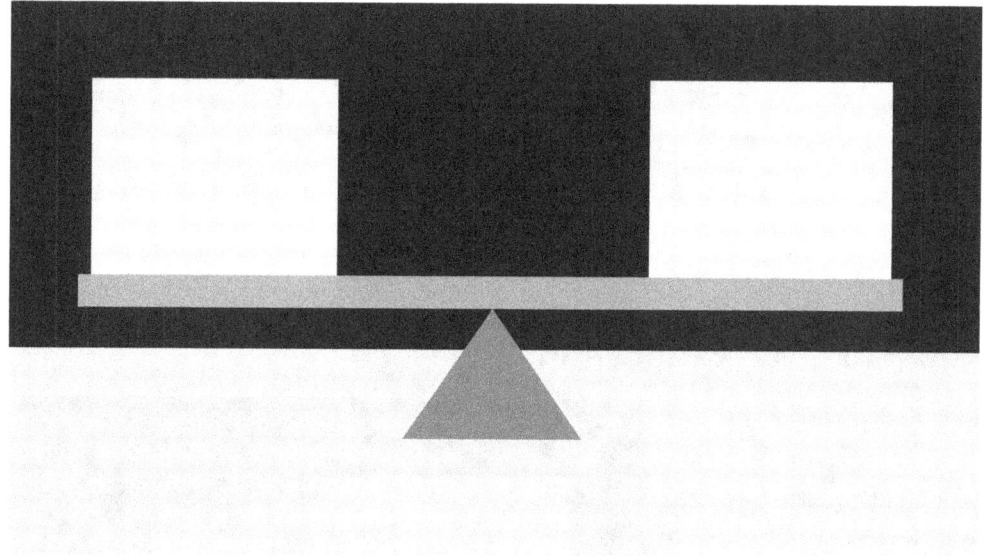

Principle of symmetrical equilibrium

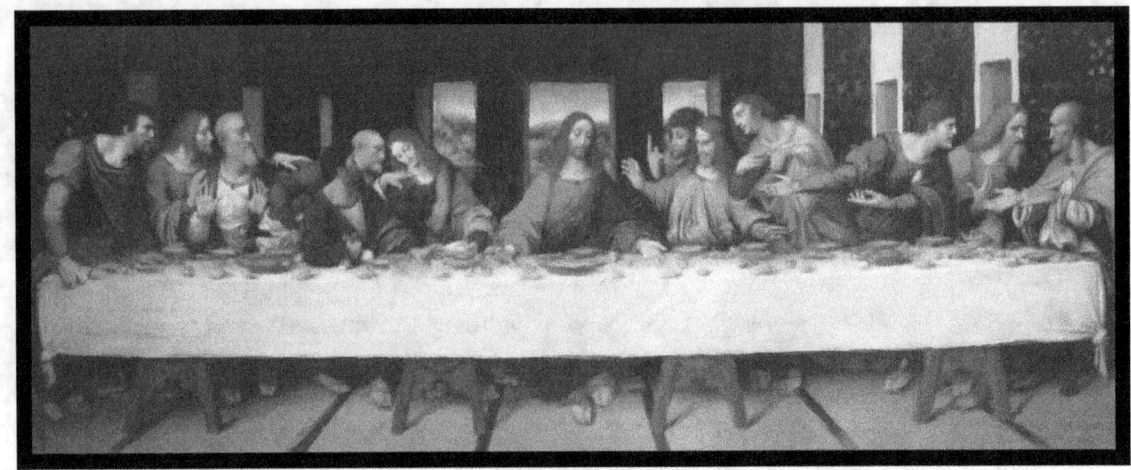

State of equilibrium through symmetrical distribution of the individuals
Painting: "The Last Supper" (copy)/Original: Leonardo da Vinci, 1494 to 1497

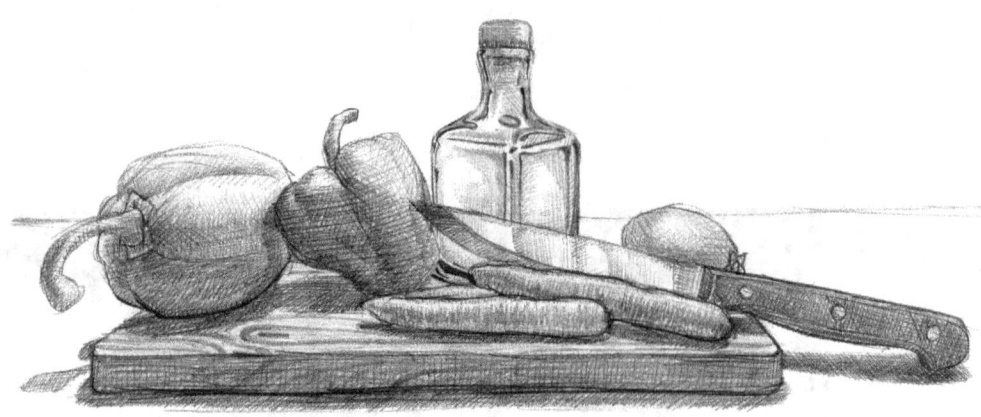

Still life with relatively symmetrical equilibrium

Asymmetrical equilibrium

With asymmetrical equilibrium, one has to deal with image objects of different size, weight, or strength. Here, a balance of forces must be created by cleverly positioning the different elements of the image in relation to one another.

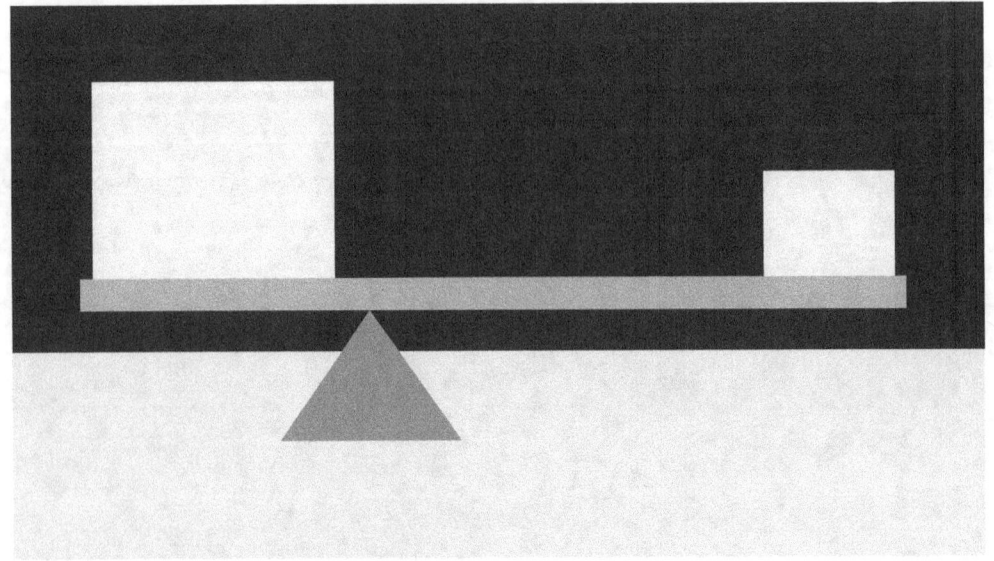

Principle of asymmetrical equilibrium

118   Further Design Elements

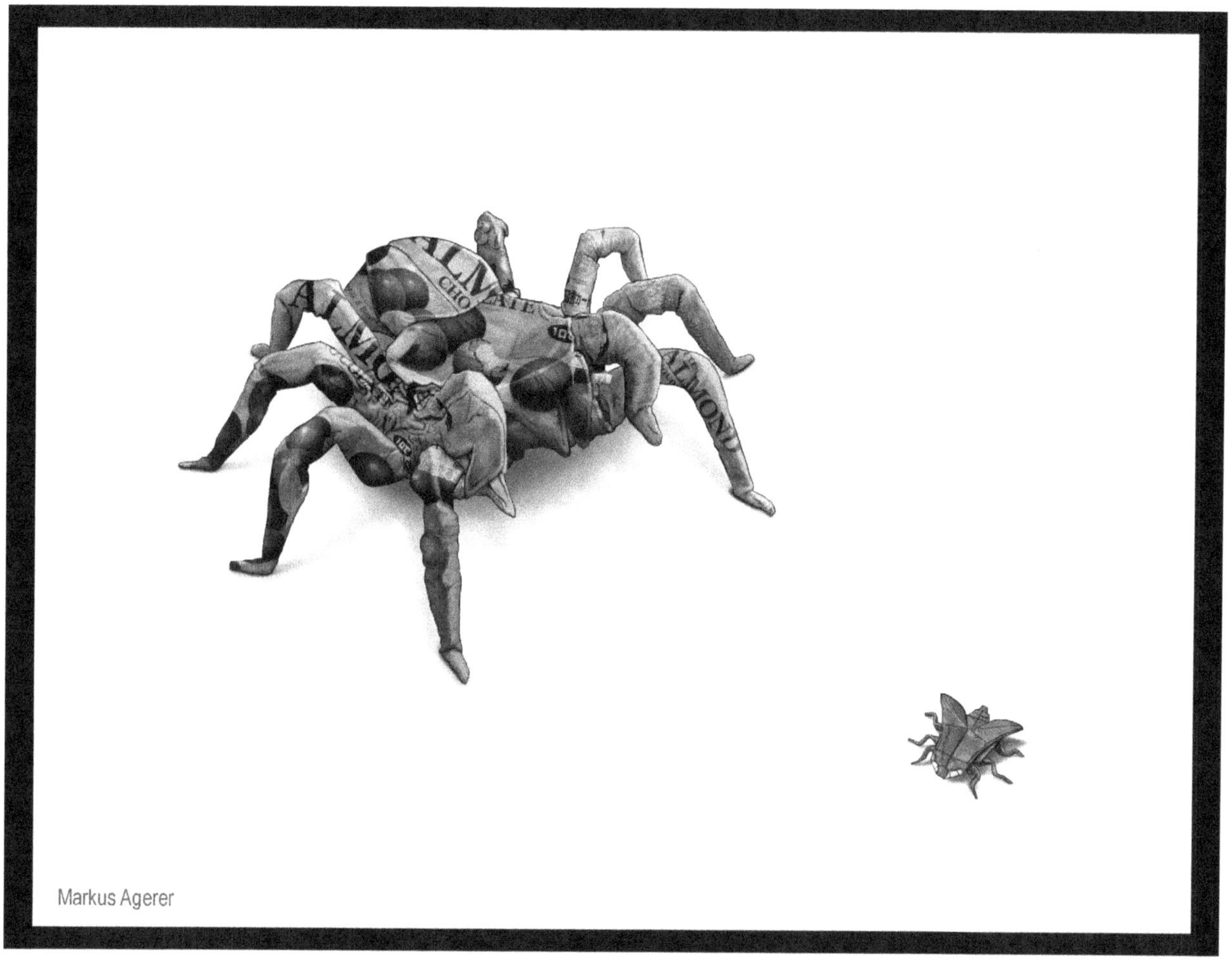

Markus Agerer

Obvious asymmetry in equilibrium through a clear difference in size of primary and secondary motif

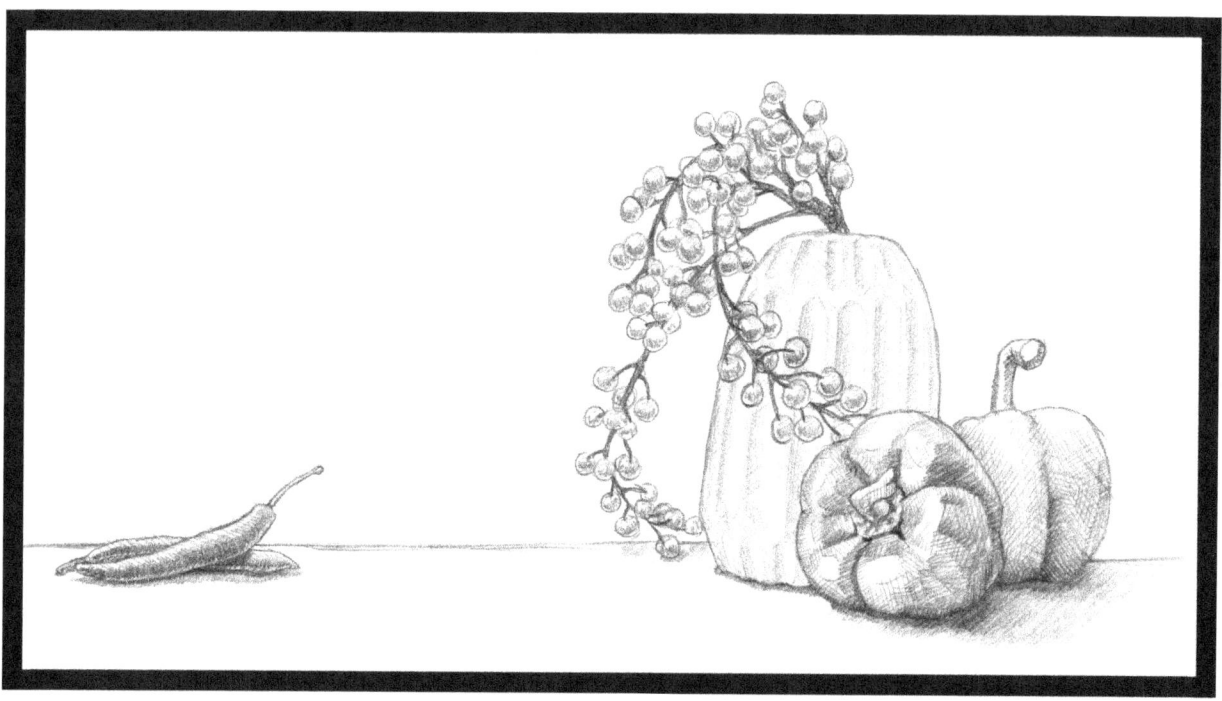

Chili peppers and vase with bell peppers form an asymmetrical equilibrium

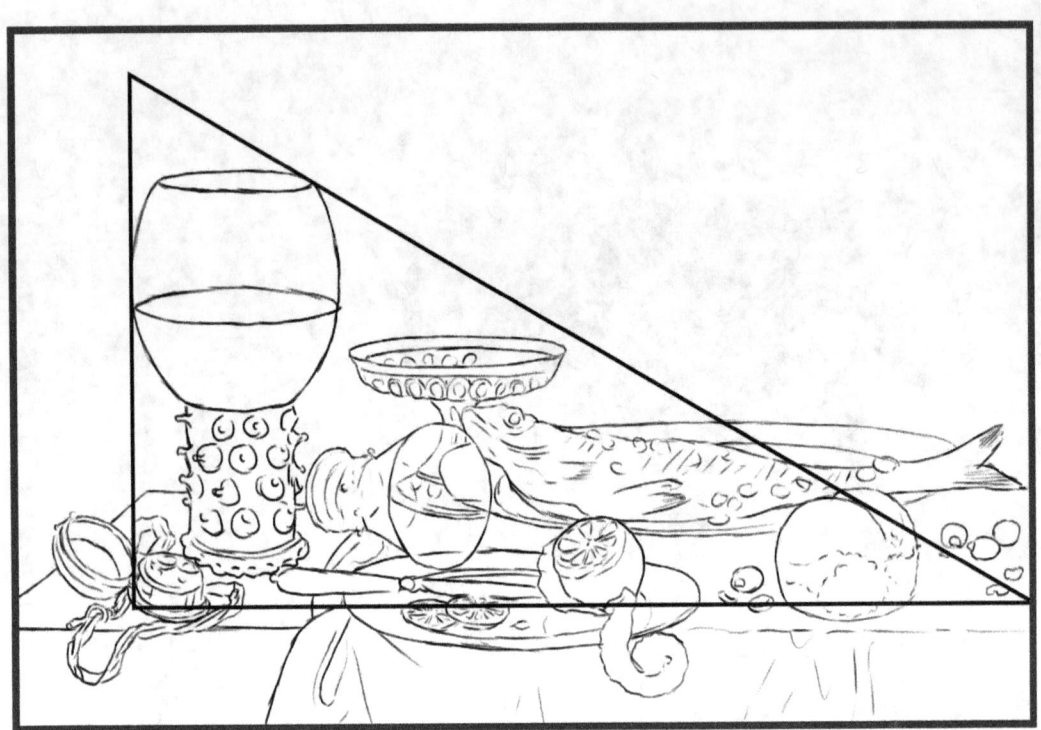

An asymmetrical equilibrium emerges by inserting a non-isosceles triangle as a compositional aid
Sketch of a still life by Willem Claesz Heda

Since symmetrically structured pictures are often perceived as boring by the viewer, asymmetrical equilibrium is particularly suitable for creating exciting works. To find such a balance as an artist, one does of course need a great deal of sensitivity, experience, and a trained eye.

On the other hand, it is also possible to create tension in a painting precisely because of the lack of this balance. The eye is looking for it and if it cannot be found, a feeling of insecurity and tension can arise.

Closing Remarks

» *The old saying "The first step is always the hardest" is only valid for skills. In art, nothing is more difficult than ending – which at the same time means perfecting.* «

- Marie Freifrau von Ebner-Eschenbach -

CLOSING REMARKS

With the chapter on Balance in Pictorial Composition, we have reached the end of this book. I hope that you have enjoyed it and, above all, that it has helped you. Certainly, reading and working through the book will not make you an ingenious artist, but the book should convey the most important basic knowledge about composition. Through the chapters, I have tried to convey various methods and give you many tips. The examples are intended to make it easier for you to understand how to apply this theoretical knowledge to your own artworks.

Parallel to all of our theoretical efforts, the most important thing for drawing is, of course, practice. You do not have to start immediately with complex compositions; rather, it is better to try and represent simple motifs. Put this book to good use whenever you arrive at a point where you are having difficulties. The methods that you have worked with here should cover many types of composition.

As you have seen, creating a picture of your own can require you to be extremely versatile, and there are several things you will need to think about beforehand. In order to further improve your skills, a lot of practice will be required. Let your surroundings inspire you to create your own pictures. You can always practice your compositional skills and gain experience in creating appealing pictorial compositions.

And if you have enjoyed this book, I would also be very happy if you would recommend it to friends, acquaintances, or on the net.

You can also visit me at my website. There you will find more instructions on learning to paint and draw and many of my own pictures:

www.art-class.net

Thanks and greetings to all readers and all who have supported me in creating my book!

Markus S. Agerer

Source

Books:

„Baustilfibel - Bauwerke und Baustile von der Antike bis zur Gegenwart"
Autor: Herbert Kürth; und Aribert Kutschmar;
Verlag: Vok und Wissen Volkseigener Verlag Berlin

"Underweysung der Messung mit dem Zirckel und Richtscheyt"
Autor: Albrecht Dürer der Jüngere; Nürnberg 1525

„Perspektivisch Zeichnen: Grundlagen zur Darstellung des dreidimensionalen Raums"
Autor: Gernot Störzbach; Verlag: Christophorus Verlag GmbH & Co. KG., Freiburg

„How to Draw: Drawing and Sketching Objects and Environments from Your Imagination"

Autor: Scott Robertson mit Thomas Bertling; Verlag: Design Studio Press

Internet:

http://www.kunstkurs-online.de

http://zeichnen-lernen.markus-agerer.de

http://www.wikipedia.org

http://www.pharmawiki.ch/perspektive

BOOK RECOMMENDATION

Start Drawing
Landscapes, Still Lifes, Figures and more

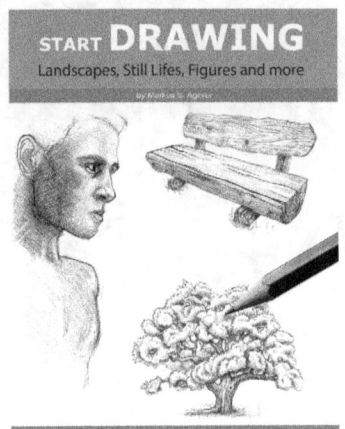

ISBN :979-869169967

The World of Drawing
Subjects, Techniques, Step-by-Steps

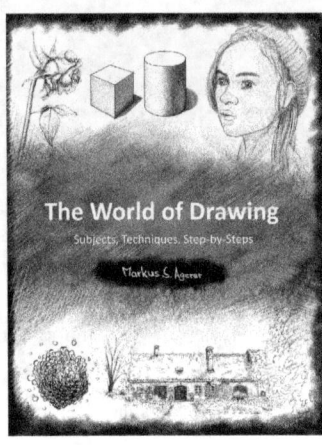

ISBN : 979-8446424313

Start Drawing Landscapes
Basic Principles, Composition and Exercises

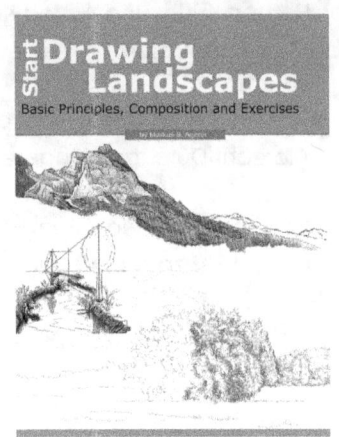

ISBN : 979-8612822158

How to draw Architecture
Illustrating Buildings and Cityscapes

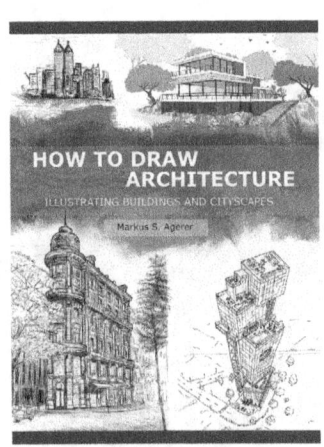

ISBN : 978-3982393223

Drawing Perspective & Space
Basic Principles of Drawing in Perspective B/W

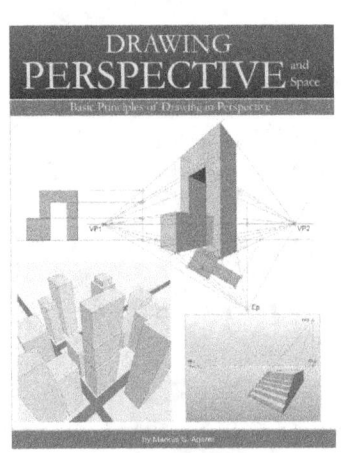

ISBN : 978-1095730065

Start Drawing Still Lifes
Techniques, Composition and Exercises

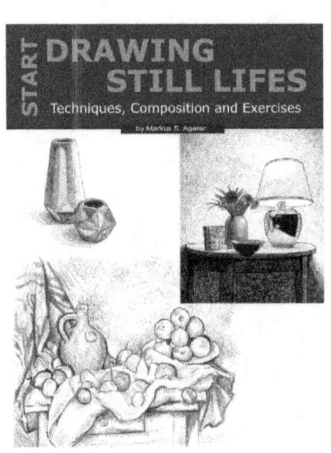

ISBN : 979-8679648319

www.ingramcontent.com/pod-product-compliance
Lightning Source LLC
Chambersburg PA
CBHW081433220526
45466CB00008B/2366